CITY POLITICS

CITY PSYCHOS

From the Monte Carlo Mob
to the Silver Cod Squad:
Four Decades of Terrace Terror

Shaun Tordoff

MILO BOOKS LTD

First published in October 2002 by Milo Books

Copyright © 2002 Shaun Tordoff

ISBN 1 903854 13 X

Typeset by Avon DataSet Ltd, Bidford on Avon B50 4JH
Printed and bound in Great Britain by
Creative Print and Design, Ebbw Vale, Gwent

MILO BOOKS
P.O.Box 153
Bury
BL0 9FX
info@milobooks.com

Contents

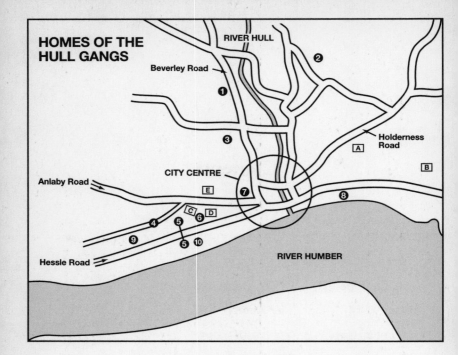

HOMES OF THE HULL GANGS

RIVER HULL

Beverley Road

❶

❷

❸

Holderness Road

CITY CENTRE

Anlaby Road

Ⓔ

❼

❹ ❺

Ⓒ ❻ Ⓓ

❾

❺ ❿

Hessle Road

RIVER HUMBER

Ⓐ

Ⓑ

❽

KEY

1 Orchard Park and North Hull Estates
2 Bransholme, home of the Selworthy Mob
3 The Avenues area, birthplace of the City Psychos
4 Boothferry Estate
5 Gypsyville Estate
6 Woodcock Street, home of the Woodcock Martyrs
7 Paragon Station and the site of the fabled Monte Carlo Cafe
   and Albermarle Youth Club
8 East Hull Docks area
9 Hessle area, home of the Hessle Road Mob
10 Original Hessle Road fish dock area

A Site of Craven Park, the former Hull Kingston Rovers rugby ground
B The modern location of Hull KR's ground
C Boothferry Park, home of Hull City Football Club
D The Boulevard, home of Hull FC rugby league club
E The location for Hull City's new stadium

Foreword

THE 1960s CONJURE up different memories for those who lived through them. To some it was the era of free love, a liberation of the mind and spirit, a right to protest against injustices around the world, Ban the Bomb and stop the Vietnam War. Protesters marched *en masse* to Grosvenor Square, where the crowd swayed and pushed against the thin blue line and chanted as one, 'HO ... HO ... HO CHI MINH!'

To us, that same decade meant living in a two-up, two-down, inner-city terraced house, with no hot water or inside toilet, having to trudge down grey dead-end streets to grey dead-end jobs or sit in cold, drab, Victorian schools without a blade of grass in sight. But we also had something to keep us going, something to look forward to all week: Saturdays, when *we* could march to the ground, with *our* crowd swaying and pushing against the thin blue line and chanting as one, 'A ... G ... A,G,R ... A,G,R,O ... AGGRO!'

Such were the times we grew up in: two different worlds and never the twain shall meet. Or so we thought. Football then was the people's game, affordable to all, with grounds positioned among the homes of the fans who attended religiously. They were part of our lives, filled every Saturday by working class heroes.

Now, with sterile, all-seater, multi-functional stadia sprouting up among the retail trading parks on the outskirts of the city, the average supporter is from a comfortable two-car family environment and sits there clapping in the right places but doesn't shout too loud for fear of offending someone. Those of us who still attend and try to instil the passion and fervour of times gone by are chastised by faceless stewards who threaten you with life-time bans for daring to swear out loud or even, God forbid, stand and abuse the opposition.

It wasn't always like this. The years leading up to England's 1966 World Cup win were little different from the 1950s style of supporting: young lads at the bottom of the terraces waving rattles, with the occasional club song thrown in. Then things changed. At the forefront of this altered mood were the teenage fans who began to band together and imitate established 'ends' such as the Spion Kop or Stretford End. Every club would witness this change, with the younger element moving up the terraces and claiming areas traditionally populated by their fathers and grandfathers. These groups of lads sang popular football chants of the day, pinching them from other clubs and making up their own. The thrills of a Saturday afternoon were to vocally support your team and, if any rival fans were present, to out-sing them.

It was the introduction of these rival fans that took the weekend ritual to another level. With the fifties employment boom, the man in the street could afford to travel to matches other than local derbies on readily-available cheap travel. By the sixties, teenage fans could afford to do the same, and began to organise coach trips or pay on the 'special' trains to follow their heroes all over the country.

From this came the tradition of 'taking ends', with the away fans duty-bound to infiltrate the home fans' terrace end and humiliate them, pinching their scarves in the process. This was like taking a scalp, and the scarves were trophies. Many early triumphs by lads taking liberties away from home set up retaliations the next time the teams met. Before long, inter-club rivalries were born outside the derby scene, rivalries that persist today.

The skinhead craze of the late sixties began in the East End of London, and this more hardened look was quickly adopted by sets of fans throughout the UK. Gangs were now wrecking trains and damaging property as well as fighting the opposing fans in and around grounds. Here, many reputations were made and certain teams stood out for their expertise at 'getting a result'.

The skinhead look was the first that could be described as terrace fashion, with hordes of like-minded teenagers copying styles and creating an identity that proclaimed: *Look at us, watch what we do, see how we behave, get out of our way.* Previously, teenagers had joined the ranks of Teddy Boys, Mods and Rockers. All of these fads were based on a certain look and noted for their violent behaviour, but this was different. The young skinheads weren't just posturing on street corners or going out of their way to impress the girls. This was a statement to the world, showing you were more than just affiliated to the district you lived in, but that you represented your street, your club and your city.

This is the story of one such city, of its youth gang culture and of its football fans and their opponents who, in the days of the late sixties, decided on a certain path, a way of life which for a few remains to this day. The path of the hooligan. The path of The Minority.

★ ★ ★

In recent years, this 'minority' at Hull City has been more active than at any time since the mid-eighties. It is fair to say that for the past ten years at least, no-one has come close to 'having one over' Hull's firm, even though the past six or seven years saw a distinct rise in hooligan activity throughout the leagues, with many an 'old school' lad returning to action.

On the whole, firms may not be as large as in previous eras but the ferociousness and intent is still there. Gone are the days of weekly mass disorder, to be replaced by well-organised meets involving like-minded individuals. Cunning and guile are now required as the present day hooligan strives to keep one step ahead of Robocop.

It was around 1999 that I first had the idea for a Hull City hooligan website called Hulltras. I wanted to provide a site that concentrated on past events and my own personal memories. With the help of a mate, Tony, I formulated each section bit by bit. It was a slow process but the finished article gave me great satisfaction, compounded by the amount of hits the site has achieved since (current average, 950 per week). Considering it is a provincial club site and not a national site, I'd say it has been a success.

Admittedly, the furore created by regional news pro-grammes has helped in its notoriety, but its best feature to my mind is the link to the Silver Cod Squad message board (which unfortunately has nothing to do with me). Lads from many teams frequent the board and the quality of the posts is second to none. We've had some crazy accusations thrown at us; apparently people involved in paramilitary organisations run the site. This statement was read out on a local radio news broadcast after some lad from Linfield had left a post saying he supported Hull City!

The Hulltras site was a springboard to this book, catapulting me into the realm of hooligan author and supposed 'bad lad'. I guess this is the point where I declare that I'm a reformed character and I haven't been involved for years. Well I'm sorry, that's not what this book is about. Over the course of a year I have collected memories from different people, all of whom have one thing in common – they have been involved in supporting Hull City and the hooligan scene that runs hand in hand with it.

I must apologise for disguising many names, but I've had

to compromise to report past events. This book goes as far back as the mid-sixties and, for some of those who talked to me, that part of their lives is dead and buried. I have to respect that. Other names have been omitted because, yes, that person is still involved, and it's not for me to point the finger and say, so-and-so did that. Suffice to say, those involved know who did what; and as far as the independent reader is concerned, the names probably mean little.

The structure of our 'firm' was and is such that no one can ever claim leadership. Most anyone can have their say; it doesn't matter if the spokesperson is 19 or 39, if the idea is a good one it will be implemented. Hull people don't beat about the bush and if anyone tried to claim leadership and kept on issuing orders, you'd soon hear, 'Shut up, soft cunt.' That would be the end of it. Years ago, as you will read, a few people did come to the forefront but more often then not it was a specific area or gang which took over the leadership role, not by ordering others around but by example.

Remember also, that everything you read is only one version of a specific event. If you read anything here and think, *it didn't happen like that at all*, well that's life. Some people are selective in how they remember scenes from the past. Hopefully this book will not be guilty of that, but you can be the judge.

Lastly, for any males who may read this with a replica shirt on and a *Roy Of the Rovers* football quiz book to hand, as well as for all those middle class psychologists and anyone else with a testosterone shortage, don't bother analysing us, or attempting to. I will leave you with this:

FOR THOSE WHO HAVE BEEN INVOLVED, NO EXPLANATION IS NECESSARY,
FOR THOSE WHO HAVEN'T, NO EXPLANATION IS POSSIBLE.

CHAPTER ONE

Bricks, Boots and Bovver

OUTSIDERS PERCEIVE HULL as a small city full of fishermen in sou'westers and large waders, a dead-end place with deadbeat residents. Certainly we have always been out on a limb. Though Hull is geographically a part of Yorkshire, I and many other residents have never shared the 'Yorkshire Republican Army' mindset or felt that we have anything in common with other cities in the county. Hull people down the years have been a defiant bunch. It was here that the seeds were sown for the English Civil War, when Charles I was refused entry through the town gates as he came to relieve the garrison of its armoury. Three hundred years later, the stout residents of Hull resisted the attempts of the Luftwaffe to pound the city to a standstill. Over 85 per cent of Hull homes were bomb-damaged, yet amazingly no working days were lost in this 'North East City', as it was known at the time.

The truth is that modern Hull is far removed from its dour historical image. Kingston upon Hull, to give the place its official name, lies at the junction of the Hull and Humber rivers. It is a big city, with a travel-to-work population of 450,000. As I write, it is undergoing a massive change for the better and is fast becoming an 'in' place to visit for a weekend break. I admit that wasn't always so. Before the slum clearances of the mid to late sixties, Hull had more terraced houses than any other city in the country. Many of these homes didn't have running hot water, never mind a bath or inside toilet.

(The council would eventually move thousands of families from their traditional neighbourhoods and place them in modern homes on the sprawling estates of Orchard Park and Bransholme, said to be the largest council-owned estate in Europe, with over 35,000 residents.)

The Hull folk who resided in those original two-up, two-down dwellings were hard-working people. Many made their living off the docks. Traditionally those living east of the River Hull worked on the dry docks, where the dockers and small industrial units benefited from the Eastern European timber ships and grain barges that plied their trade up and down the Humber. To be brought up west of the River Hull usually meant your family had some connection with the fishing industry, either by going out to sea or working shore-based in the many fish factories around Hessle Road. These trawlermen were a different breed from your coastal fishermen; yes, they both earned a living from the sea, but the hardships endured by the trawler crews during their three and four week 'trips' as they battled freezing winds and roaring seas made this the most dangerous profession in Britain.

Both areas of Hull are proud of their heritage, and rightly so. I say both areas and that's what it boils down to: talk to anyone in and around Hull and they will profess an allegiance to east or west. It may stem from their own upbringing or even from where their forebears lived, but more often than not is decided by which of our two professional rugby league clubs they support. East Hull is Hull Kingston Rovers (who play at Craven Park) and West Hull is Hull FC (Boulevard) and rarely the two shall mix. Support for one or the other was often shared with a passion for Hull City Football Club, who play at Boothferry Park. Some would go to see two out of three, but rarely to all three.

Out of all this in-built rivalry came the gangs. I'm not just talking about mobs of lads fighting at football grounds, but gangs of young men who roamed the cobbles and ruled the back street pubs of a different age. My grandad told me stories from his youth in Edwardian Hull of hatchet gangs who fought for territory around Porter Street (Hessle Road/ Town area). Tales were relived of factions clashing head-on in the town centre in the late forties and fifties, settling their differences in the dance halls and public houses, gangs of tearaways who hated the fact that those bastards from Hessle Road came to 'Town' throwing their money about and that their girlfriends fawned all over these 'Flash Harry' seamen with three days at home and three weeks' money to spend.

Many of us grew up knowing nothing else. I was brought up in West Hull, born into a family of 'bobbers' (dockers who work only on the fish dock, unloading trawlers) and fish workers in the Hessle Road of 1958, a tough, no-nonsense place with long-established links to the sea. By the time I was old enough, I was a member of a gang down our road, Eastbourne Street. Gangs were joined when you were as young as five or six, and by the time you were eight you were proficient in brick-throwing and fighting with other streets, especially during the bonfire season, when taking the wood off another street was a victory. During the 'raiding' season, hundreds of kids all over Hull fought with each other for the ownership of horsehair settees, old 'pissy' mattresses and backyard doors. Revenge raids were planned, ambushes were implemented and small gangs of urchins took liberties on their rivals' manor. To many of us brought up like this, football violence was a small step away.

Each street had its own gang, and most supported Hull City – 'the Tigers,' a nickname adopted for their amber and black striped shirts. Founded in 1904, the club were elected to the Second Division of the Football League a year later. 1909-10 was the nearest we have ever been to top-flight football: we came third, losing out on promotion by goal difference to runners-up Oldham Athletic by an agonising

0.29 of a goal. Hull stayed a solid but under-achieving Division Two side, somewhat in the shadow of the city's rugby league clubs, and were relegated in 1930, despite having our best-ever FA Cup run (reaching the semis) that same year. A bit of a yo-yo spell followed before war intervened.

The years immediately after World War Two saw a new ground at Boothferry Park (on the site of an old golf course), a new board led by Harold Needler, a new manager, Major Frank Buckley, and the arrival of Raich Carter, one of England's greatest-ever forwards. Carter led the club to a record-breaking Third Division (North) championship that included an attendance of 49,655 for a top-of-the-table game at home to Rotherham on Christmas Day, a divisional record that still stands. A cup run saw an even bigger crowd, 55,019, witness a home defeat by Manchester United, a Boothferry Park record that will never be beaten.

By the early sixties we were back in Division Three and a new manager, Cliff Britton, undertook a wholesale rebuilding of the team. It would lead to one of the most exciting periods in Hull City's history, at a time when soccer was booming and England was gearing up for 1966 and all that. It was a period that also saw the roots of what would become known as the 'English disease' – modern football hooliganism.

To describe those formative years, I have enlisted the help of Montie, a leading Hull lad who is older than me and can tell with accuracy how the gang scene took off.

MONTIE: The 1965-66 season was arguably Hull City's best ever. The club stormed to the Third Division championship, breaking every existing record. A huge cash investment by the chairman, Harold Needler, paid off and brought together the feared striking partnership of Chris Chilton and Ken Wagstaff, who tore opposition defences apart on a weekly basis. No two Hull players since have become national household names, but Waggy and Chillo were, and made Hull City fashionable in an era when being fashionable was everything. The match programme for a Chelsea v Hull City sixth-round FA Cup tie in March 1966 described us as 'the Third Division club with the Second Division outlook and the First Division ground.'

City made national media headlines that damp March afternoon by scoring two late goals (Wagstaff) to earn a replay with the mighty Londoners at Boothferry Park the following Thursday. Such was City's reputation in those days that everyone expected them to knock Chelsea out and march into the semi-finals. Regular and long-time followers of the Tigers will no doubt know that things like that don't happen for us, and Chelsea ran out 3-1 winners in front of over 40,000 expectant City fans. Chelsea brought approximately 100 supporters; they stood in the 'Well' chanting something about Peter Osgood being good. I have hated Chelsea ever since.

In my small world, my football club was everything, and you could say that went for a large part of the population of Hull, because home crowds that season were enormous, and we always won, except for one occasion of two home defeats in a week (QPR 3-1 and York 4-1). We scored goals for fun and romped away with the championship. How was I to know that my first full season would never be bettered?

City attracted huge numbers home and away all season: noisy, enthusiastic, original, and totally innocent. The only crowd trouble was cramming all the people into the ground. Vocal support was thunderously loud from the South Stand 'choir', but often drowned out by the deafening roar of thousands of away fans packed under the low East Stand roof. Wolves gave us a singing lesson that year, followed closely by Huddersfield and Derby County. This impressed me and made home matches against the bigger clubs very memorable, if only for the atmosphere. We were, unconsciously, learning fast from the big boys at this time, copying everything they did. On the pitch, the team was a match for anyone; off it we still smacked of that Third Division innocence.

The first club to exploit this was Crystal Palace, of all people, the following season. City were cruising the game and Ian Butler had just put us in front. The South Stand were loving it, teasing a small band of Palace supporters with a chant of 'Can you hear the Palace sing? No-o-o. Where's me handbag?' Very tame by today's standards, but highly amusing then.

There was a sudden surge from the back of the South as a dozen or so Palace fans wearing hob-nailed boots and full-length, dark blue raincoats fastened up to the collar burst into the stand, sending the unsuspecting City fans scattering. An empty space appeared, with the Palace lads giving us the 'come on boys' gesture with their hands. One was waving a knife about, another had a chain, and as boots and fists connected, Hull City's South Stand lost its innocence.

I was fourteen at the time, and copped for a full-blown punch to the back of my head from a bloke twice my size. Such was my disgust that I later wrote to Bert Head, the Palace manager. He printed part of my letter in the Palace programme, and I received a parcel with a signed apology from the manager himself. Little did I know I had given Palace the publicity their boys wanted, but from then on it was never going to be the same.

March 22, 1969, and City fans had a baptism of fire at Ayresome Park, home of the 'Boro Boot Boys'. In another goal-filled game, ending 5-3 to Boro, mayhem broke out just after half-time when, unbeknown to us, the Boro fans changed ends and laced into our fans behind the goal. It was my, and probably many of the younger lads', first visit there, and we thought it strange our numbers began to thin out at half-time. Then this huge surge of Boro, many wearing miners' safety helmets and heavy steel-toe-capped boots, came straight at Hull, now down to about 40 in number, pinned us against the back of the stand and gave us a good hiding.

Not one copper in sight, nowhere to run, scared shitless, all we could do was fight back – and some of us did. All the lads who had travelled by coach stood together for the first time and got battered. I remember some City fans lighting a small fire in one corner of the stand in defiance, or was it a cry for help?

Not that it ended there. In a melee after the game, in pitch darkness, Boro picked us off one by one as we limped back to the coach; someone smashed half a brick into my face before I boarded the bus. Windows went through and the bus screeched out of town while the Old Bill stood idly by saying, 'Well, what did you expect?' We hadn't expected that, but from that day on, we did. Football was changing.

I felt humiliated after Boro. It hurt that my club colours meant nothing outside my small circle of mates. Attending City games no longer meant simply shouting as loud as you could for your team, we were now fighting for our club's honour, for our own safety and to put some respect back into the Black 'n' Amber, so I went out and bought a pair of steel-toed boots from the Army & Navy Store on Beverley Road and began plotting my revenge the next time Boro came to Hull. Some big games followed – Millwall, Birmingham and Villa at home – but none left an impression like the one at Ayresome Park, an evil place.

As 1969 drew to a close, my little gang, all in their final year at school, were desperate to get together a mob to rival the Boro Bootboys. It wasn't easy living on a paperboy's wages; we couldn't even afford a pint. Our 'patch' was just as restrictive, a wedge starting at Orchard Park, a sprawling new council estate that stretched from the northern edge of the city to the town centre.

We spent most of our time involved in petty crime and spraying 'Bootboy' slogans on highly visible walls. Our world was made up of getting pissed on a Friday night on Olde English cider, football on Saturday, and the rest of the week skint, idling time away roaming the streets or keeping warm in various youth clubs. My club haunts were Appleton Road and, for a bit, Setting Dyke.

This pattern came to an abrupt end when a rival West Hull gang ambushed five of us one Friday night. The youngest and most innocent of our gang, Bri Stainton, suffered a fractured skull when he was smashed on the head with a lump of concrete. 'Stag,' as he was known, was near to death for days. I felt particularly guilty because I had let myself become detached from my mates, walking a bird to a bus stop. Stag's older brothers also blamed me when I faced them at Hull Royal Infirmary, and I felt guilty as hell, but it was the comradeship-type thing developing. We were no longer schoolboys but young men, and we knew we had to stick together no matter what the odds against us. From that day on we did, even though that scrap was not football-related.

I bumped into his attackers one Tuesday night at City v Birmingham. Hull had just chased a few Brummies out of the old North Stand and I was at the top of the terracing looking for stragglers when Jeff Bone, a giant of a bloke who was part of Mike Wolffe's Hessle Road Mob, offered me out. He had about eight lads with him and they kicked me up and down the East Stand terracing. No one came to help me but I fought back as best I could. They jumped me again after the match and I took another beating. The next time I saw this mob was at a rugby match at Hull KR v Hull FC. I shit myself when I saw them all, but I wouldn't run; anyway, there was nowhere to run. To my surprise Bone came towards me and shook my hand. After that we were best mates. Mike Wolffe was later killed by crocodiles in the Indian Ocean (true), but his mob were the hardest I have ever come across.

By late '69 the skinhead culture was taking hold in Hull. The city then was a very different place to the modern, 'top ten city' it claims to be today. Hull had been a bit of a Sleepy Hollow, the most vibrant area being the large fishing community on Hessle Road. Here, the trawlermen were kings; they were know as 'three-day millionaires'. These lads, home for a few days from the deep-sea fishing grounds of the Baltic and White Seas with pockets full of money, would rule the roost. It was a Teddy Boy mentality: flash suits, DA hairstyles and violence to match, with brawls aplenty come last orders.

It was a violent place, especially if you were a stranger who happened on the wrong pub at the wrong time. But these fishermen were a dying breed. The next generation of Hessle Road youth didn't flock to the sea with the same enthusiasm or in the same numbers as their forebears. Instead they looked for shore-based jobs, shaved their heads and laced up their boots. These skinheads would virtually wipe out the fishermen culture along with the after-effects of the Cod War, which decimated the industry in Hull.

The 'lad culture' which was emerging was very much in its infancy, with many a fresh-faced, streetwise school-leaver scouring the pages of the national Press for tips and bits of information on the latest fashion craze sweeping the nation. We read of the London Skins, the Kilburn Aggro and the Willesden Whites. The Press coverage gave this new craze all the credibility it craved and we copied every aspect greedily.

Football fans were at the forefront of this craze, as we had seen the Cockneys parading all the garb. Levi Sta Press, blood-red Doc Marten boots and sheepskins were the fashion down south, so we copied it. The best shops were Arthur Masons on Carr Lane and Milletts down Whitefriargate, where we all bought our Harrington jackets. I had teamed up with a lad called Dobo by now and we left the suburbs and started mixing with the town lads at the Albermarle youth club, which was full of City lads who all felt the same as us and hung out at drinking dens like the Star and Garter down Portland Place and the Broadway on Ferensway.

Late '69 saw City improve on the field and they went on to lose only one of their last twelve matches. It also saw me get my revenge on Boro. They came late in the season, by coach down Beverley Road. Dobo and myself hid in bushes just outside Hull with catapults, and we each put several coach

windows in. Inside the ground I stood among the Boro fans,
awaited my chance and, when Boro scored, smashed a brick
into the face of the nearest Boro fan. Welcome to Hull, you
bastards. I had gone before they realised what had happened.

Cowardly? Maybe.

Revenge? Yes!

★ ★ ★

We were Hull City barmy and had been for two years, but this
was only the second time I had seen my heroes playing a First
Division team. The talk at school all day had been about the
forthcoming match with the mighty Liverpool and how City
would cope against players of the calibre of Roger Hunt and
Ron Yeats.

I walked to the ground with three of my best mates, Alan,
Rob and Les. We lived down the same street and always stood
together at the bottom of Bunkers (the South Stand), right
behind the goal. We walked over Hessle Road flyover and, as
we chatted, the conversation turned to whether or not any
Liverpool fans would be at the match. The Beatles were at the
height of their fame, the Scouse accent was very much in
vogue and we wanted to stand among them and see if we
could pass ourselves off as Scousers. So we abandoned our
usual position in the ground and entered the turnstile under
the old North Stand.

We positioned ourselves behind the goal Liverpool were
defending. Near us was a group of 20 Kopites, singing away.
We moved nearer and nearer to these lads until we were
among them, and before long we were talking to them, asking
stupid irrelevant questions and probably getting on their
nerves, but we were enjoying the whole experience.

Half-time came and these Scouse lads told us they were
moving behind the other goal – you could walk around the
ground in those days – and began to make their way towards

Bunkers. Now we knew this was Hull's end but we just tagged along with our new friends. They stood midway up the terracing to the left of the goal and soon they began chanting. Their songs had the local Hull lads looking round for infiltrators, and within five minutes of taking up a position on the home turf, all hell broke loose, or that's how it seemed to us. The Hull boys began pushing down on the Scouse lads and, once their prey was surrounded, they attacked. A few kicks and punches were thrown and the Liverpool lads retreated back towards the North Stand behind the other goal.

The whole thing lasted all of 30 seconds but has stayed with me over the years. None of us was hit during the fight but that mixed feeling of both fright and unbearable excitement had us hooked. From then on we knew where we had to stand every match, and our long and eventful apprenticeships began. All the lads in our area would eventually adopt the skinhead/ suedehead look and stand together on the South Stand. Ages ranged from younger members at twelve (of which I was one) to older lads in their late teens – our heroes.

The seventies had arrived. Just saying it brings back so many memories: skinheads, suedeheads, bootboys, smoothies, punks, soul boys, scooter lads, all variations on a theme and all seen on terraces up and down the country. The speed of change was amazing; as a style came into vogue in one area, it was being abandoned somewhere else. Terrace fashion for the first time was becoming big business and how a 'firm' looked was as important as how it performed.

This decade would see the birth of the superfirms, with teams like Manchester United, West Ham United and Chelsea coming to the fore and thousands of young thugs rampaging through town centres wherever they went. All this was played out to an eager audience of like-minded young supporters of every provincial team in the UK. They lapped up the newspaper reports and televised footage and soon this type of behaviour became widespread. Pandora's Box hadn't just been opened, it had exploded. Lads were now seeing for the first time how powerful a mob could be. The police were sometimes hard pressed to keep control and it wasn't un-common to see mobs of literally thousands fighting up and down streets around our football grounds.

It all began with the skinheads. The movement was introduced to Hull around late 1968, when a lot of the lads that watched City noticed that rival supporters, especially from the larger cities, were coming to matches with shaven heads and sporting 'bovver boots' – not so much Doc Martens but more often army or hob-nailed boots, worn with rolled-up Levis. After being on the receiving end of a pair of size nines and getting kicked up and down the South Stand terracing, you either stayed well away or you began to plot your revenge. This was how many inter-club rivalries began, and some teams are still hated thirty years later.

It wasn't until 1969-70 that the fashion really kicked in and people started wearing the better gear like Doc Marten boots, Brutus and Ben Sherman, and even Arnold Palmer shirts, depending on what you could afford. These clothes weren't elitist; they were made for and sold to the masses. Nobody was frowned on for not wearing the best gear, fashion was not so transient, and certain styles stayed in for a year or more. Clothes were bought from shops like Northerns and Arthur Masons in the city centre and Clothing House on Hessle Road. Most bought their boots and jeans such as Wranglers from their local Army & Navy stores.

The first set of skinheads to emerge in Hull were mainly lads who knocked around in the town centre. Most lived centrally, around Beverley Road, going as far as Orchard Park Estate, Anlaby, Hessle and Holderness Road. These lads started congregating around a coffee bar called the Monte Carlo Café off Osborne Street, to the bottom of Midland Street, a rundown area of cafes, dirty-looking shops complete with the obligatory cracked, flaking paint, and King Arthur's tattoo parlour; not a nice place to be, especially if you weren't local. This was their territory, where on match days they met and waited. Here they were in an enviable position, hidden enough to escape detection from rival fans but only 500 yards from a side entrance into Paragon Railway Station, ideal for ambushing.

They called themselves the Monte Carlo Mob and you knew you were all right when these lads were around. I can still picture them walking over Anlaby Road flyover, bouncing as they walked with that telltale swagger which radiated confidence. They were violent, they looked mental, nothing phased them. Names like Sinbad, Dobbo, Doyley, Tarzan, Brains, Fez and Ginner trip off the tongue; these were 'the boys' and their exploits were the stuff of legend.

The lads who frequented the Monte Carlo gained a massive reputation around Hull. They all sported skinhead haircuts and were distinguished by their unique markings: a tattoo of a black boot, with a number underneath it to show your standing in the gang. Number One was the legendary Sinbad. Whenever you were in the presence of these lads you felt invincible as you walked to the ground in a serious mob. They acted as a magnet for other boys to attend and congregate, but only for matches; midweek the café was the domain of the 'town skins' who divided their time between hanging out at the 'caff' and relaxing in the newly-built Albemarle youth club. The majority of skins circa 1970/71 were still underage for pubs, so the local YC played a big part in the planning, recruiting and mobilising of 'the troops' before an important game. Clubs that stood out were Albermarle, Setting Dyke, Ainthorpe, Sydney Smith and Amy Johnson. These were all predominately West Hull locations, but the support for City was widespread.

The Albermarle Mob were arguably the leaders, as they encompassed the entire city, with east, west, north and town lads frequenting the club. Setting Dyke and Ainthorpe lads were mostly from north-west of the city, around the Bricknell

Avenue, Willerby and Wold Roads areas. Sydney Smith was the domain of the Boothferry Estate boys and Amy Johnson pulled in the lads from Hessle/Anlaby Roads and the Gypsy-ville Estate Crew. The OPE (Orchard Park Estate) Boys congregated around Holmes's 'beer off' (off licence) and the notorious Voodoo Disco, while the lads east of the River Hull danced the skinhead moonstomp at their weekly disco at Jarvis School (now Andrew Marvell) on Bilton Grange.

We were Hull City, we were as passionate about our team, our players and our city as anyone and we were soon able to show this. Many lads were now gaining notoriety around the town and were looked on as heroes to the younger element hanging on their coattails.

MONTIE: The centre of Hull was slowly dragging itself into the Twentieth Century, with the new disco and nightclub scene developing. Although Sundays were still as dead as a wet Wednesday in Withernsea, the place did start to come alive with hundreds of youngsters flocking to 'town' on a Friday and Saturday night.

The big meeting place had become the Monte Carlo Cafe on the corner of Midland Street, a real skinhead haunt. Round the corner was the Midi Cafe and the barbers, where we all went before a match to have our heads shaved. Monte Carlo was run by a West Indian called Mohammed, a larger than life character who gave the place atmosphere. All the Hessle Road skins met here, honest lads like Sinbad, the Sivewright brothers, Ray, Tony, Jacko, Huddy, Ronnie, Gerald, Peo, Woody, Dave, Andy, Dobbo, the McNallys, Mulloy, etcetera. On a good day more than forty lads would be there and it would be impossible to name them all, also a little unfair as they were only kids then and some have gone on to lead very successful lives. Some of course went the other way with the law, and for the same reason it would be unfair to pinpoint them. 1970 was a very different era to today.

My own gang of skins were new to this scene but we had already stamped our authority on the few 'greasers' who frequented the North Hull youth clubs and wanted more action. It was with great trepidation that we met up with these city centre skinheads, not least because of the fierce reputation of one of them: Sinbad. There was a lot of trouble in the city centre that year – virtually every Saturday – with Sinbad's lads usually at the forefront, clashing with greasers. It was usually smash, bang, wallop, with greasers running all over, battered and bruised, and the Old Bill arriving ten minutes later with Sinbad long gone.

We had yet to meet this elusive Sinbad character, but his reputation went before him and he wasn't looking to win any popularity contests. He was a bit secretive, a cut above us really; he was heavily tattooed, with a gold earring long before it became a fashion necessity. He didn't mix freely and was usually seen with three or four other lads, also heavily tattooed. They had hundreds of stars tattooed on each arm and hand. Sinbad also had the famous bovver boot marking with No 1 underneath. He was from a large, well-known Hessle Road family, was very muscular in build and usually dressed in faded Levis and Doc Martens; a fearsome looking character, not to be crossed. We followed like little lapdogs: to Cleethorpes, using the now defunct Humber Ferry, to fight the Grimsby Skins or any other groups who came our way or, if they showed their faces, the elusive greasers.

With Monte Carlo the meeting place, and Sinbad's reputation growing, more and more skinheads were drawn there. Yet as it became more popular, Sinbad and his close mates seemed to outgrow the place and became even more elusive. Looking back, it was probably because the police were on to him. It was obvious the Saturday afternoon battles could not be allowed to continue; it was bad for business. Retailers were up in arms, complaining of the loss of revenue due to unruly youths battling in the city centre. Add to this the trouble at Boothferry Park, mid-week gang skirmishes, queer-bashing, muggings and street assaults. If Sinbad wasn't directly responsible, it mattered not; he usually ended up with the blame.

He was eventually jailed after an assault on a Humber Ferry steward. Sinbad tried to escape before the boat docked in New Holland but was held up in the Humber mud and caught. Part of his charge sheet read that he had been found with an ice pick, which had been used in an earlier clash as his skinhead gang had rampaged down Whitefriargate in Hull and assaulted a group of greasers. Sinbad's court case appeared on the front page of the *Hull Daily Mail* and enhanced his reputation further.

Much has been said locally about Sinbad. Remember though that this all occurred a very long time ago, in a very different social climate. Many of his exploits were probably myth or exaggerated, but I speak as one who was there, on the very edge of the Sinbad-induced skinhead movement, and for someone to be still talked about over thirty-three years later says much for the man's character.

As Montie says, the skinheads fought not just in town but at the match. The football terraces had become a venue for these young Tigers to flex their muscles and bare their claws.

MONTIE: The summer of 1970 was Hull City's coming of age. We had signed Terry Neill, the former Arsenal and Northern Ireland captain, as player-manager. The World Cup in Mexico gripped the nation and Mungo Jerry's 'In the Summertime' captured the atmosphere of that wonderful summer. Scooter boys became fashionable and now Sundays meant trips to Bridlington to chase the West Yorkshire boys up and down the promenade. I can't recall ever seeing a proper punch thrown at Bridlington, but it was all good fun.

It was also the year the Hull police force was merged with the much larger Humberside Police, which brought with it much empire-building and new brooms to sweep clean. So the emerging skinhead cult, coupled with the increasing football hooligan element, met head-on with a 'new' police force out to prove a point.

The first sortie of the '70/71 campaign was a tie in the pre-season Watney Cup at Peterborough. We travelled on three coaches, with many more going by train. We fought, took the London Road end and returned home 4-0 winners on the pitch. That was easy. Now for the Red Army! Combined with the Neill signing, a mouth-watering draw at home to Man Utd on 5 August 1970, in the next round of the Watney Cup, set the City alight.

Man Utd at that time were at the height of their notoriety, top of anyone's hooligan league, and we wanted a shot at them. It was a night match but trouble started as early as 2pm as Man U began arriving at Paragon railway station. Running battles took place in the basement of Hammonds department store, down Paragon Street and around the Paragon pub. City lads were all over town and for the first time we used a 'spotter'. He was high up on the top floor of Hammonds in the Picadish restaurant, which in those days employed doormen! A huge battle took place at 5pm at the corner of Midland Street and Anlaby Road when City poured out of the two cafes and chased United onto the building site that is now Great Thornton Street flats.

Nearer the ground outside the Three Tuns pub, City more than held their own against superior numbers from Manchester. Inside the ground, both sets of fans stood shoulder to shoulder, separated by a thin line of police. Hundreds were ejected, myself included, missing extra-time and the after-match excitement. The police holding cells beneath South Stand were so full that constables reverted to clipping lads round the ears and shoving them down the South Stand steps. The aftermath took days to die down, with complaints to the paper from local residents, and the league season hadn't even started.

A coachload of lads left Albermarle for the first away game at Charlton. We had no idea where Charlton was and expected no trouble at all. We got plenty when we got on their kop end, held our own for a while but were hopelessly outnumbered, with some saying Charlton had brought in outside help from West Ham. Either way we put up a good show and were definitely 'getting there'.

The games came thick and fast. August 22 saw Middlesbrough at home, with hundreds battling down Anlaby Road as far as the EYMS bus depot. Boro always brought a huge mob and the police found it hard to control the mayhem in a crowd of over 20,000.

September 5, Bolton, always up for it. October 3, Birmingham, who in those days had nothing like the massive shows of the later Zulu years. Finally October 14, Hull Fair Week and a mass battle with Sheffield United. The Blades brought an army who fought with City before, during, and after the match. The *Hull Daily Mail* gave front-page coverage to this trouble, as by now football hooliganism was getting serious.

It was part and parcel of the game back then, and no matter how liberal one might be, the facts were that if you went to a game and cared for your club, you would eventually get dragged into some sort of crowd trouble. It was inevitable; it was everywhere. Every club brought huge away followings and amongst them maybe three quarters were out for trouble. You had to mix it or get battered every week, plain and simple. It probably cost the club thousands of fans in later years, as people stopped going 'because of the trouble.' I believe the true reasons for falling attendances were that the team stopped winning and it became too expensive. Undoubtedly, however, hooliganism would leave a mighty imprint on football throughout the decade.

CHAPTER TWO

The Kempton Fusiliers

BY JANUARY 1970, I was the proud owner of my first pair of Doc Martens, which cost the princely sum of £5 15s 6d from a local Army & Navy store. Along with a pair of Levi jeans and a visit to the local barber, I was sorted.

Our gang called themselves the 'Woodcock Martyrs' – after Woodcock Street – and numbered around 20. We loved Hull City and the romantic idea that we were part of the City mob. We suffered delusions of grandeur. At best we were tolerated and used for spying; we were the early warning system outside pubs such as The Broadway and the Punch Hotel. As long as we didn't get in the way, we could stand on the fringe, but the fringe of a mob was a dangerous place to be, especially when under attack.

One of my mates, Colin, stood with us one Boxing Day in South Stand as we were being pushed and shoved up and down the terracing while fights kept erupting around us. We were playing Sheffield Wednesday and both sets of supporters were side by side. One minute we were well away from any action, then due to the swaying of the crowd we were in amongst it all. Luckily for us we were only twelve or 13 and not seen as a threat. Wednesday were cruising 4-1 until City began to fight back, this time on the pitch. Chris Chilton led from the front and, with little time left on the watch, we equalised. With this, all the Owls fans still congregating on the South Stand went mental. My mate got caught in the middle of a big scuffle and ran blindly into a crash barrier, which laid him out. He was carried off to the St John Ambulance station, where he was left till he recovered. It was quite a while before he was keen to return to Boothferry Park and get back into it.

I was too young to be involved at the time, but it was great to watch, with police sirens going off all over the place, seeing lads from other teams causing havoc one minute and the next running off down Boothferry Road and through Gipsyville Estate with a mob of Hull Skins in hot pursuit. We had the best of both worlds: we wore the gear but weren't seen as a threat. Our youth was a passport of neutrality, giving the bearer access to places and incidents without any danger attached. We could follow the Hull lads into battle and if a retreat was necessary we were bypassed without any form of retribution.

Yes we were young, but we were learning fast. You quickly absorbed who to follow, who were the main faces, and how to be of service. Many hours were spent looking out over the exits of Paragon Station from the confines of Picadish Café in Hammonds department store, yet these hours weren't wasted. We talked of the times when we'd be old enough to 'run' with the lads and follow City away, which teams we hated, and exaggerated tales of our own derring do.

One year on and we were accepted. Our real apprenticeship was beginning. We were still cannon fodder to the older lads but associations built up with the Gypsyville Skins at Amy Johnson youth club, and the younger elements of the Boothferry Estate boys through school, meant that we could get involved in confrontations with the enemy. At a match against Sheffield Wednesday we were encouraged to get a boot in: 'Come on young 'uns, christen your fucking Docs.' This was the start of the long road to acceptance by the older skins. We would soon be going to away matches with lads who were too old for us to knock about with during the week but would tolerate our presence at weekends.

Oh, the joy of being noticed. We once went to Mecca on a Monday night, all of our young troop bedecked in our finest Ben Sherman shirts, sleeveless jumpers, olive Levi Sta-press, black brogues (complete with 'segs') and Crombie coats with the obligatory cardboard-backed hankie and pin. We were razor sharp. We paraded back and forth looking for some form of recognition from the Town lads. Everyone else just stood about, with the dance floor empty apart from a group of Town lasses dancing in the corner, all smartly dressed in their three-quarter length Trevira coats; that was until the sound of the current number one record filled the air. Two hundred Crombie-wearing lads massed together, arms aloft, repeating the chorus over and over again: 'Son of my Father. . .' Once started, that was it; the DJ had to play the record repeatedly, or face the consequences.

I felt privileged to be part of this scene; after all I was still only 13 and the majority of City lads in attendance were at least five years older, with a good few of them the brothers of boys in my year at school. The funny thing was, my friends and I were amongst it all and yet my peers wouldn't allow their siblings entry into the inner circle, which many of them found galling.

The best was yet to come. As we prepared to leave, we passed by a group of main faces, and one of them, Doyley, piped up to his friends, 'Out of the way lads, it's the Hessle Road infants.'

Taking the piss? Yes. Were we bothered? No! We had received a massive compliment. Our small gang had arrived. As we rocked back and forth on the back seats of the No 73 bus, we chatted excitedly, with Doyley's comments taking centre stage: 'He fucking knows us . . . he fucking knows who we are!' The self-satisfied feeling I had that night has stayed with me all this time.

The Woodcock Street area was our home, stretching from Hawthorn Avenue to St George's Road, with Westbourne,

Eastbourne and Somerset Streets in between. Here we were
kings and, as young as we were, people didn't take liberties.
Our Gypsville neighbours to the west were our closest allies
and planned away trips were often a joint exercise as a coach
or specific train journey was attended by both sets of lads.
Again these Gypsyville gang members were three to four
years older than us, but what we lacked in years we made up
for with our enthusiasm and willingness.

Weekdays were taken up with nightly visits to the local
youth club, named after the famous 1930s pilot Amy Johnson.
Here we sat and planned our movements for forthcoming
games, against the backdrop of table tennis, TV room and
draughts. Friday night was disco night; time to break out the
cider, down as much as you could, then bring it all back up,
with remnants of your last meal clogging up the toilet sink.
Happy days.

Drinking was our vice, along with a packet of ten No.10 or,
if sophisticated and flush with money, twenty Embassy. Christ,
if it wasn't for John Player coupons, some of the lads would
never have had any money for away games. Drugs weren't
thought of – to us all that crap was part of the loathed hippy
scene – until we were introduced to Lady Esquire Shoe
Conditioner, known as 'buzz'. Buzz was spread on hankies
and sniffed with much the same outcome as using a bag of
glue. A few put it onto the lapels of their Crombies and stood
in dark recesses with their noses stuck to their coats. I even
heard of a lad who put it on his pillow most nights. All the old-
fashioned cobblers began to stockpile it just for our use. A girl
who frequented the youth club started sniffing at every
opportunity and developed bad sores around her mouth; that,
coupled with the violent headaches which were common after
a sniffing session, was enough to put us all off. Our dabbling
in the 'drug scene' had lasted all of three weeks. Back to cigs
and Woodpecker.

There were other painful experiences, including one that

still hurts when I think about it. My usual Saturday routine meant that I would start to get ready around 10am. My Docs would be polished ready for action, my pewter Sta-press trousers were cleaned and pressed and all I had to decide on was what shirt to wear under my Levi denim jacket.

On this particular day, Rob, Alan and the lads came over. I picked up my money and was just about to walk out when my mother called after me, 'Shaun, come here and let's have a look at you.'

I looked at my mates, then up to the skies and tutted. My first thought was, *for fuck's sake mam, don't say ought to show me up.*

'Come here, your face is all chapped, put some Nivea Cream on.'

'I'm all right.'

I then heard the dreaded lines that we've all had to put up with at one time or another: 'Put some on or you're not going out.'

I had to give in and lather my face with the fucking cream; the whole scene was played out in front of my mates. *Typical, why couldn't we have had this argument before they'd called for me?* I stepped out of the house and expected them to rip into me and really take the piss, but all I got from Rob was a wry smile.

We made our down the street and met up with the other lads, who were stood waiting for the 73 bus to town. *Here we go, they've been waiting for a bigger audience.* But not a word. *I've got away with it.* I began to relax and thought no more of it.

As usual, we paid into the East Stand and stood among the faithful crammed into Kempton; once more we were part of the swaying masses, singing the praises of our footballing heroes while hurling abuse and vicious threats at the enemy. I didn't expect what was to happen next.

Around us stood older lads and one of these looked about and said, 'Who's wearing fucking perfume'?

'It's him, he's got Nivea on.'

I was grassed by three of my so-called mates. Now, what you have to remember is that this was 1971; Kevin Keegan and Henry Cooper hadn't even smelt Brut yet and smelling nice wasn't on, as I found out. I was dragged along the floor, punched, kicked and stomped on; all the while I could hear these lads shouting, 'He's a puff, fucking hit him.'

For a minute or so I was kicked down the terrace. I scrambled up and darted through the crowd. My mates came running to me, crying with laughter. I was glad they'd enjoyed the spectacle: *you know me I'll do ought for a laugh*. Like fuck I will.

I was hurting all over, my nose was bleeding and I had a massive graze on the side of my head where it had scraped on the floor. I looked a complete mess, yet out of all this I managed to come away with some pride; I had taken a beating from lads a lot older than myself and came out of it full of anger. I hadn't curled up and cried; instead I shown to my friends that I was made of sterner stuff – something I was to prove time and time again down the years.

★ ★ ★

By the 1970/71 season, City were riding high, crowds were witnessing the Terry Neill Revolution and the South Stand choir sang the praises of Chillo and Waggy. Our cup run that season was special. A 3-0 mauling of Charlton was followed by a 2-0 win over First Division strugglers Blackpool. The Seasiders brought a trainload of lads who bounded down the steps of the East Stand towards the City faithful but were stopped in their tracks by two Hull youths who stood partly balanced on the railings, kicking out at all and sundry. City fans mocked their Lancashire foes: if they couldn't get past two Hull lads, what chance did they have against the rest?

The fifth-round tie again gave us home advantage, with

Brentford the visitors. It was one of our hardest games of the season, with Chris Chilton bearing the brunt of some dubious challenges, yet we still came through, setting up an un-believable quarter-final draw against Stoke City, with Gordon Banks, George Eastham and Co. Even then, Stoke were renowned for trouble. I can't remember much going on before the game, but we had headed to the ground quite early, as we knew there would be over 40,000 fans crammed into Boothferry Park.

Two-nil up yet we went out 3-2, missing out on a semi-final against Arsenal (who would win the Double that year). After the match, City fans, pissed off with the result and the controversial way it had been resolved, were hell-bent on revenge. The ferocity of the fighting down Boothferry Road had to be seen to be believed, with ordinary fans as well as the skins getting their two penn'orth.

My first away game was not long after, against Sheffield United on 9 March 1971. Both teams were up for promotion and this result could make or break our season. Although I had experienced regular 25-30,000 crowds at Boothferry Park, I was still excited to be in a strange town at the age of 13, herded to the ground, eyes darting everywhere as the terraces filled. These were alien surroundings and I could feel the hair bristle as the sights and sounds of Bramall Lane washed over me. An estimated 10,000 Hull fans made the trip to the old three-sided ground. Loads of City were singing in the Shoreham, with gaps appearing every now and then as fights broke out. City won a scrappy game 2-1 but it was the occasion, not the result, that was memorable.

It became known as the Battle of Bramall Lane, and was followed by an even more eventful game at Bolton Wanderers.

MONTIE: As our promotion hopes faded towards the end of the '70-71 season, the notion that hooligans only went for the trouble was put to the test at Bolton on March 27. We had been knocked out of the FA cup in the sixth round by Stoke, another epic football day overshadowed by some sickening violence: running street battles and, in a 42,000 crowd, thousands on each side up for fighting. If this sounds like exaggerated numbers to those too young to remember those days, try to imagine no surveillance, little or no segregation, few arrests, police not clued up, and not the family atmosphere encouraged now. Then imagine how many young men were in a crowd that size and it doesn't seem so improbable, does it?

Bolton became a 'must-win', as we had won only one of our eight previous games, the Battle of Bramall Lane, another famous terrace war that received more headlines than a fabulous football victory. For the Bolton match, a football excursion train took a large part of the 1,000-plus City following. Of the 800 or so on the train, we had upwards of 200 lads. It was a damp and foggy Lancashire day and Bolton were a good team, that's why we were there, falsely thinking good away support would help lift the team.

We camped out in a large pub across the road from the ground, until it got a bit rowdy and the Old Bill turfed us out and forced us into the ground early to stand in pouring rain on an open end. Bolton's lads congregated on the car park, slapping the supporters' club types and then making a charge at our turnstiles, throwing bricks and bottles over the wall at us. I was hit with a bottle that brought a fountain of blood spurting from my wrist. As it needed stitches, the St John Ambulance led me to their place at the other end of the ground. I decided to take a short cut back across the pitch, gesturing, as you do, at their fans. Three of them came on the pitch, so I waved the Hull lads on. They swarmed on and chased Bolton back into their stand. They came back on in greater numbers and toe-to-toe fighting broke out all over the pitch. City ran them and I was arrested, missing a 0-0 draw and getting fined at court. Eight other Hull lads joined me in the cells, making a crap end to a good day out.

We headlined on *Grandstand*, made all the Sunday papers and went down in football hooligan folklore as one of the first reported pitch invasions.

We drew that day and would end up fifth, just missing promotion to the old Division One. Rarely had we come closer to the top flight.

It was around this time that our traditional end was abandoned in favour of the old Railway Stand, renamed the Kempton by the lads due to the stand being positioned in front of Kempton Road. The area was ideal for singing, as it had a low roof that gave a deep echo and was a much darker and more sinister place than the roomy South Stand. I was still too young to be involved in out-and-out violence but stood on the edges, watching and waiting for opportunities to stick the boot in, and by the early seventies these came thick and fast. I take my hat off to whoever thought about moving to this dark, unforgiving section of the ground. It meant the police were split into smaller groups, as they now had to consider implementing crowd safety measures on three fronts: controlling the away fans, the home fans and a group of nomadic skinheads who would turn up wherever the mood took them.

From this humble beginning was born the Kempton Fusiliers. Many flocked under the banner. Hull united against the common enemy, in itself a miracle of gigantic proportions, as lads from different areas traditionally hated each other. Petty squabbles were put aside when an organised firm was due to visit. In the Second Division at that time were teams like Sheffield Wednesday, Sunderland and Middlesbrough, with fanatical supporters who travelled to away games in their thousands. They always showed up at Hull and always tested the home supporters as they tried to infiltrate the Tigers' end. Incidents in and around the ground were commonplace when we entertained these teams and you had to have your wits about you before and after a game.

The lads who fought and sang as Kempton Enders came from all over but the main group were from the West Hull area, which was split between the Hessle Road, Anlaby Road, Gypsyville and Boothferry estates. The most notorious were the Monte Carlo Mob, Orchard Park Estate Boys, the Gypsyville and Boothferry Skins, East Hull Boys and the lads living around the Avenues area. Inter-gang rivalries between these different factions meant it was sometimes volatile at home games, especially if the away fans were few. But away from home everyone closed ranks and fought for the cause. The traditional leaders of the City Boys were members of the Monte Carlo Mob.

Many teams came to Boothferry Park expecting to walk straight onto our kop, just as they had back in the late sixties, when most 'offs' consisted of running the other fans and taking scarves and quite often no punches were thrown unless there was a stand-off. Now they were attacked in the street as they stepped off their train or coaches, with running battles commonplace as teams like Sunderland, Boro, Leicester and both Sheffield clubs arrived ready and willing to mix it with the local youth. It's hard to comprehend if you weren't around during this time but most of the teams mentioned would bring 5–15,000 fans to games, depending on the time of year and their league standings. Among these were a healthy abundance of bootboys, not just the small minority the establishment portrayed.

The skinhead look was now old hat and the suedehead style soon followed suit, although it was infinitely smarter than the previous 'hard' look, with the wearing of Sta-press, Crombie and all-leather brogues, and no self respecting 'lad' would be seen without his rolled up, pointed brolly, which was never used for its intended purpose and remained fastened even during downpours. By late '71 there was a discernible shift from the suedehead look to the bootboy scene. People still wore Docs but with 'skinners' – parallel jeans with wide legs and stitched-on turn-ups. Jumbo-collared shirts would soon be all the rage, rather than buttoned down, and along with the infamous football jumpers, the look was complete.

I had seen my first pair of skinner jeans when on a trip to Blackpool in October 1971, and in the summer of '72 I saw a shop selling them while on holiday in Scarborough. I couldn't wait to buy them, as I knew of no shops in Hull at the time selling them. I also went to a shop called Scene One, owned by a Scottish guy who sold one-off jumpers. I bought a football jumper from him that zipped up and came complete with collar and breast pockets, and thought I was the business. Even then, it was all about one-upmanship and going home wearing gear that nobody else had. One lad took this to the extreme. He was mad keen on Prince of Wales check, and he bought trousers, Crombie and Harrington jacket all sporting the famous design. These items were worn both separately and as a three-piece combination, which was quite dazzling: he became a danger to the public, as you couldn't see him on a zebra crossing.

My second away game was a trip to hell on 4 December 1971. This was the day I would be travelling to Sheffield to see my beloved Tigers against the Owls. If I'd known what lay in store, I wouldn't have bothered. I have never experienced anything to match how I felt at Hillsborough that day.

The previous home game, against Millwall, had seen the South Stand singing, 'If you're all going to Wednesday clap your hands.' The stand erupted as they all proclaimed as one that they'd be there. So our little mob paid on a coach, got there okay, went into the Leppings Lane, walked down the tunnel chanting at the top of our voices, and expected to see thousands of Hull massing behind the goalmouth. What we found was terracing empty except for a group of Sheffield lads, who proceeded to surround our shell-shocked crew. Half-time came and we were looking round for help but no one noticed our predicament, or nobody cared. The Sheffield boys allowed us to walk back down the tunnel. Maybe they weren't so bad after all.

They were.

They were far more clued up than us and only let us through so they could do the damage without any witnesses. We were systematically picked off one by one. Three were followed into the toilets and smashed to bits, while a couple more scared witless at the refreshment bar had to buy the aggressors a meat pie before getting slapped. The rest of our group fought with each other as we dived over the turnstile to the safety of the street.

It was frightening. Still, myself and a kid called Kev tried to no avail to get back into the ground to watch the second half. We had to wait until they opened the gates and went in Wednesday's end, just for a look. It was very impressive. The whole trip was an eye-opener, the first time things had not gone to plan on the violence front. And it hadn't ended yet.

We had to run the gauntlet to get back to our coach, which was near a park and some public toilets. Some of the lads were already on the coach but by the time I arrived it was surrounded, with Sheffield lads banging on the windows, baying for blood. I had to think fast and decided the best tactic was to join them, and banged on the window for all I was worth, hurling abuse at the petrified prisoners inside. I slowly made my way to the door and then screamed to be let on. Luckily I managed to get on with only a few punches thrown at my head. I was frightened of being dragged back and taking a kicking, but I'd made it. Then a brick came through the side window. We all bobbed down, expecting more, but this signalled the end of our siege, with the police coming to our aid. We had a cold journey home, but were just glad to be back in one piece. It taught us that you didn't mess about at Wednesday, or if you did, you had better go with plenty of game lads.

The same season, we had another pretty good cup run. We

beat Norwich in the third round and had a good turnout of lads at Carrow Road: lots of coaches and two trains full meant there was little or no resistance as we took The Barkley and basically took the mickey all day. We were then matched against Coventry City, who had recently signed Chris Chilton, one of our heroes, so it became a bit of a grudge match. City's reputation must have been spreading, as the police there were arresting anyone who stepped out of line. They took the laces off lads wearing Doc Martens and even made some stand in the ground in stockinged feet, reasoning that you were not going to kick out if your boots would go flying or you had no boots at all. It made no difference; there was still a lot of crowd trouble in the packed stand behind the goal, with Hull lads making huge inroads into the Coventry section and picking off the home fans all match.

The return game against Sheffield Wednesday saw hordes of their fans arriving by train and they wrought havoc around the town centre, fighting with Hull lads all the way to the ground. Reports started to reach the home fans that some Owls had turned over a Mini with a young girl driver inside. This incident and the liberties the Sheffield lads took before the game incensed the Hull fans, and they made plans to leave early and mob up outside to attack the visitors as they trekked back to the station.

Inside the ground, our gang was stood on the edge of Kempton. Unbeknown to us, in front were several Wednesday fans all well into their twenties. Les P, nicknamed 'Kono' (he looked like the detective off *Hawaii Five-O*), was directly behind one of these infiltrators and, as they raised their arms and began shouting 'Wednesday', no one prompted him: he instinctively lashed out, catching the unsuspecting Owls fan with a karate chop to the back of his neck. The bloke's legs buckled and, as the crowd pushed down onto them, they broke ranks and ran for cover. We were helpless with laughter. Les stood there with a daft smile on his face; a fourteen-year-old lad had managed to instil panic in five grown men with a Kono chop.

The game over, Boothferry Road was awash with Hull lads. We now began to overturn the results the Sheffield youths had achieved two hours earlier and ran them all the way back to the town centre, with many being picked off and done over. During one clash a teenage Sheffield youth was thrown through a shop window and rumours soon got round that he had a punctured lung. By the time all the City crew had reached town, they were satisfied they had got a result.

But the Hull lads hadn't finished for the day. They mobbed up, ran through the town and began to smash store windows and rampage through shops, kicking in display units. This was a totally new experience for me, though over the next few years events like this became the norm. It wasn't long before I felt like a seasoned veteran. I have been involved against Sheff Wed on a number of occasions, but Hull really took it to the extremes after that game, and I bet a lot of Owls had second thoughts about venturing into Hull again.

After the mini riot, a few mates and I were walking past Willis Ludlow's store and noticed a couple of police coming towards us. We had run them ragged all day, so they didn't take too kindly my piss-taking question, 'Have you got the right time?' With a solid punch to the stomach, I was lifted off my feet and left in a crumpled heap, without the copper even missing a stride. I learned a painful lesson that day: don't gob off to the police, as there's only going to be one winner.

★ ★ ★

By 1972, the Monte Carlo Café had closed down and the skin/suedehead look had been replaced by the bootboy fashion. The closure of the Monte Carlo meant the meeting place for younger members of the gangs changed to local youth clubs, with the Albermarle YC taking over the mantle as the most prominent. These clubs became fervent recruiting grounds for newcomers to the football scene, and the one I went to was part of this culture.

The youth clubs gave us somewhere to hang out, away from street corners and the inevitable attentions of the local police. Gangs of youths were constantly being moved on their way by officers with nothing better to do. A friend of mine was actually done for loitering outside a chippy while he waited for his mates to be served; this was the seventies version of zero tolerance, Hessle Road style. We were stopped on a daily basis: 'Where've you been? What are you doing?' You began to answer automatically. The less lip you gave, the sooner you'd be on your way.

The champion of this was a certain PC Nesbitt. It seemed he'd made it a personal crusade to rid the world of the gang culture in our area. He had the knack of turning up at the right time (or wrong depending on who you were), patrolling the city centre, Hessle Road and most of the troublesome estates. Somebody once commented, 'How many Nesbitts are there, he's everywhere, are they using cardboard cut-outs?' He was the thorn in the side of all City supporters, so much so that they even sang about him. No need for video evidence, riot gear, batons and gas in 1972, just send for Nesbitt.

I wonder were he is now, probably shaking his head, tutting with disgust as newspaper reports tell of arson attacks, burnt-out cars, smackhead thieves burgling homes and youths attacking an innocent couple returning from a New Year's Eve party. Where are the police when all this is going on (within a mile radius of Boothferry Park)? Over-worked and under-staffed is the cry, but come Saturday you'll find vanloads of them trying to do the job that one man seemed to do 30 years earlier. That's progress for you.

While younger members frequented Albermarle, those with money in their pockets started drinking in The Broadway (now the Shire Horse) and the Star and Garter, a scruffy little back street hostelry. These pubs, and others such as Punch, became the meeting points for the older members of the crew, as all gave easy access to any away fans arriving in the town centre. Such clashes with away fans, however, were few, with most action still taking place around the ground, while inside the focus was still on taking the opponents' end, not their town centre.

For me, one season stands out: 1972. Our numbers were massive, over 1,000 for key games. Kempton would be overflowing with bootboys, chanting and fighting, and the streets around saw scenes of violence on a scale never to be repeated.

The season began with much promise. At 14 years old, I at last got involved at the front end of an off, at a match which had nothing to do with my team: York City versus Grimsby Town in August 1972. The York lads had associations with some Hull scooter boys and had asked for assistance, so it was agreed that we would turn out, and word spread that an away day had been arranged.

Some Hull lads went over on the Friday night. Some dossed where they could while the lucky ones had arranged to stay with their York hosts. The main group arrived by train on the morning of the match. We were told to meet at the Golden Fleece public house, where we congregated before making our way through the town centre, then on to the ground. Much to our annoyance, I and a dozen mates were ordered out of the pub by the landlord for being underage. We had to put up with the pisstaking of the older lads as they sent over some crisps and a bottle of lemonade.

By the time we were ready to move, the mob had reached over 300, with upwards of 200 from Hull. On the way to the ground, the group played cat and mouse with the local police as they tried to control our movements. The mob split up into smaller groups and got up to all kinds of mischief, smashing windows, running through crowds of shoppers, all the usual antics of football thugs at that time. We mobbed up again behind the Pop Stand and most sat and awaited the arrival of the Grimsby coaches. It wasn't long before we could hear the distant chanting of fans heading our way. Everyone stood waiting for the signal, then the shout went up and we steamed round the corner straight into a mob of Grimsby fans. The ensuing violence was short-lived, as the pressing numbers still coming round the corner forced the away fans to retreat against overwhelming odds. One-nil to us.

The next step was to get in the ground, take up a stance on the terraces and hopefully continue the ruck inside. Small pockets of Grimsby fans were dealt with as we searched them out, with one lad getting a severe beating by the toilets (in the wrong place at the wrong time). This was the first ambulance case I had witnessed at close quarters and I was relieved it wasn't me on the end of the beating. Our attention then focused on the Grimsby fans stood behind the other goal. As the fencing was only a painted picket fence, we soon made our way onto the pitch and ran at the Grimsby end. They responded and the police had two factions trying to kill each other as they battled to restore order. The police baton-charged both sets of fans and sent in the dogs. Panic set in as we all scrambled back over the fencing to the safety of the terraces. A mate, Johnny Hutch, screamed in pain; he had misjudged the height and landed squarely in the middle of the small fence. He was dragged into the crowd and away from the grasping arms of the chasing police. The next step taken by the police defused the situation completely: they rounded up as many of our lads as they could (myself included) and marched about 200 of us straight out of the ground. The known York lads with us were sent one way while the rest of us were escorted straight to the train station and home. We were actually on our way before half-time.

The next week, we were at home to Nottingham Forest, who had just been relegated. They brought hundreds of lads.

Our little group bumped into a mob of them straight away as we turned the corner of Wheeler Street onto Anlaby Road. We ran back down the street in panic, as we knew we were no match for them. There was no point in us hanging around near the ground, so we walked up towards the flyover and sat waiting in the August sunshine for the lads from town to arrive. Before long, Hull fans were visible on the horizon. The massed ranks of City boys meandered down the western slope of the flyover, resplendent in their short-sleeved shirts, jeans and boots, and soon were over the crest and walking towards us. We couldn't wait to give them the information.

'We've seen em!'

'Forest, they're here on the car park!'

We repeated this to whoever was willing to listen, adding bits on each time. By the end, we'd had a go with them, been chased up and down Anlaby Road, but 'couldn't do nowt cos there were too many for us.' Pathetic, I know, but we didn't want to admit bottling it.

The lads at the front congregated outside the Silver Cod pub near the ground, waiting for the stragglers to catch up before moving on towards the car park. Cod was not the football pub it is now; its clientele were more likely to be middle-aged rugby fans, hard-drinking types who wouldn't stand any crap from teenage hooligans. It would be another six years before the pub would be used as a base.

Forest were sat on the old gravel car park waiting for the turnstiles to open, and were taken by surprise as City poured round the corner, their shouts echoing off the walls as they came from under the bridge. This was perfect, no police. City ran straight onto the car park, creating dustballs as their pounding boots skidded on the hot, dry surface. A brawl-cum-brick fight ensued. 'Welcome to Division Two, you Forest bastards.'

Some Forest fans were trapped in the corner at the entrance to Boothferry Halt. The rest quickly retreated towards North

Road to escape the bombardment of bricks, concrete and gravel. Police reinforcements arrived and pushed us back under the bridge, allowing the Forest fans to return and reclaim their original position on the brick-strewn forecourt.

Fans were now beginning to arrive by train from Paragon Station, all of them City. Recognising they could have trouble on two fronts, the police managed to force the reluctant Forest boys into the ground, where they stood, watching and waiting, on the East Stand terracing overlooking the car park. Job done, the police left the area, back to their cups of tea and biscuits, thinking they wouldn't be needed now for two hours (football intelligence, circa 1971).

The City mob feigned to go to the home end and passed by the watching Forest fans, who must have been impressed with the numbers filing by. By now trains full of supporters were arriving every fifteen minutes, and the Forest fans moved away from their vantage point and further into the ground so they could abuse the incoming Tigers supporters queuing on the train platform. Forest had played right into our hands: we could now pay into the North Stand, wait till everyone was inside, then charge up the slope and take over the Kempton. If Forest had stayed overlooking the car park, the same trick would have been impossible, as any Hull seen paying to get into the away end would have come unstuck inside.

The Forest fans were now deep inside the Kempton, jeering at the home fans arriving at Boothferry Park Halt and those already positioned on the South Stand. There were few or no police near us, just a few old stewards. Suddenly the City chants resounded under the North Stand and we ran straight up the terracing into Kempton. Forest did not even fight, which was great for us younger ones. Some scrambled into South Stand whilst the rest occupied the open terracing between.

Afterwards bedlam ensued around the ground. The away fans had to walk up to Fiveways to their coaches and vans.

Hundreds of Hull lads had reached them also, nipping down the side streets of Gypsyville Estate and up Askew Avenue. This was now a full-blown police operation, with dogs and horses trying to control both sets of supporters. We were everywhere, mobs of lads lobbing bricks and glass from old allotments that looked onto Pickering Road and the parked coaches. Others, myself included, were running through Costello playing fields hoping to ambush the coaches further down Boothferry Road, but instead had to shake off the attentions of a couple of dog handlers, while the canny Gypsyville lads had taken their time, gathered as many bricks as they could carry and entered the eastern section of the park via Lakeside Grove; no police to worry about, just straight up to the fence and let rip. The popping of coach windows was seen as fair game. You knew the compliment would be reciprocated at their place, and the more you put through, the better the result.

The next two home games brought differing numbers of away fans to Boothferry Park. Bristol City arrived with a small but very game bunch, and Burnley came over the Pennines with a big following, many on special trains. Bristol had two options, stay together under the North Stand or enter East Stand and feel the wrath of the Kempton Mental-men. They chose the latter and managed to repel the inevitable onslaught well into the second half. This coachload of lads solidly stood their ground. The funny thing was, they'd managed to evade detection until the game had started; surprising, you might think, considering they were wearing red and white scarves, but it wasn't unusual to see Hull lads wearing them also: a group of Hull lads calling themselves 'the Disco Mob' often wore these to games, as they were a mixture of Man United and Hull Kingston Rovers supporters (both red and white).

Among us this day stood a lad called Steve Perrins; not the brightest spark around, but very handy with his fists. We had sussed they were Bristol City fans, but he wasn't having any of it.

'Are they fuck Bristol, it's Disco Mob.'

'Steve, it's Bristol.'

'You lot know fuck all. I'm off down there to stand with Disco Mob.'

He made his way through the crowd and moved amongst the alleged Disco lads. Punches flew at him and he was soon wading head-down back towards safety and us.

'THEY'RE FUCKING BRISTOL' he shouted, his face red and swollen from West Country fists.

'Yes, we know, Steve!'

The Burnley visit saw more trouble. Rob, Alan, Les and I sat on Silver Cod wall before the game. We could see a large mob approaching, walking from town. It was difficult to pick out who they were.

'It's City.'

'No, it's Burnley.'

Many of the lads we could see were wearing 'football jumpers'. The most popular style for these was claret and blue, which happened to also be the colours of West Ham, Aston Villa, and the team we were playing that day. We still presumed they were Hull lads, but as they got closer realised they were Burnley fans. They were less than 200 yards away when we decided it would be prudent to beat a retreat, running back towards the roundabout and down Meadowbank Road, where we hid looking out from a ten-foot. A lot of their lads were "grebos" or greasers, rocker types with long hair and leather jackets. It must have been the fashion for the provincial Lancashire teams, as Blackburn were the same.

As we waited for the Burnley to pass the top of the street, a car pulled up and five Hull lads got out. Among them was one of City's top boys, Fez. He asked what we were doing and we told him. He replied, 'Fuck 'em, you four come with us.' I was terrified, yet more frightened of what Fez would do if we didn't follow him. We proceeded to walk right through the Burnley, hurling abuse such as, 'Get some soap and water, you scruffy cunts.' A few punches were thrown and some lads outside Three Tuns witnessed it and came over to back us up. The Burnley fans didn't want to know. I couldn't believe it, but I still wished I had been across the road observing rather than stuck in the middle of it all. There were loads of them, yet they did nothing. It was the first time I had witnessed a smaller group being able to intimidate much larger numbers purely by having the balls to do so.

After the match, quite a few Hull made their way to the town centre, as they now knew Burnley had come on train. Another first for me as, to give Burnley their due, when City ran into the station, they came charging to meet them and backed City out and onto the street. I wasn't particularly proud of running, but if the lot of you are on the back foot, it's a collective thing. All you can do is make amends the next time.

CHAPTER THREE

Golden Bootboys

THE DANGER OF our early encounters meant little to us young lads; it probably didn't occur to us that people could get seriously hurt. Yet, of course, they could, and did. While the use of weapons was relatively rare in those days, anything could happen in the anarchy of a mass brawl.

One of those who discovered this to his cost was a rising young terrace terror, H from the Orchard Park Estate. This sprawling housing area was built in the sixties to accommodate the demolished sections of the inner city, and many of the people that moved there were from Hessle Road. It was a land of high-rise flats, pebble-dashed walls and dark and dangerous underpasses, with slogans spray-painted on the walls like 'Doc's Red Army', 'A Clockwork Orange' and 'City Psychos'. Violence was commonplace, and Sunday nights at the Voodoo disco were legendary – it was for under-18s only, but some of the cider-fuelled brawls could turn really nasty. Like myself, H became attracted to the hooligan scene while still at school – and it almost cost him his life.

H of OPE: I had never really bothered with going to football until I left school in 1970, but as soon as I started earning I was off up town checking out all the clothes shops: Arthur Masons, PR Davis and Royce. On one of these Saturday jaunts, I decided to go to Boothferry Park with a few mates. Before long, we were going to City every home game. We already knew a lot of the City lads from school and our skinhead gang from Orchard Park had a good reputation in the town. The team was doing well and the atmosphere was electric. Round that off with a bit of seventies-style aggro and you had the lot.

Trouble came thick and fast in those days, and you always had to watch out for weapons. It was common to see people using various types of weaponry at games and during inter-gang fights around the estates. I've seen many used in street battles and finished up on the wrong end of a knife myself. One lad used to carry a docker's hook, while others favoured the old cutthroat; this was useful at close quarters, as a poor Sunderland fan found out during a pitched battle near Paragon Station. An FA Cup game away at Stoke saw hundreds of us running amok as we got off the three special trains; a Stoke fan was hit in the back by a Hull lad with a hatchet as we hurtled through the station. These were violent times indeed and the sentences handed out didn't always match the ferocity of the crime, as I found out only to well.

City had arranged a pre-season friendly at Scarborough and it seemed a good idea for a day out. Many others thought the same and the train leaving Paragon Station was packed with lads. We aimed straight for the seafront and caused chaos amongst the weekend daytrippers, brawling outside the amusement arcades with anyone not associated with us. It was obvious who we were and why we were there and word must have spread among the locals, as the terracing was full of lads ready for trouble. This was fine by us and the lack of police inside the stadium added to the attraction. Fights started, and I was in the thick of the action.

I turned round after feeling what I thought was a punch and saw a young lad stood there with a big bread knife.

'I've been stabbed, I've been fucking stabbed.'

Bri and Gordon, the nearest lads next to me, held me up and steadied me in case I fell forward. Mad George came over and Gordon let go and went berserk: he flattened the kid with the knife and went for anyone else stood there gaping at us. It was quite surreal, everyone stood open-mouthed, not knowing what to do until George broke the silence, screaming at them to get out of the way as they carried me towards the turnstile, which they dragged me over.

We were now in the street. Blood was gushing from the wound and I kept thinking I was going to die. One of the lads tried flagging cars down and, luckily for me, one stopped. I never did find out the driver's name nor got the chance to thank him but it was his quick thinking and knowledge of the area that saved me. He drove like a man possessed, mounting kerbs and taking shortcuts down side streets and back alleys, and reached the local hospital with me in the back, semi-conscious. I was too far gone to appreciate the seriousness of the injury. They were going to airlift me back to Hull but the decision was changed, as they felt I was too weak, and I was operated on at Scarborough. I'd lost four pints of blood by the time I reached the hospital. Thank fuck the lads reacted as quick as they did, and I'll be eternally grateful to the bloke who stopped to help.

The incident made the back pages of the national Sundays. They described the events and the fact that 50-odd fans were ejected or arrested. I spent two weeks at Scarborough before transferring back to Hull. A couple of days later I was asked to do an interview by one of the papers that had picked up the story, but I didn't want to know, it was still too soon after the operation. It was hard enough trying to contemplate that I nearly died without having to answer idiotic questions from some reporter from London.

You may wonder what happened to the youth with the knife, well the police found him, shall we say 'a bit worse for wear', laid out cold on the hot concrete terracing. True to form, the courts imposed a massive six months sentence; six months. . . the twat nearly killed me.

Funny thing was, because I had been stabbed, my reputation increased, whether I wanted it to or not. I also started to get more attention from the local bobbies. To them I was just a trouble causer. Mind you, the police took a fair bit of stick at that time. We were always causing trouble either at home on the estate or out and about with City.

Kempton wasn't the favourite haunt of the boys in blue either: they were wary of entering unless they were in large numbers. Mounted police had to be used inside the ground on more then one occasion when things started getting ugly. One game, the police were present at the bottom of the stand. Someone had a score to settle and now was the perfect time to do it. The old tune went up, 'Oh we all go marching down, marching down together.' This was the signal for the lads to pile down the steps. The Old Bill at the bottom were bowled over, smacked, stomped and ripped. If I remember correctly, eight of them were put on sick. They gave us plenty of stick week, in week out, and now it was our turn.

Attending away games often meant hitchhiking; we didn't always have the money for travel so this was the next best thing. We often turned up in towns with rolled up sleeping bags (doss bags) that would be deposited in the British Rail left luggage office before we ventured any further. Games like these often took all weekend. We normally set off Friday night and returned sometime Sunday, often dishevelled, wet and hungry but you'd always had a good laugh.

Weekend dossings to places like Bridlington or Scarborough were always popular in the summer and often ended in violence. A concert by Slade at 'Brid' Spa provided us with more then a singalong session with the group. The violence inflicted on members of the audience was as vicious as anything I've witnessed before or since. Our gang of lads had got an early Saturday train in, and wandered up and down the seafront, checking out the most likely places to sleep. The favourite spot was deemed to be the old Victorian glass shelters, which ran at intervals along the front. Satisfied our sleeping arrangements were sorted, we deposited our doss bags in the back of a mate's car.

We enjoyed ourselves at the many watering holes around the old harbour area before leaving for the concert. Our group were the first to arrive and set up camp at the top of the stairs and waited for the doors to open. All the time more and more fans arrived, and our small bunch from Hull were calling the shots. We began chanting City songs and pushed down on the people stood below. Insults were exchanged but no punches were thrown. Not yet.

Inside we positioned ourselves next to the bar entrance, this was ideal as we could see the ever growing numbers of locals and Leeds lads massing together. We knew what was coming. It was a pity they didn't. Our small group of ten was looked at in disdain. A small gap on the dance floor separated both sets of lads and we could see them trying to egg themselves on. A scuffle broke out to the left of us and this was the signal for the rest of them to come bounding over, boots and fists flying. It was all we could do to drive them back. We ran into the bar area and began throwing glasses at the doorway. This stopped them doing any further damage. We knew there were two coaches of Hull lads on the way; we just hoped they'd get here soon. I think the locals were still wary of entering the bar. So would I have been. They were happy to wait outside; after all we couldn't stay in their all night.

The two coachloads arrived and caused uproar in the hall. As our reinforcements started pushing the Brid youths back, a skinhead bird from Albermarle ran in and pushed a glass into a lad's face after she'd seen him knock down her boyfriend, P**** Mc. Lads were running into each other from all sides, pint glasses flew through the air and people were being dragged backwards and forwards. Some were struggling violently so as not to end up amidst the wrong set of lads. To end up on the floor among strangers wasn't the place to find yourself, not if you wanted to stay conscious.

A local youth came forward waving a flick knife. I made sure I was well out of reach, as did everyone else. Stalemate was broken when a Hull boy ran in and hit him with a chair and once again all hell broke loose. The dance floor by now was awash with beer and blood, the bar was wrecked and the concert hadn't even started. Chas Chandler, Slade's manager, appealed for calm and things began to get quieter but this had more to do with the police dog handlers positioned around the inside of the hall then anything Chas could say.

The concert itself was fairly entertaining, with Noddy Holder in fine voice. Both factions kept well away from each other but those of us dossing out for the night couldn't relax; we knew the only way to avoid getting turned over was to leave early and keep out of sight. As the band went offstage before returning for an encore, we began to leave separately so as not to be noticed. The rest of the night was spent hidden from view, laid out on the floor of the shelter talking in whispers. The last thing we wanted was to draw attention to ourselves, not with marauding locals after our blood.

My trips to Boothferry Park became fewer and fewer. I was now earning more money and began to travel the country watching Man Utd. They were my boyhood favourites and after my first visit to Old Trafford I was hooked. The team were really struggling on the field but the violence off it was something else. This was a real eye-opener and once sampled it was hard to imagine doing anything else. Our estate had quite a reputation amongst other United fans; all the lads had heard of the Hull Reds and in some ways it increased the rep of the city itself. It did, mind you, create problems back home in Hull, with many of the City lads seeing us as traitors. I didn't see it like that. I was still fiercely proud of Hull and Hull City but I chose not to go, or at least not as often.

By 1973, I'd had plenty of practice fighting for United. The Hull Reds had led a charge into the North Bank at Highbury and from this we started meeting up with the Salford boys and the Cockney Reds, especially the Peckham crew. It felt good knowing that lads from both these firms used to wait for our train before

moving on. As I said before, it was good for us and good for
Hull.

* * *

Bootboys were the new order and this terrace look stayed with
us in some way or other right up to the start of the eighties.
Skinners flapped around the legs of the new terrace terrors
and 'Ruperts' were also as popular with the Doc Marten
brigade. Although some of us kept our hair at suedehead
length or a little longer, many of the lads aped David Bowie's
Aladdin Sane look, with long hair cut shaggy down the back
and spikey on top. I think this was prevalent in Hull for the
reason that Bowie's backing group, The Spiders from Mars,
were from the city. It was also the early part of the glitter
scene, and some of the lads had got some really smart made-
to-measure shirts from Glasgow that were totally different to
anything being worn at the time, Ben Shermans still being
popular with the masses.

The boys who wore these new shirts were the real in-
crowd, and I managed to get hold of one, secondhand but that
didn't matter to me. An indication of how sad I was at the
time was that it had the previous owner's initials, 'K.P',
monogrammed on a pocket and all the lads used to take the
piss: 'Are you into fucking nuts?' and so on. But it was an
Arthur Black, it was mine, and that's all that mattered. People
used to ask, 'Have you got five of them fuckers?' as I never
had it off my back.

During a trip to Blackpool, I also decided to get my ear
pierced. I came out of the jewellers with one gold sleeper in
my ear and the other in my pocket, complete with an ear that
now looked like a swollen Quaver. That was the least of my
worries. Although I thought I was grown up (14), my father
wasn't what you'd called 'up with the times'. He seemed as
though he was from a distant age and probably missed out

adolescence and moved straight onto adulthood. I knew he'd object.

I entered the house sheepishly, not wanting to draw attention to myself, and sat down waiting for the inevitable onslaught. I didn't have to wait long.

'Are we gypsies?'

'No.'

'Are we pirates?'

'No.'

'THEN TAKE THAT FUCKING EARRING OUT.'

That was my first fashion disaster. Looking back, I had many others. Sometimes I was so eager to get an item before anyone else that I just had to come home with something, and often bought stuff I would wear once and then hate. Among these items was a half-length leather coat bought from Northerns. I wanted a three-quarter one but there was none in stock, so I took home what they had. It cost £70, a lot of money to waste in the mid-seventies.

That same year I had seen a three-quarter length denim coat with a fur collar in my mother's catalogue; it was sort of Huggy Bear/New York pimp style and I remember walking into the local Hawthorn pub, where the lads hung out, thinking I looked a million dollars. Everyone stopped what they were doing and fell about. I was gutted. I turned round, went home and flung it at my mother, saying, 'Fucking send it back.'

In 1973 we regularly hit the national headlines, with write-ups galore in all the major papers. Hooliganism was beginning to reach a new level in Hull. The old-school skins were now in their early twenties and City had upwards of 1,000 lads. The Kempton Enders were a force to be reckoned with, not many tried to 'tip-toe through the Kempton' and trouble was beginning to move away from the terraces as firms began to target town centres as well as the areas around the football grounds.

MONTIE: And so it continued throughout the seventies, big games, not so big crowds and better and better policing of matches. Every time we played a club from West Yorkshire or Lancashire, the local paper ran a report on the arrests on the Monday night. Custodial sentences started to be given out for the most trivial of offences, and this put a lid on some of the spontaneous trouble. You had people thinking, *Now, do I want to spend three months in North Sea Camp?*

By early 1973 football hooliganism peaked in Hull. We drew Stockport away in the FA cup third round. Influenced by glam rock and the film *A Clockwork Orange*, City fans turned out in their hundreds dressed as butchers in long white coats and with Doc Martens sprayed silver. We ran riot in Stockport, dancing on car bonnets, smashing shop windows and terrorising the locals. Greater Manchester Police had never seen anything like it. City fought with the police inside the ground while Stockport fans took cover. It was mayhem, absolute mayhem.

The Stockport game is one of perhaps half a dozen matches that have gone down in folk legend among the followers of Hull City, and perfectly encapsulates the mindset of the early-seventies hooligan. We wanted to be different. We wanted to shock, as well as frighten, our opponents. Some lads were seen at games wearing bandages, bandana-style, emblazoned with the term 'MAD' copied from the popular American magazine of the same name. New names appeared such as Kempton Axemen and Kempton Mentalmen. But none of these ideas took a mass hold.

Then a few lads bought some glitter, spray-painted their Docs silver or gold, and soon everyone looked like roadies at a Sweet concert. The look was finished off with silkscarves tied to their heads, Indian-style, and a few even went to the extremes of painting their faces, inspired I suppose by Stanley Kubrick.

This hybrid of the bootboy was unleashed on an

unsuspecting public at Stockport County. The word had spread that a heavy turnout was required, as Man Utd could be out looking for revenge for events at the Watney Cup clash three years before. On the day they were too busy dealing with Wolverhampton Wanderers, but still fifteen coachloads and two special trains arrived in Stockport, spilling these Golden Bootboys onto the streets. Eight hundred lads travelled over the Pennines that day; not 100 lads and 700 thermos flask carriers, but 800 painted, screaming bootboys, and the familiar sounds of smashing glass and police sirens were heard all round the area adjacent to the ground.

For eight hours Stockport would reel from an onslaught of violence that at times the police were powerless to prevent. The locals must have wondered, why them? It wasn't personal; it was one of those days when everything seemed to fall into place. We had the right setting, people intent on causing trouble, all the main faces there as well as lads from just about every area of Hull. It was like the gathering of the clans.

Among them was H of the Orchard Park Estate Mob. He usually followed the Red Devils but this day had decided to go with his Hull mates.

H of OPE: Although I had experienced life in the First Division running with some of the most feared group of lads ever assembled, nothing prepared me for what I witnessed at Stockport County.

I had the option of special train or coach. I knew plenty of lads travelling on both but decided on the coach, as it was setting off earlier. We arrived just after 11am and the area around the ground was already crawling with Hull lads. It felt strange for me at first, I seemed to be watching events from the outside. I was there but not really part of the scene.

On the way down, lads on the coach were handing round cans of paint and spraying their Docs either silver or gold. 'What the fuck's this all about?' Other lads were tying their silk scarves around their heads and applying glitter and gold stars to their faces. Trust me to pick the wrong bus, I thought. But I hadn't. This bus was no different from every other one that unloaded hundreds of City youths all togged up the same. The pubs were full of these Golden Bootboys singing the praises of the team and raising the roof with a rendition of 'The Kempton Fusiliers':

Eyes right, foreskin tight
Arses to the front (bum,bum)
We are the boys, who make no noise,
We're always after cunt,
We're the heroes of the night
And we'd rather fuck then fight
We're the heroes of the
Kempton Fusiliers

The atmosphere was electric, and aided by a few pints I began to feel at ease. It seemed as though Stockport had been taken over by Hull City and as we left the pub, I realised it had.

My own group was no different. We booked a coach through a local company and set off on the day of the match at 7am. We arrived well before pub opening time, so everyone had a wander round the town centre. Some of the lads on our coach ended up outside a local museum/art gallery and brightened up the place by spraying the walls and paintings with modern art, Hull style – 'HCFC OK' – before doing a runner.

Fans were seen arriving as early as 10.30, ready for the pubs to open. Many public houses and off licences did a roaring trade as they met the demands of the thirsty visitors. We managed to sit ourselves in a pub just up the road from the ground. Still only 15, I left it to the older lads to stand by the bar and fetch over the drinks. One young fan (aged 13) who was asked his age by the pissed-off landlord, turned, looked him in the eye and proclaimed at the top of his voice, 'See, I told you I shouldn't have shaved my beard off.'

Some Stockport lads entered the pub, realised we were Hull and made for the door. One of them didn't make it and was dragged back into the bar, were he stood waiting for the onslaught of fists and boots. Instead he was made to sit under the dartboard while a game of darts began. Only a few darts were thrown at the board before one of the players told him not to worry, he could go. His face had been a picture.

Out in the streets, things had gone haywire.

H of OPE: Hordes of City fans were running amok. I could see lads jumping up and down on the top of cars, both parked and ones being driven. Others were fighting with police and chasing any Stockport fans they could find. They were hunting the poor bastards down in packs. You'd turn a corner and meet up with different mobs of City fans. It was very intimidating.

The police took the main brunt of all this aggression inside the ground, they were now literally brawling with the Hull bootboys. I had to keep reminding myself this was Hull City. Mob rule had taken over the terraces. I'd witnessed many things but nothing as severe and anarchic as this.

After a goalless draw, the crowds emptied onto the streets of Stockport. This time I was in the thick of it. Running across wasteland with a brick in my hand one minute, the next I'm being led away with my arm up my back. I didn't see him till it was too late; the copper stepped out from the shadows of a shop doorway. I was gutted. Mind you, I think he was relieved, as nicking me got him away from the full-scale riot going on around us.

I had to appear at Stockport Assizes and came away with a small fine. A reporter from the *Daily Mail* turned up and took us all in a pub and interviewed us. It was big news at the time; nobody had heard or seen anything like it on that scale before.

Even the Manchester Evening News called us barbaric. This was a year and a half before United's Red Army really hit the headlines.

Inside the ground, the police had penned the City fans into a section of the side stand. This prevented any further clashes with the home fans but meant the police now took the brunt of the Hull fans' displeasure. During the game, a procession of Hull fans were constantly being escorted out of the ground to be ejected or arrested.

After the game, large gangs of Hull lads roamed round looking for trouble. Our coach had four missing, all arrested, so after finding out that they wouldn't be bailed till late in the evening, we set off home. Our driver, who by this time was well upset, warned us that any further trouble encountered on the way home would result in all of us being dropped off at the nearest police station, so we settled down for the drive back to Hull.

It was agreed that we would have a toilet stop in Barnsley bus station, where we got off to stretch our legs. A small group got involved in an argument with some Barnsley lads, who were chased off only to come back with reinforcements and bricks. The ensuing deluge forced us back towards the waiting coach. The driver set off sharpish but not quickly enough, as two side windows were put through. The coach rounded a corner, where the driver stopped and said, 'Right, you've got twenty minutes to get the bastards.' So we all piled off, some armed with bricks, and steamed round the corner into the locals. They were so surprised that we had them on their toes straight away. The perfect end to an extraordinary day.

This was one newspaper's report of the aftermath:

Wearing boots painted with gold and silver, with gold stars and sequins stuck to their faces, some Hull City supporters brought chaos to Stockport last Saturday, a court was told today.

There were 15 coachloads of them and special trains.

Insp. Michael Miskell said: 'The majority of these people were young men who were obviously not here simply to watch the game but were bent on trouble.' He told the court today that chaos broke out from the time the pubs opened and there was trouble all over the town.

Det. Insp. Kenneth Etchells said he got behind a group of Hull supporters who were identifiable because in addition to scarves, they wore gold painted boots, gloves and clothes.

'We have never seen anything like it,' said another officer. Some fans had streaks of red paint on their cheeks and wore their amber and black scarves tied around their heads, Red Indian fashion. I had been to many City games, and in the mid-seventies started going to Man Utd as well, when the Red Army was at its headline-grabbing peak, but the violence and destruction at Stockport was on a rare scale. Everybody seemed to be of the same mind, running mental, and that feeling would last throughout the season.

The next home match was West Ham, who brought three football special trains. The police had to be on their toes for this one, and were, as all the West Ham specials dropped their passengers off at Boothferry Halt, minimising the risk of pre-match trouble. The West Ham fans, starved of 'aggro' before the game, turned their attentions to the Hull fans in South Stand and made their way towards the no-man's land section, just standing off from the fence separating both sides. It was obvious to us what was going to happen next, and sure enough the Cockneys ran at the fence. I thought City would bottle it, but they didn't. A kid called Chris Johnson, only a year older than me, ran at the fence and knocked a Hammer down. A lot of City did the same, and after a while West Ham gave up and went back into their end. The amazing thing was, most of our main lads were not even in the ground and we'd still done all right.

H of OPE: Hull was really buzzing after the Stockport game, especially as West Ham were the next visitors to Boothferry Park. None of our lot would miss this. We all met up in Sandringham at 10.30 on the morning of the match. We sat and waited for their special trains to arrive but the police had the town centre sewn up. The Londoners were redirected straight to the ground, so that's where we went to meet them. Fifteen of us paid into Kempton and stood with the Hammers fans; at first we began talking to a few of them. We discussed fights with other teams and before long Man U were mentioned. Someone said, 'Fucking Man U's here now' and whacked this Cockney across the mouth. Well it all kicked off then. We were fighting for our lives, and they were straining to get at us. We backed off and split up, melting into the crowd to re-emerge at the corner of the North Stand.

Just before full-time, about 30 or 40 of us lined up outside the exit for Kempton. We had some right good lads, all ready for an off. The departing Londoners sussed us straight away and made a beeline for our group. The few police around were otherwise occupied and both sets of lads made full use of the opportunity to mix it. We ran at them and met them full pelt, bodies charged into each other, shouts of encouragement came from both sides as the boots and fists flew. We pressed on and a few Hull got behind them and attacked the backs of their heads. This was enough to spook a few of them and they began to back off. It was futile to give chase into the massed ranks of claret and blue. Instead we headed away from the ground. We had to be back in the town centre before they were.

By 5.30, town was heaving with lads. Any West Ham foolish enough to wander from Paragon Station were set upon. All us Orchard lads were targeting the Cockneys with carry outs: unsuspecting lads laden down with cans, cider and crisps ready

for the long journey home were rounded on. They got battered
and we got sloshed.

After the match, incidentally won by us 1-0, there was a lot
of trouble, with City taking it to the Londoners. This
surprised me, as a lot of the older lads had told us about
West Ham's reputation, and I, like thousands of others,
had read all the *Skinhead* books. We were all giving it
'Where's your Joe Hawkins now?' I know what West Ham
have been from the sixties through the ICF days, so don't
think I am claiming City have a better mob or would have
repeated that result on other occasions, but on that night,
that's how I saw it.

H of OPE: Coventry beckoned and once again hundreds of Hull
Golden Bootboys took up the challenge, I had to see this
through and decided to hitchhike to the game, setting off on
the Friday night with a few mates. We got as far as Sheffield
and gave it up as a bad job. We were frozen solid – it's no fun
hitching in February. Instead we warmed ourselves in Sheffield
Station, sat in a waiting room all night.

Our journey continued by rail, and on approaching Derby we
spied a train full of Chelsea on their way up to play Wednesday,
Fuck me, if they weren't all wearing glitter and had their
scarves tight around their foreheads. Trendsetters or what!

★ ★ ★

We were now at our peak. In the first three years of the
decade, we had grown into one of the most feared firms
outside Division One, and a match for anybody. Surely it
couldn't get better than this?

It didn't. Within three months the crew had all but
disbanded. The cause was our old bugbear, inter-gang rivalry.

MONTIE: By this time City's mob was at its peak, numbering well over 1,000, but it was getting a bit 'old hat'. If even West Ham couldn't trouble us, there was some of the excitement missing.

The away game after West Ham was Burnley on February 10. Another football special train took 1,000 or so City to Turf Moor. We had a sizeable mob, looking splendid in our sheepskins, and stood unopposed on the Burnley kop. This time, however, the team let us down, getting thumped 4-1. Burnley made a show at the train station but a handful of City ran them off. We couldn't be bothered. We wanted to be home.

The train was subdued. Our thoughts were no longer on football but on getting home for a night round Hull. The town centre had some decent nightclubs by this time and we all had a few bob in our pockets, so we arranged to meet in The Georgian at 9.30 and go on to Malcolm's nightclub later.

There had been a few skirmishes in the city centre leading up to this night and the police had locked up several of us the week before. It was obvious some police top brass were on another 'clean-up campaign' and the Albermarle lads seemed targeted as the culprits for everything over the previous year. About ten of us enjoyed a late night drink at Malcolm's. One of the lads had just returned home from sea with a huge knife and was showing it around when people started telling us there was a mob outside waiting for us. Why? I still don't know.

One of the lads said there had been a ruck the previous week but most of us missed it as we were locked up. Was it another mob, full of bad blood from earlier weeks, or just a bunch of drunks wanting a row?

We all left together football-style, stood together and fought together. It resulted in a near-fatal stabbing, and one of our lads stabbed through the leg. It was nasty and vicious and I still do not know why it happened. The 'Battle of Dock Street' ended up at Crown Court and some heavy custodial sentences were handed out.

Looking at a cell door shut in your face, football hooliganism is soon put into context. I still follow my club and I watch the lads from both sides posturing. It's still there but not a fraction as important or violent as it was in the seventies. For a short while Hull was up there with the 'big boys'. I for one wouldn't want the sterile, family, all-sat down atmosphere (or lack of it) at some football grounds today.

H from Orchard Park was also involved in the Battle of Dock Street. He says that both the aftermath of that fateful night, and the links of some Hull lads with Manchester United, led to the break-up of the mob.

H of OPE: The fight was a follow-on to events from the previous Saturday, when a fight had started as we were waiting for the late bus. I'd noticed this bloke run up and kick this young kid off the bus. I didn't know the lad who ended up on his arse but he was in the thick of all the fighting outside the nightclub along with his mates before he was near-fatally wounded.

Most of the main faces at City got pulled for this one. The Old Bill were rubbing their hands, especially as a good few ended up with custodial sentences. One funny thing though, was where a few of them were when they got arrested on the Sunday: they were actually playing football at Everthorpe Borstal for Albermarle YC.

I was dragged out of my house that same afternoon. They told us we could be looking at a murder charge. The lad was in intensive care, he'd been stabbed through the lung and it was touch and go. I was only kept in for 24 hours, they had nothing on me. I'd only been involved in the earlier scuffles but because I was known, I got dragged into it all.

The local police had the bit between their teeth now. The force was in a transitional period, moving across to the larger Humberside Division, and it seemed as though they were trying to sweep away all the old problems together. The football lads were a target and so were the street gangs. Larger sentences were handed out and six- to nine-month terms became the norm. Lads who were used to £5-25 fines suddenly faced the possibility of losing their jobs and freedom. This was enough for many of the lads and they just quit the scene altogether.

On Orchard, they tried to break up the gangs but found it far harder than policing the terraces, I remember some of them as though it was yesterday: Ostler, Bennett and Nesbitt (local Old Bill), we led them all a merry dance. They never managed to break us, we lasted longer then they did.

Among the many gangs in Hull, OPE had a big reputation. But we were ostracized for following United. This all came to a head after the Reds were relegated in 1974. We were now in the same division as City and the hostility worsened. It didn't help matters when a pre-season friendly was arranged on the back of the Stuart Pearson transfer. Pearson was a classy centre-forward who had gained a reputation playing for Hull in the lower division and was signed by Tommy Docherty to help kickstart Manchester United's return to Division One. Rumours circulated that the Orchard lads were meeting up with other Reds to come and do City. It was complete bollocks, but a few people with old scores to settle made us out to be bad bastards. After this, the rift never really healed. None of us went again.

The Battle of Dock Street left 15 members of City's elite crew imprisoned. Along with the fallout with the Orchard Park lads, it signalled the collapse of one of the most feared firms outside Division One. With their leaders on remand and the heavy police presence at games, the hardcore began to break up. By the time three-star jumpers hit the shops, we were a spent force, the West Ham victory just a distant memory. Those of us left were to endure years in the doldrums, a tiny crew facing thousands of visiting supporters who were after our blood.

CHAPTER FOUR

The Dark Ages

HOW QUICKLY THE empire crumbled. What had been a citywide mob of lads was soon just a group of 15 to 18-year-olds from the Woodcock Street, Gypsyville, Boothferry and Hessle areas. These lads had no-one to look up to, no older figureheads to egg them on, stop them from running or shout words of encouragement. They often had to run the gauntlet of different firms who came to town and took liberties. Oh how the lads from Sunderland, Boro, Wednesday and Sheff United laughed as they strolled to the ground unopposed.

'Can you hear the City sing? I can't hear a fucking thing.'

The average age of the crew fell from 20-plus to about 16. This propelled friends and myself into the firing line and the weekly task of trying to mix it with big beer bellies. It was men against boys. Christ, three-quarters of us weren't even shaving. Some of the Albermarle lads still turned out for the big games, but it was mainly left to those of us who lived in West Hull to try to maintain our dignity.

We also had to contend with many Hull lads supporting other teams, of which I was as guilty as the rest. I divided my time between watching Hull and travelling all over with Man United. This was common in Hull. As we had never managed to reach the dizzy heights of the First Division, many instead learned their trade as thugs supporting teams like Man Utd, Liverpool, Leeds, Chelsea and Spurs. The seventies football fan didn't travel away to England games in the numbers that they do now, so these jaunts to the more fashionable clubs meant that the Hull lads could add to their experiences and enhance their reputations at the same time.

September 1973, Leeds United at home to Manchester United. City were away, so many lads were enticed by the fixture. The 9.45 from Paragon Station was heaving, standing room only and, surprisingly, full of lads you wouldn't normally expect to turn out. Orchard Park Estate was well represented (as always) but the surprise package was the Albermarle crew; they had a massive turnout, with all the main faces in attendance. The Orchard and Albermarle lads hated each other and, for me, living amongst one group but travelling with the other made for an uneasy journey.

Was there an ulterior motive? Had the Albermarle lads come to support Leeds? My thoughts were soon answered as our mob of Hull lads, numbering 200-plus, made its way down the slope of the railway station. Across the road by a statue stood a group of Leeds fans. The shout went up and we piled into them. Traffic halted as fighting ensued. Our superior numbers soon had them running down the street towards the Corn Exchange. We were Reds for the day, we'd taken over the city centre and it wasn't even 11am.

The attraction of following a team like United was obvious. The 1973-74 season was pretty dire for Hull City. Although finishing a respectable ninth, the players were not as cavalier in spirit as their predecessors. The public voted with their feet and crowds dropped below 10,000. Our own numbers reflected this shift. Only six months before, 1,000 voices could be heard exalting our footballing heroes. Now here we were, teenagers looking for leadership, in fact looking for a mob to back us up. Our numbers had been decimated and we considered ourselves lucky if we could raise 150. For our biggest rivals, it meant payback time.

We had to grow up fast. The first thing we did was to abandon Kempton and return to the safety of the South

Stand. My own band of brothers still persevered, and our original 20 from two years before increased to well over 50 lads, all living within a ten-minute walk to the ground. These lads, from Walton, Granville and Sandringham Street as well as the younger Gypsyville gang, all frequented Amy YC. Hull's reputation was now on our shoulders. It may tarnish slightly over the forthcoming seasons, but it wasn't for want of trying.

When we played Forest a season on from the routing they'd received at our hands, they brought thousands, many after revenge. We decided to do our own thing and not even try to match their superior numbers. It was guerrilla warfare. We realised the only way we could be effective was by attacking other groups of equal numbers. We had to be selective, give teams like Sunderland, Wednesday and Boro a wide berth, let them take over the pubs and the town centre. We had a plan and stuck to it.

We would gather in the South Stand, making our way into the ground in small groups to avoid any confrontations, and then watch the away enclosure to see how many fans were being thrown out, the normal policy of the day. We knew by experience that any lads thrown out wouldn't venture far. Encouraged by the fact that any police on duty would be inside, at half-time we would leave the ground and go hunting them.

We weren't cowards or bullies, we didn't go after ones and twos. Their numbers would often be equal to ours, or greater; the numbers ejected in those times were very high. Sometimes you would underestimate the numbers or quality of those thrown out, and end up getting chased all over Gipsyville Estate yourselves. That's just the way it was, a massive learning curve. If we felt the opposition didn't pose too much of a threat, we met in town, frequenting the White Lion (now The Gingerman). Those of us looking old enough to drink would bring out refreshments to the rest standing by the pinball machine. We normally had only a couple of drinks before moving on. We didn't want to spoil our fortnightly jaunts by being banned for underage drinking.

This particular Saturday, we were at home to Aston Villa. Our fortnightly pub ritual completed, we headed for Paragon Station to get the train to City. As we walked across the Yorkshire Electricity Board (YEB) car park ten-strong, a coach of Villa supporters pulled up. We jumped over the wall and began banging on the windows, beckoning the Villa youths to get off the coach. They sat staring, not even responding to our taunts.

'They're a set of knobs'

'They're shitting it.'

As we stood around the coach laughing at them, we didn't see the two cars emptying behind us, nor hear the sudden rush. I certainly did feel the spanner hit me, as the pain shot up my arm. I turned to see an Isaac Hayes lookalike smiling wildly with spanner raised, ready to strike again. Dave, a good mate of mine, whacked him on the back of the head, giving me time to get out of range. A few punches thrown, a couple of bloody noses on both sides, then a Mexican stand-off. Meanwhile the Villa fans on the coach were jumping up and down. I knew what they were thinking: *Who are the knobs now, eh?*

We bunched together near the old wooden taxi office while our ambushers were over by the coach, which was now emptying. A swift retreat to the safety of the local bus station looked the best bet. We didn't take the train; instead we got the bus back home, as more lads would be needed if we were to get any sort of revenge. After banging on a few doors, we made our way onto Anlaby Road with a bit more confidence. We still numbered only 14 but we had one last stop, Parkers pub on the corner of Walton Street. The lads in Parkers listened to our story (minus the bit about us running as the coach emptied) and agreed to come in Kempton with us, as we knew that's where the Villa would be standing. We were now a respectable 25.

On entering the ground, we realised they hadn't arrived, so we spread out leaving the original group together, hoping they'd think we were the same ten lads they'd met beforehand. We could see Isaac and his mates walking towards us. Our eyes darted about looking for their back-up; the coachload was nowhere in sight. Good. This time we moved across to them. Mr Hayes was bigger than I remembered and had a mean look about him. We soon found out why. He began to unravel a bandage on his arm and you could see a knife emerging. *Fuck that*, I thought, *I'm not going anywhere near that cunt*. A quick movement to the side of me made me jump. Suddenly Isaac was on the floor, being pummelled by Hutchie, who sat astride him. Whilst the rest of us stood like frightened rabbits, Hutchie had acted, hitting him before the bandage was fully unwound. Isaac's mates ran, leaving him to his fate. He'd been well and truly *shafted*.

Late June, 1974, saw our forthcoming fixtures printed in the local paper. In previous years this would have met with the nods of approval as the important games were etched in your memory banks. But on this occasion you looked down the list and decided on which areas of Hull you had to give a wide berth so as not to endure total humiliation. This season would pitch us against the likes of Man Utd, Sunderland, Forest, Villa and the Owls. We knew what lay in store.

November, and United were in town. Surprisingly many of the old heads turned out. Maybe it wouldn't be so bad after all. It was. A mini invasion of the pitch by a solitary Red (incidentally a Hull lad) sparked off a series of fights within the South Stand. Other United fans in amongst the Hull faithful took the initiative and began lashing out. Many panicked and rushed to the sides to escape a beating as the Reds, led by Black Sammy, moved up the empty terracing. But not everyone ran. A small group of Albermarle, including

Alex S, Ray J and Killer, greeted the onrushing army. The watching Reds cheered as both sets clashed, but it wasn't going all their way. Spurred on by the actions of a few, more Hull lads joined in, and by the time the police moved in neither group was giving an inch. The United infiltrators were led away as 12,000 Reds howled in anger and spat venom towards the police and the South Stand. The Albermarle lads had managed to avert total humiliation. This alone was seen as a small victory on a day of near total domination by the Red Army.

The final league game of the season threw up a treat: Sheffield Wednesday were to play out their last game in the Second Division at Boothferry Park. They'd had a nightmare year and were doomed to relegation. Oh how we gloated. One of our closest rivals, the mighty Owls had sunk to the murky depths of the Third Division (if only we'd known what was in store for us in later years).

The *Hull Daily Mail* ran a series of articles leading up to the match, quoting the police on their zero tolerance tactics and warning fans not to misbehave or suffer the consequences. Many thought the Owls would stay away, not wanting to witness the death throes of their dilapidated team. They felt the Sheffield supporters would abandon their team, but I knew better.

Over 40 Wednesday fans arrived on the Friday evening. Fights broke out as the town centre pubs emptied at closing time. Satisfied with a good night's work, the Wednesday dossed down in their vans and cars, only to begin roaming the town centre by 7am looking for a café and a much-needed bacon sandwich. They were unfortunate to meet up with equal numbers of OPE Reds taking the early train to Manchester for the Championship party match against Blackpool. The poor Owls didn't know what hit them and were soon on their toes as the Orchard lads gave chase down Mill Street. One unlucky Sheffield lad was caught, grabbed while he ran, steered straight into a parking meter and left in a heap.

Apart from this altercation, the day was theirs. Each train arriving in Paragon Station seemed full of Sheffield lads. It was their day of defiance, a day to show how passionate they were, a day to sing the praises of the team they loved. And a day to run us all over the place!

This wasn't the time to begin to spread your wings and embark on perilous away journeys, but even though our numbers were low a few new members still rallied to the cause. One was Mark Jackson, known as Cockney Jacko. His story not only explains what it was like during those bleak times, but also reveals how it was for many young fans bitten by the football bug in the mid-seventies.

COCKNEY JACKO: Why me? I've often asked myself this question. Why Hull City Football Club? It's not as though they were the first team I had been to watch. West Ham United were my local team when I was little, which I still am, incidentally. As a child of eight, for a Christmas treat I was taken to Upton Park, the home of the 'Happy Hammers'. The game was against Tottenham but I wasn't bothered who won; though West Ham ran out 2-1 winners, I knew I wouldn't be coming back for a while. West Ham were a glamorous club at the time, containing three of the World Cup-winning side, but I just didn't like Upton Park. It struck me that there was a very nasty atmosphere about the place. It was pitch black when we left and I can recall thinking to myself, please don't make me come here again, dad. I loved football, I loved the way West Ham played, but I didn't like Upton Park or the surrounding district. It scared me as an eight-year-old and it still does to this day: me and thousands of others.

What I didn't know was that my parents, bless them, had also bought me a kit for Christmas, complete with a crossed-hammers cloth badge. Not many eight-year-olds spend Christmas Day sobbing in the snow but I didn't want to be a

Happy Hammer. I thought that claret and blue were cissy colours. I would sooner have eaten snow until February then wear the kit. Everyone at school was astonished; a West Ham kit in those days was the equivalent of a Manchester United replica shirt now, a star prize indeed. I sometimes look back, in view of the fact that later I took the hooligan path, and wonder what might have happened if I'd put on that shirt. Instead, from that Christmas morning in 1967, Tottenham Hotspur became my 'bit on the side'.

This was, of course, accompanied football, sitting with your dad on your best behaviour, which is different altogether from going to a match by yourself. This I first tried two years later, in 1969, by which time we had moved to a little village in Lancashire called Blackburn. It's just outside Burnley somewhere as far as I can remember. The only claim to fame Blackburn Rovers had at the time was a grossly-overrated left-back called Keith Newton who somehow fluked his way into the World Cup squad of 1970. Watching Blackburn was then, has been since, still is, and always will be a dire experience. Walking down the road from where I lived, with their squalid little ground surrounded by *Coronation Street*-type houses, I never could have imagined then that one day this set of chancers would actually buy the Premier League trophy and go a long way to ruining football. I could have jumped on that glory hunter's cash-driven bandwagon and been one of those Blackburn fans who could say, " I've bin coming 'ere sin' 1970, lad." I could have been to Europe, seen a Championship trophy, gone to Wembley. But I didn't. I have never once regretted this decision.

Fate had decreed we were to move on yet again to a place called Hull. Being a little Cockney in Blackburn had not been funny. The white kids had called me a Cockney bastard and decided it was best if I hung out with the other foreigners, i.e. the Asian lads. Some of the Asians weren't particularly keen on this idea and even some of them called me a Cockney bastard. Being a little Cockney in Hull was pretty much the same except there were no other outsiders to hang out with. Football was now at a place called Boothferry Park, a ground so groovy it even had its own train station which brought fans from the city centre, close to where I lived. I loved the place from the first time I saw it and soon struck up friendships that have lasted till this day. I was only a Cockney bastard six days a week now; I got Saturdays off.

Soon after my arrival, one of the biggest games for many years took place. It had a profound effect on me and sparked a love for the Tigers that I will have until my dying day. I had already been to a couple of games at Boothferry Park and knew I would have to be there early to have any chance of getting to the front, the only place from which a tiny eleven–year-old would be able to see. On match day, my tactic of arriving at the ground at 11am paid off and I was able to secure a place exactly to the right of the goal at the South Stand end (Bunkers Hill to you).

You could walk completely round the inside of the ground in a circle if you wished – segregation was unheard of – and large gangs of Stoke City supporters who had also gained entry early were doing exactly this: marching round and round the terraces in a circle non-stop for four or five circuits. On the fifth time round, they had the misfortune to enter the South Stand just after a full train had pulled up at Boothferry Halt from Paragon Station. The South was now full of skinhead types from Hull and the inevitable happened. A massive brawl broke out right in front of me. People were running away in all directions while others were surging down to the front or even fighting on the pitch. It was chaotic for about five minutes. I stood there mesmerised. I was scared stiff but would not leave the place I had queued so early for.

I did not understand the politics of it all, like the 'who was who' and why should they wish to fight, or why in the South Stand? I assumed everybody went along to see a good sporting contest and may the best team win. On this day everything changed. Something happened before my eyes that hurts till this day: the legendary Gordon Banks, he of World Cup-winning fame, pulled the ball back from over the line and claimed a save to deny Hull City a draw and Ken Wagstaff his hat-trick. As one brought up with Sunday school, cub scouts and Boys' Brigade, I was appalled, and I kept shouting at Gordon Banks to go and tell the referee the ball was in. Among such a massive crowd he was hardly likely to hear my tiny little voice: the official attendance figure that day was 41,452; that's right, forty-one thousand, four hundred and fifty-two.

Thinking he wasn't able to hear me, I walked to the goal line a few feet away. He heard me this time all right but politely ignored me and headed to the edge of his penalty box. It wouldn't have surprised me if he'd turned round and called me a Cockney bastard like everyone else did. Maybe Gordon had heard I got Saturdays off now.

When I said my prayers at bedtime that night, I remember praying for Hull City to win the FA Cup the following year to make up for this travesty, and maybe promotion to Division One. These prayers were never answered but I was a Tiger from that day. I still missed my London roots but decided then that Hull was where I lived, Hull City were my team and it was not ever going to be negotiable. At eleven years of age, full of innocence, you actually do believe that your team will go on to win the FA Cup in the next couple of years. The top division was the only one above ours and we were usually at the right end of Division Two, so obviously one season soon we would go up and from there it would only be a matter of time before we would win the Football League. Easy.

I started to watch City regularly from the age of 13, the same age as starting senior school and having my first paper job. I kept the same routine on Saturdays when City were at home: under-18s disco at Mecca club on the Saturday morning, hang round town for an hour or so, and then get the train to Boothferry Park and straight in the ground. Neither of these pastimes were too expensive; away matches were not for me yet but missing a home game was not even considered. Missing the odd one might not have been such a bad idea, though, because Hull's fans at the time were a bit of a soft touch for having their home end taken. All manner of teams would stroll up, run across the pitch and clear the South Stand.

This didn't affect me much; no one was going to attack me because, despite my teenage years, I was still very small. The louts that swarmed into the stand ignored me, while some of my school mates often got belted in the mouth. Some stopped going for this reason but lots of others didn't. They got slapped about and chased a few times for it in the next few years but many of these lads have kept the Tigers faith.

The 1974/75 season had quite a few significant events for me. I turned 15 at the beginning of the season and acquired a second income as a cellar boy at a town centre pub. This involved starting at 7.30am Saturday and Sunday mornings and working three hours on the Saturday – which left exactly the right time for the Mecca – and four on the Sunday. I got £3.50 for this on top of the £2 paper round money, so away matches would soon come into the equation.

However, I was in a quandary. Away matches meant time off work, and no work meant no money for away matches. My trips would have to be carefully planned. Another obstacle was parental consent. When I had sneaked off to an away match at Mansfield the previous year, my mum had not been happy at all. It was made clear there were to be no away games until after I had left school, preferably at 18. Partly my mum was worried about her young son wanting to spread his wings, and partly there was the Manchester United factor.

They had been relegated the previous season, amongst growing discontent. The United faithful had not taken it well and had taken it out on all and sundry. The newspapers were full of stories of United's Red Army rampaging up and down the country. We had a taste of it in a pre-season friendly. There were less then 9,000 at this game but a large United contingent made for a hostile atmosphere. They invaded the pitch on several occasions, took the South Stand a couple of times and caused damage in the town centre. There was nothing unusual or even personal in this, it was what they always did. Every week. Other teams had started to imitate this behaviour but United were masters of it.

Everyone who has written about football violence has pinpointed this season and United's contribution to it. As other clubs copied them, so the South Stand end was taken over regularly. The Hull City supporters just weren't up to it. When Manchester United came back in November it was noticeable that a lot of regular faces from school were missing. People were scared to go. There had been some hype in the paper about the possible outcome of this event, and there were even people in Hull hoping City wouldn't do anything stupid like beat them. Of course we did beat them, 2-0, in front of 23,000 people. There were probably about 12,000 United fans at Boothferry Park that day and as usual there were pitch invasions and wrecking in the town centre.

There was also fierce fighting in the South Stand. While a lot of the younger element was missing, the same did not seem to apply to the older lads. If anything there were more of these types than had been seen before, and when United's fans streamed across the pitch and into the home end, as they did at the beginning of most matches, they were met with fierce resistance. The South was taken in the end but instead of the usual scattering in all directions at the sight of the advancing hordes, City's fans ran to the bottom of the South and fought hand-to-hand. I had not seen anything like this since that Stoke game in those non-segregated days of '71. The sheer weight of numbers swayed the confrontation United's way, as it always did in those days, but just for once it was good to see a few people showing the right attitude. It wasn't the last time the South Stand was taken but at least after that it was always fought for and never just given up.

They were a mighty power, Manchester United, and the Red Army was a massive invasion force. I wanted to be part of such a force, and I wouldn't have long to wait. The following month, Hull City played their Christmas Saturday away fixture at York. British Rail were running several football special trains and every man and his dog would be there. Six thousand City supporters made the short journey to York and I was one of them. I didn't bother asking either of my parents. When I left work that morning I simply walked across the road to join some mates in the train queue, which was already hundreds of yards long and several deep. It was a magical sight, so many people decked out in black and amber on the way to see the team who had recently crushed Manchester United 2-0.

York City had just come up to our division and it was expected by most on the journey that two points were there for the taking. On arrival, we were made to wait in the vicinity of the train station by horses and dogs until all the trains had arrived. We were to be taken down to the ground in one big escort. When this got moving, it took us over the River Ouse on the way down to Bootham Crescent. As you cross the bridge over the Ouse, you have a vantage point both in front and behind. As far as the eye could see in front were Hull City supporters. It was the same behind. This was something special; you had a feeling of invincibility. This was obviously a team that was going places and I was going there with them. Final score: York City 3 Hull City 0. It was not the only bad news of the day.

I might have got away with the trip but for a bit of bad luck. My parents were under the impression that I had gone to see a girlfriend to take her a Christmas present and stop for tea, and would return about nine o'clock. I'd even wrapped two of my best City scarves in Christmas wrapping paper as I left for work in the morning. The bit of bad luck I had would repeat itself many times over the coming years. I was arrested. One away match, one arrest. My mum and dad were informed at seven o'clock that I was at the police box at Paragon Station, held for committing the offence of disorderly behaviour on British Railways. I had being hanging out of the train window singing City songs for all I was worth on the way home and was the only person grabbed out of hundreds doing the same thing. This sort of luck was to dog me over the years. I wasn't the only person arrested; an older lad who was drunk and disorderly was also there and we talked football until a very irate dad came to take me home. As I was leaving, the lad I'd been with shouted, 'I'll see you at Fulham next week.' Despite the trouble I was in, I did see him at Fulham the following week. The bug had truly bitten me.

After the inquest at home, my parents wrongly assumed I wouldn't be doing anything like that for a while. The following Saturday I left for my pub job at the usual time, only I didn't go near the place. I went straight to Paragon Station, bought a platform ticket and joined a rough-looking bunch carrying cans of beer. I got on the train and walked up and down, looking to see where the ticket inspector was and maybe hide if necessary. I didn't know Martin was going to be on the train but there he was, my drunk and disorderly friend from the police station. He was also carrying cans of beer; they seemed to be quite a fashion accessory. He was looking for some of his mates and when I mentioned the other lads with scarves and beer at the other end of the train, he suggested we head for a look. A lot of people must have got on at the last minute, unseen by me, because when we got to the first two carriages they were full of City fans nearly all drinking from cans.

On most Saturday mornings at eight o'clock I would have been emptying beer bottles into skips and then into crates. This week I was emptying full cans down myself on the way to Wembley via Fulham. I was also on my first jib, although I did not know it was called jibbing then; it was more like playing hide-and-seek at that age. My new buddies looked after me pretty well, though I don't have much recall of it. I have vague memories of being carried drunk by various people through the Tube network and not being able to focus too much on the finer points of the game. I spent hours hidden under the train seat on the journey home and only surfaced at Doncaster to change trains. At this point I was now free of the worry of train guards. I drank more beer on the last leg of the train journey and even got invited to go to the pub they used in the town centre. This was a non-starter, as I wouldn't look old enough for public houses for another ten years. Home time for me. I had been grounded the previous week and only let out on the Saturday because of work. Turning up drunk and dishevelled at nearly ten o'clock sent my parents into a fury. After the previous week's episode, they didn't need drunkenness. I told them a story about drinking beer and cider at a friend's house and I don't think it crossed their minds to wonder about faraway places such as Fulham.

I was grounded once more and missed the replay on Tuesday night, which again ended in a draw. In those days second replays were on neutral grounds and ours was to be at Filbert Street, Leicester, the following Monday. This would not involve skipping work and I would have enough money out of the weekend wages. Of all the naughtiness I got caught up in at that age, it never included twagging school. I went every day; I didn't even twag the odd lesson. But I found it easy to feign illness at dinnertime, and by mid-afternoon I was on my way to Leicester.

That bit was easy. Explaining where I had been to my parents, who had the police out looking for me, was less so. Football was now completely off limits, effort was to be made towards forthcoming exams, and the next few Saturday afternoons were spent at the kitchen table doing homework. I was gutted. Still, I couldn't blame my parents. In a few short weeks I had been to three away matches (of which they only knew about two). I had been arrested once, got drunk once, was caught twagging school once and was grounded three times, the latest for a month. The Manchester United away game was just over a month away, time to behave. Not that there was any chance of me getting permission off my mum and dad for that fixture. No chance, none, nil, zero. Its just that, well, I knew I would be going no matter what.

This was another game that did not involve any time off work. I could leave as normal at 10.30am and still have time to kill before the football special left. By the time match day, came football had not been mentioned in our house for a while. Getting to work and sneaking off to the train station the way I had done for the Fulham game should have been easy. I hadn't reckoned on my mum's sixth sense. The night before, I had hidden a scarf, three pound notes, some food and a bottle of cider, items that would be essential the next day. My mum woke me at a quarter to seven the next morning. She was wearing my best City scarf, the one I had hidden. She wasn't just on to me; I was completely captured. 'You won't be needing any of this lot today,' she said, as she waved me off to work. There were tears on the way to work that day I can tell you, floods of them.

All week at school the talk had been of the United game. The funny thing was, despite the special train (fare £3.25), I hadn't found one single person who was prepared to make the journey with me. Everyone was too scared. I had been telling everyone all week that I was going and now I wasn't. Boy, was this going to make me look a twat at school. Well ladies and gentlemen, that was my excuse for not going to Old Trafford that day. What's yours?

Things didn't improve when, on arrival at work, Roger the landlord informed me that my dad would be picking me up from work at ten-thirty. With my £3.50 wages and £1 I was owed from the previous week, it was still just about possible to go, but this latest news put the tin hat on it. Work was not going to be any fun today. Roger told me to go and do the upstairs bar first and downstairs second. It was usually the other way round. When I got upstairs, the bar was as bad as I'd ever seen it. Well it wouldn't clear itself, so I made a slow start gathering in the debris. I found a reasonable amount of change laid about, which wasn't unusual. There was something unusual though: three £1 notes in the middle of an empty table.

Loose change was considered a perk of the job, but notes were different. Any I had found before had been handed to Roger or Chris, the under-manager. When I took these notes to Roger, he told me to see Chris about them. Chris told me they were mine to keep. 'A City fan might need a few extra quid today,' he added. I told him I wouldn't be going and returned to finish off the bottling up. At ten o'clock, Chris buzzed me on the intercom and asked if I could pop down for my wages. When I got to the office, both Chris and my dad were there. It was obvious dad was taking no chances. Chris handed me my wages and told me I might as well get off and he'd do the rest for me. Cheers Chris, half an hour of extra homework. Great.

'We'll go across to the station for the taxi,' said dad. On arrival at the station however, he guided me to the buffet and ordered tea and sandwiches. Outside, through the glass windows, I could see people gathering for the special train. A special train I would not be on . . . until my dad produced from his inside jacket pocket my three £1 notes and my City scarf. I could go! There were no pies to be seen, no alcohol was to be drunk at all, and on arrival back at Paragon Station I was to get a taxi straight home so that my mum wouldn't be worrying. But I could go. Oh deep joy.

If I'd have known what I was letting myself in for, I'd have gone straight home with my dad. I boarded the special, a train packed with City fans on the way to take on the mighty Manchester United − or so I thought.

Despite the fearsome reputation of the Red Army, there was another thing that distinguished them from other fans − they dressed like clowns. Many possessed Leo Sayer hairstyles and most of them wore scruffy Wrangler jackets. On these jackets, which were never washed, there had to be sew-on Status Quo patches and a 'wings' patch on the back. They wore half-mast trousers – preferably white skinners but Wranglers would do – revealing major domo boots. The trousers and sometimes the jackets were often finished with a bonny tartan trim just like the Roller girls had. This wasn't compulsory, just popular. The outfit was always finished off with two or three United scarves. (If I have offended any real circus clowns by comparing these people to you, I apologise.)

This was the bizarre sight that greeted me as I got on the train: clowns, hundreds of them. Something was not right; maybe I was on the wrong train. Walking the length of the train I realised it was the right one but had been hijacked by United's Red Army. Along the entire length I spotted only 20 City fans and most of them belonged to the flask of soup and tartan blanket mob.

I had thought carefully about my attire for the day and was dressed in a tasteful 'newish' Levi Strauss red tag jacket, Sta-prest trousers and all-leather loafer shoes. My silk Hull City scarf stayed firmly in my pocket. There were only three other City supporters who I knew on the train and we sat round a table playing cards. We all had to agree that City's supporters had let the players down badly. The same could not be said for United. This special train, with its cut-price fare, had been a gift for the many local United fans. Quite a few had started travelling to Manchester to see United and this gave them all a chance at an affordable price. They took it with both hands, to the tune of approximately 400 United fans on the train.

There where 44,000 others inside Old Trafford, where we arrived after an uneventful walk. Hull City were greeted with the song 'We All Hate Bananas' as they took the field. As football wit goes, this put them right up there with those other masters of repartee, the Scousers. Later in the game, when

they were very luckily 2-0 up, they managed 'Thank you very
much for Stuart Pearson,' to the tune of 'Aintree Iron'. Neither
of these songs, nor any others, received a reply, as there were
no away supporters to sing back. Not even 30 surrounded by
the police in the Scoreboard Paddock like other teams managed.
None. All the City supporters I knew of had hidden their scarves
and split up in ones and twos, pretending to be United daytrippers. We left the ground with heavy hearts after a 2-0
defeat.

I don't think an ambush crossed anybody's mind as, in our
ones and twos, we'd had an uneventful time at the ground and
hadn't brought any attention to ourselves. We were happily
strolling along, not too far from the train station, when BANG.
Hordes of United appeared out of nowhere from two directions
and came in on the attack. Our group of ten or so, some of who
were young, stood no chance. Some of us were lucky enough
and quick enough to get away with only minor injuries but
others were not. Paul and myself managed to get to the train
and get a seat. We had twelve minutes to wait before the train
left and there was no sign of Dave or drunk and disorderly
Martin. With two minutes to go, Dave turned up minus the
sleeve of his Afghan coat, which had been pulled off, deliberately,
after his beating. He looked a sorry sight and we had to keep
him awake on the journey home. The train left without Martin
and we had no way of knowing what had happened to him. We
found out weeks later that he had been in hospital due to his
injuries and was going to be off work for a while. His doctors
had forbidden him alcohol but he chose to give up football of
his own free will.

The '74/75 season ground to a close with both Cardiff, and
Sheffield Wednesday on the last day, taking the South Stand.
The Wednesday supporters were irate because they were being
relegated that day. Nowadays on relegation days, of which
there have been plenty for the Owls, the average Wednesday
supporter sits glued to his seat sobbing uncontrollably, to the

delight of the football-supporting world. There are many other team's fans that cry on the telly, notably Liverpool's, but nobody can boo-hoo like a Wednesday-ite. How we mocked their plight. It was a joy to tatty-bye them from our division. They in turn run us out of the South Stand and chased us all the way to town, handing out punishment beatings as they went. Good riddance. Enjoy the Third Division.

The next couple of seasons passed without any major incidents. By now we were used to seeing teams like Nottingham Forest infiltrate the South Stand – which they did in both '75 and '76 – but there was a difference: we were actively looking for them and weeding them out. Slowly but surely, little victories snowballed as good lads started to come through. Confidence was returning and numbers slowly increasing. We made a conscious decision that no one would take our end again. At least inside the ground we could maintain our pride, and we did. Chelsea fans were spotted in our end and were dealt with before they could group together, most opting to jump over the barrier. The Londoners began to mock us as they were led away, but we'd done enough to spook them and give them second thoughts and that was enough for us.

We knew we couldn't compete with visiting firms like Chelsea in the streets. For us it was still easier to arrive late or by the back door, skirting around the area and entering via Hessle Road. Even this route gave us problems. Sunderland in '76 brought thousands to a promotion bash. They were everywhere and we had to dodge them as soon as we walked over Hessle Road flyover. They sat all along the wall of Gypsyville Library, drinking cider, so we skulked through the small back alleys which ran through Devon Street along to Marlborough Street. Our only move was to walk through Pickering Park and make it to the ground via Lakeside Grove. We couldn't believe the sight before us as we entered the park; they were all over there as well. Talk about out of the frying pan, into the fire. Over by the fleet of coaches, we could see hundreds of lads running round in their butchers' coats, playing 500-a-side football while the boating lake had over a dozen rowing boats full of singing Wearsiders rocking from side to side.

'Brick 'em, fucking brick 'em,' shouted JBS.

So we did. Six of us stood by the side of the lake throwing bits of concrete and stones at the Sunderland sailors taking part in the Black Cat Regatta. They were fuming; in their haste to reach us they were banging into each other and it looked like a few would capsize. Instead they were off like crazy trying to reach us, as we ran along the path laughing till it hurt. There were still many laughs to be had during these lean years and most scary moments on reflection gave you something to smile at. A classic moment in time again featured Sunderland when Trogg, later to become one of the original City Psychos, performed one of the most talked about actions in the late seventies. He ran from out of the South Stand, resplendent in his cut-down sheepskin, and dived into the massed ranks of Sunderland fans packed into Kempton. Trogg disappeared from view until he was dragged out, kicking and punching, by two incredulous police officers.

CHAPTER FIVE

City Psychos

BLACKPOOL AWAY, NEW Year's Day, 1976, was a turning point, though the seed laid on this trip would not reach fruition for another couple of seasons. A coach left Hull that day full of young lads. This was one of the earliest trips featuring the Hawthorn pub and Bransholme boys (Woodcock Street and Selworthy Mob respectively). These lads began to meet in the Hawthorn Hotel, a local spit-and-sawdust hostelry situated a few hundred yards off Anlaby Road. This was our area. We knew the layout and felt secure there.

After a while, lads from other estates like Boothferry and Bransholme started using the pub. If it hadn't been for these lads at the time, we would have had nobody at all. Although these were lean years, it was a learning experience and made you more determined to recruit. A lot of the young lads coming through from the local estates were game as hell, and everyone started to come closer together, as much from necessity as desire. The alliance between West Hull and the Selworthy Mob was due in no small part to three brothers who were originally brought up near the ground but had moved to the sprawling council estate that was Bransholme. The Simpson brothers introduced both sets of lads to each other and before long they were seen as one mob. Certain members of this alliance were later instrumental in ensuring the formation of a new gang called the City Psychos, and are still active 27 years later.

After a while, we became a tight little unit. We began taking coaches to away games, and holding our own against most clubs. Out of all the teams we played on a regular basis, I believe one stands out as our main rival: Sheffield United. They usually came to Hull in the seventies in large numbers and took the piss. During these lean years I can only remember one moment when we turned them over: August 1976 in the Anglo-Scottish Cup.

After watching the game, around 15 of us were walking back down Anlaby Road when two groups of Blades began mouthing off at us. The main group began to quickly move up behind us, with the rest walking on the grass intersection almost alongside. They numbered approximately 60, four-to-one in their favour, and began to move in for the kill. 'Hold tight City, nobody run, stick together,' all the old clichés came out as our hearts pounded and the adrenaline kick took over. We tensed ready for them. 'Turn and straight into 'em,' someone said. A Sheffield lad booted me in my back, so I turned and propelled myself into him, arms flailing, knocking him backwards. The rest of the Hull boys followed my lead and, to my surprise, had the Blades backing off. James was rolling around the floor with a young black kid.

'Get off ' I shouted.

'He won't let go,' replied James, with the Blade holding tight onto his jumper. I could see the Old Bill coming our way.

'Jimmy, get off him, the coppers are coming.'

There was only one course of action. I ran over and jumped on the black lad, and Jimmy was able to join up with the rest of our lads. I wasn't particularly pleased with my actions, and I still can't bring myself to join in when the odds are heavily stacked in our favour, but Jimmy is a mate and I wasn't going to see him arrested, not if I could do something to prevent it.

Sheffield, smarting from that initial encounter, regrouped

under the Green Bridge, ready to have another go with us. But they never managed to get the upper hand, as we now felt invincible. If they run once, they'll run again. They came at us again just before we'd reached Silver Cod and one of the Hull lads ran over to a secondhand scooter dealer's, came back with an old exhaust pipe and clipped a few Blades with it before they took off again. This was the last bit of action for the day as the Old Bill moved in and pushed us away. We were buzzing for days. After being run by them for a couple of years, we had got a result. All of a sudden they no longer seemed invincible, and people started talking about going to Bramall Lane, which would have been unheard of a year before.

It was the same with Millwall. They might only bring 30 lads, but when they ran at you, if you let their fearsome reputation get into your head, you were already half beaten. At that age, we had to keep reminding ourselves that reputations cannot fight, and that 30 game lads in their late teens were the same as 30 from a similar background anywhere in the country.

★ ★ ★

'White riot, I wanna riot . . .' screamed The Clash. Anarchy was in the air. Carnaby Street was swinging again, the Kings Road was the place to be seen and once more the mood was changing. Against this backdrop of teenage angst, the football authorities were losing the war against the hooligan firms. Fenced terraces hadn't helped, while the shutting of grounds only moved the problem elsewhere. Attendances were decreasing at an alarming rate.

Yet to us it was exciting. We were supposed to be this small minority, but try telling that to the shopkeepers and house-holders of Sheffield as the boards went up before a Leeds–Manchester United FA Cup semi-final, or to Underground workers who would go on strike rather than face the hooligan elements battling it out on the platforms. The national newspapers fuelled the frenzy, running endless spreads on this English disease. We lapped it up. What I'd give to be 19 again and so full of yourself.

The mid-seventies had been bleak for us but by 1977 things were picking up as younger teenagers again 'wanted to know' at football matches. New faces were seen on the terraces as a large contingent of Bransholme lads, along with some Avenues boys, began to come up. With lads from east and west of the river (including the Gypsyville, Boothferry, Hessle, Anlaby, Holderness Road and Longhill/Bilton Grange estates), we again began to organise decent turnouts away from home and to take revenge on some of the clubs for the batterings received during the lean years. Even though the club teetered on the brink of relegation to Division Four, our reputation was growing once more. A lot of the younger lads were filling out, and were no longer mismatched against beer monster types in a fight.

One small thing that gave an indication of the way the climate was changing happened at a night match at Sheff Utd. Previous visits had seen us run a gauntlet, with Blades picking you off in and outside the ground. This time we got off outside the John Street Stand and, instead of seeking refuge inside the ground, decided to go for a wander. We turned down a side street and saw a pub full of United at the bottom. They saw us and started to move towards us. I am not claiming it was their top boys, but at that time it had never needed their top lads to do Hull; we had our hands full with their scarfers and beer monsters.

We ran at them, and the first few we caught soon realised we were there to hurt them. For years we had been a doormat to the Sheffield teams, and it was heartening to be on the giving end and watch them scramble over each other to get back in the pub. That was a key moment that led me to think, *Yes, City are back.*

I know teams like Crewe, Rotherham and Chesterfield are not massive scalps, but there was guaranteed trouble every week, if not at the match then at services or at train stations. There was a lot of trouble on rail journeys to matches, as there aren't many places to hide in a station or on a train. I remember one journey back from somewhere when a few Leeds fans from Grimsby approached us. They had been battered by some Geordies and asked for our help. It was one of the old-fashioned trains with separate carriages off a corridor. We sent lads in ones and twos to the other end, tooled up with table legs pulled off the train's tables. We planned our attack for just before we got off at Doncaster, as we didn't want the Old Bill to have time to arrive before we had scarpered. We ran in and battered three carriages of Geordies. The cleaners had quite a bit of blood to shift that night when the train went in the sidings.

Poor results on the pitch had helped chip away our support, along with the threat of violence at matches. We had gone down from an average of 25,000 in 1968 to a paltry 8,000 ten years later. We felt these 17,000 lost souls who now made alternative arrangements on a Saturday afternoon were fickle fans that only dusted off their black and amber scarves when it suited. We were made of stronger stuff. We continued to support our team home and away, vocally and physically, enhancing our reputation along the way.

We travelled by double-decker, sang out our allegiance to the Tigers and stared relegation in the face. I now understood how the Owls had felt in 1975. We were saddened at the decline of our club but found solace in the fact that we would be carving out new boundaries. We would visit grounds we'd not been to before and come up against fans we'd never met. In fact, relegation couldn't have happened at a better time for the firm. Spurred on by new experiences, we would often outnumber the home supporters and names and reputations were made weekly. Other areas of Hull were now becoming prominent, amongst them the Avenues, which had a solid crew. These lads arrived with new ideas and played a big part in renaming and reinventing our firm.

* * *

We massed under the banner of the City Psychos, a name thought up by some of the Avenues lads. It would become synonymous with Hull City. The club did not really have a national hooligan reputation at this time; any that had been built up in the early seventies had dissipated. But this was to change. Hull was no longer a place you could go and take the piss.

I am grateful to the two lads, Mannix, of the Boothferry Park Estate (1978–present), and Nick, who helped in the research into the early Psychos period. I'll let them explain what it was like.

MANNIX: In the late seventies, City had very little in the way of serious numbers. Once, seven of us went to Reading on the train and five got arrested in Doncaster station fighting with Sheff Wed. Apart from the two Official Supporters' coaches and a few other cars, that was the limit of the away support to matches outside Yorkshire and Lancashire. Getting a handful of lads back to the train stations was like the Warriors trying to reach Coney Island in the film.

At the beginning for me, around 1976, I couldn't get served in pubs, so used to wait around YEB on Ferensway in town. It was no problem in those days, as there was no police attention for coaches at all. The mode of transport was mostly double-deckers. We went to Lincoln on one around 1978 and the whole decker was detained, as someone had thrown a hammer off at a Lincoln fan. We were taken off two by two for questioning, but even the young lads kept their mouths closed, and they finally let us go four hours after the match.

Even attending home games had its dangers then. My mates and I lived on Boothferry Estate, so our walk to the ground was up the main approach road into Hull. Cars of blokes used to stop, get a bat or whatever out of the boot and chase us. I don't think they were really interested in young lads of our age, but it used to get us buzzing. A game that sticks out is Notts Forest about 1976. It was Billy Bremner's debut for us and Forest came on the pitch. All I remember is about 100 lads of school age running past me to try and get out. The effect of seeing lads, some older than me, running made me panic and we ran to the exit behind South Stand. The older lads, of course, ran to the pitch and stood toe to toe with the Forest lads, but for my age group, you honestly thought your life was in danger.

A game against Sheff Utd I remember is when our East Stand was divided into two, and my boyhood hero, Keith Edwards, had just scored. His whole career seemed to consist of being transferred between us and Sheff U, but I loved him. The East Stand, erupted with people trying to climb the dividing fence and throwing eggs injected with paint and detergent at each other. It was pure hatred between us, but I must admit they usually had the upper hand.

By the mid seventies, a lot of the main lads in Hull were into the Northern Soul scene, and drugs went hand in hand with that. I was never aware of many taking smack, it was either speed or barbiturates, and I also cannot recall ever taking amphetamine in 'wrap' form in the early days. It was tablets: Dexies, chalkies, blueys, Duramine, and so on, mostly speed and various uppers, and barbiturates as downers. Although this was the era of flared trousers, I recall vividly seeing a lot of lads at games in vests or T-shirts, heavily tattooed and wearing 'Spencer' soul bags, denim, pinstripe, patchwork, you name it. These were fashionable on the northern scene at Wigan Casino and other venues. The Hull lads I knew were into drugs and frequented all-nighters, where they often met up with lads from other clubs, in particular Sheffield United and Middlesbrough. Friendships were forged with these lads but didn't stop us kicking lumps out of each other when we met in a league fixture.

Beer monsters were still around. You would see them stood on open ends, pissed, with steam coming off their donkey jackets. For the younger lads it wasn't so cool. We couldn't get served in all pubs, hadn't much money, and had seen enough farcical brawls to realise you aren't much cop in a ruck with ten pints down you.

For lads my age, in the late seventies violence was more opportunist. The older lads may have gone with intent, but we went for the match and whatever came with the day out. I remember once we had been in a mini-van to a London game and were parked near Kings Cross. We saw a few blokes in Sheff Utd shirts buying a burger, and eight of us ran up and started punching and kicking them. They were beer monsters in their early thirties, we were teenagers and we didn't knock any of them down, but they ran. We went back to our van full of ourselves, and whose coach was parked about four spaces behind us? Yes, the Sheffield lads. A fat one was now pointing us out to the rest of his mates and they ran at us: twelve young lads versus 50 miners. We ran like fuck and had to dive into the open doors of our moving van. I laugh now, but at the time I had never been as frightened. Totally opportunist, not planned, but if you bumped into someone wearing colours that weren't your team, it went off. Lads were still wearing colours then, circa 1979.

In 1978 we were relegated from old Division Two. In our first season in Division Three we finished eighth, and things looked promising for a push for promotion after a season spent acclimatising. Nick was another who was involved in the early Psychos sorties:

NICK: Hull City v Carlisle United, 19 August 1978. After being relegated the previous season, the first game in Division Three saw City play Carlisle on a hot sunny day in August in front of 5,062 spectators. From playing the likes of Chelsea, Spurs and Wolves, we would now be playing mainly against small and (to us) unknown teams.

Carlisle brought three coachloads of fans, a typically average away following for a club 150 miles away on the first day of a new season, and went in Kempton, occasionally singing, with a few woollen scarves, centre-partings and the rest of the mid to late seventies gear. Sometime into the second half of an uneventful game, a small group of ten to 15 City appeared around the halfway line in Kempton, not far from the Carlisle gathered at the back and against the wooden barrier which ran from top to bottom, forming a no-man's land and separate from Bunkers (the South Stand).

Carlisle spotted them and slowly got ready to confront them. The City, realizing this, frantically beckoned to Bunkers for reinforcements. The first few City jumped over from the corner of Bunkers into the no-man's land, with no stewards or police to stop them. More and more City started heading for this corner, to the point where some started running diagonally across the corner of the pitch and directly into Kempton, bypassing the no-man's land. In a short space of time, a sleepy and peaceful atmosphere had been transformed into a tense stand-off, ready to erupt into a pitched battle.

The small group of City fans had now grown into a couple of hundred, and Carlisle were starting to worry. Only a few coppers separated the two factions in the Kempton. City started to advance towards the Carlisle, who were now wedged tight as sardines in the dark top corner of Kempton, against the barrier. The coppers managed to get a few more numbers in between the rival groups, but they were looking worried too. As the City advanced, out came the truncheons, an extremely rare occurrence inside Boothferry Park , and a sure sign of alarm. It stopped the advance and gave the police time to get more men in. The game finished with a stand-off in Kempton between City on one side and the police protecting the huddle of Carlisle on the other.

A small incident had almost started a major disturbance, and from that day on City again regarded the Kempton as theirs, rather than being 'for the away fans', even though this meant in effect that away fans had no designated section in the ground . The problem for the coppers was where to put away fans, as the ground was effectively divided into two standing areas: Bunkers, exclusively for the home fans, and the other three unsegregated sides for everyone else, away fans included. Now that City had decided to have Bunkers and Kempton, away fans would have to be left unsegregated with police protection in the same part of the ground as City. Over the next few seasons, this would cause all sorts of fun and games, and it all started with this small incident against Carlisle.

Tranmere v Hull City, 26 August 1978. The first away game in Division Three saw us at a place most of us knew only to be somewhere near Liverpool. A brief skirmish at Birch services with old friends Blackpool (who were at Rotherham that day) livened up the journey on another sunny August day as we headed westwards on the M62. This really was a trip into the unknown. Not unusually, the driver of the double-decker got lost in the Cheshire chemical belt, miles away from anywhere and with no one around to ask.

By the time we arrived, the game was well underway. Prenton Park was small and dilapidated even by Third Division standards. It was another world after Molyneux and Bramall Lane, and the crowd of fewer than 2,000 confirmed the fall in status. Opposing fans were separated down the middle of a low, dusty, covered side terrace by the type of flimsy fencing you might find on your local allotment. As the latecomers filtered in via the covered end behind the goal to take their places with the rest of the City fans on our side of the halfway line, scuffling broke out on both sides of the fence. Small groups of infiltrating fans from both teams spilled briefly onto the pitch to get back among their own. This disturbance over, everyone settled down to watch the game, which City won comfortably 3-1, the entire scoring spree taking place long before the end.

A complete lack of interest from Tranmere and their fans led to a relaxed atmosphere among the City, who slowly spread out around our half of the almost empty ground, many sitting or lying on the terraces as the pre-match drinking and hot sun took its toll. The game, long since over as contest, was fizzling out when, in the dying moments and with the exit gates open, a new mob of Tranmere showed themselves.

Bursting in through the exit of the covered end, about 100 of them appeared, armed with sticks and rocks. Led by oldish blokes in their late twenties, they were well organised and knew exactly what to do. They laid into any City fans they could spot, bricking others and kicking and punching anyone between 15 and 30 in what seemed a well-rehearsed attack.

With the game over, more Tranmere arrived to block the way back to the coach park behind the Main Stand, causing the scattered and disorganised City to run the gauntlet through the assembled Tranmere. This had all the hallmarks of fortnightly ritual, and the local coppers seemed to take no interest in it (the novel *Awaydays* by Kevin Sampson, about a group of Tranmere fans called The Pack, which has accounts of trouble at Prenton Park, seems to accurately describe what went on there). Although no one got a bad kicking, the bus was subdued coming out of Birkenhead. The home game against them was pencilled in for revenge in a few diaries that day, but sneakily they never showed, standard tactics for many lower division sides with small away followings.

Welcome to Division Three. Welcome to crowds of less than 2,000, where policing is minimal and where danger from opposing fans can be greater than at grounds in higher divisions with ten times the crowd, and where new faces in small towns stick out like sore thumbs. Welcome also to grounds and towns where 100 determined and organised away fans can cause mayhem, and where contact between opposing fans is almost guaranteed. The Tranmere game, like Carlisle the week before, was a benchmark. There were not many places to go more tricky than Tranmere, and even if the Fat Lady is singing, it's not over till you're back on the coach and even then the emergency exit can still be opened if necessary A cunning and unexpected ambush at the end of the game had taught us to avoid complacency and to expect the unexpected. This was not like Division Two at all, with its bigger numbers and simpler tactics. This was sneaky, vicious and effective. Now you see me, now you don't.

A few years later in an FA Cup game in 1984, City took several coaches to Tranmere and vans of lads – a much larger than usual mob to such a game. Play was held up in the first half as City took it to Tranmere in the seats. Result: dozens of seats ripped out and thrown, fighting from top to bottom in the stand, with City having the upper hand, one ginger Tranmere kid in a green Irish rugby union shirt getting plenty of attention, write-ups in various newspapers about how trouble marred the Tigers' victory. For the double-deckers of '78, it was a satisfying return.

Saturday, 15 December 1979. City Hall was the venue for a concert by fading punk band The Damned on a cold Saturday night in December. The promoters had decided to risk a large venue and their adventurousness seemed to pay dividends as the hall filled up nicely with a mix of students, suburban punks and mainstream locals. But it soon became clear that there was another group in the hall that night who had not come just for the music. Long before The Damned took the stage, a large group of scruffy punks had taken to chanting 'Boro' at regular intervals. They had come down by coach from Teesside and were part of that extremely rare subspecies, the punk football yob, spotted a couple of years earlier at Blackpool wearing mohair jumpers and winkle-picker boots. However, if Blackpool were dressers and punks into football, these Boro lads were scruffy leather jacket punks who were looking for a row, and used football to spark one off.

At first the chanting was met with bemusement. Few students and suburban non-football types knew or cared what all the noise was about. However, enough people sussed what was going on and were sizing up the situation rapidly, getting ready to handle what was coming. As the Boro punks moved in front of the stage in a large group, unnoticed by the students and the chattering classes, the loud disco drowned most of the chanting and shouting. Slowly but surely, a group of Hull lads (Boothferry Estate, Hull FC, City, Hull KR and various other small, local squads) was forming alongside them, watching their every move, getting ready. A loud Boro chant went up, audible above the music, and was met with abuse and a few plastic beer glasses, then surging and the first punches and kicks.

This continued for 20 minutes in an increasingly packed hall. Loud chants of 'Come on you Hull' and 'Old Faithful' went up as rallying calls, as more and more Hull lads mobbed up. At a certain point, it went off big style. The bouncers were powerless to stop it and just shrugged their shoulders as chairs were used to lay into the Boro. Chaos reigned for several minutes as the fighting spread over a large area in front of the stage, with about 150 people involved. The emergency exits were forced open, word having got round nearby pubs (Bass House and Cheese). Reinforcements steamed in from the side and the Boro bottle started to go as, outnumbered, they were coming off worst. They attempted to get out of the hall but found things just as bad outside.

By now the concert had been abandoned, with the scale and ferocity of the fighting emptying the downstairs area of the hall, and The Damned took refuge in their dressing room. Up on the balcony, a few City took advantage of the chaos to let off a fire extinguisher and spray it on the bedlam below. The Damned's road crew, seeing this strange indoor shower, suddenly realised the danger and ran onto the stage to stop thousands of pounds worth of equipment from blowing up, trying to disconnect it all before it short-circuited. However much the punks talked about anarchy, it was the local football/rugby lads who delivered it and who will always remember it with glee – as will The Damned, who got paid for it.

Blackburn Rovers, Friday, 21 December 1979. Six days after the Night of The Damned at the City Hall, City played Blackburn at home on a freezing Friday night to avoid clashing with the Christmas shopping. A gate of just over 3,500 turned out to see struggling City's first game since a 7-2 thrashing at Brentford three weeks earlier.

Small pockets of City fans were located in the Kempton with others in the North Stand waiting. Would any Blackburn show? Blackburn were a team who had a few at home but were no great shakes away, like many in the Third. On a night when turning up at Boothferry was a duty rather than a pleasure, no one expected many from over the Pennines – a couple of hundred at best, normals included.

But slowly it became clear that they had brought a few old growlers who had no hesitation in letting everyone know they'd arrived. In a weird silence in the semi-dark of the Kempton, before the floodlights had been fully switched on, a small group of young City clashed with a similar number of Blackburn. No one wore colours, with many Blackburn in sheepskins and duffel coats to keep out the cold. It was toe-to-toe, no-one running on either side, and slowly more sporadic fights broke out in the North Stand. The few police present didn't know what to do, so didn't do anything. The scrapping continued on and off for a couple of minutes, which seems like forever inside a football ground. Blackburn's initial confidence in their own ability to deal with these trendy young kids slowly disintegrated as the City kept at them. As Blackburn slowly realised they were risking a serious and unexpected pummeling, they tried to corral the wagons in the Kempton, leaving a few stranded in the North Stand. One of these was left unconscious, to be stretchered away to Hull Royal Infirmary.

This game exposed once again the lack of police control and segregation. Unlike most teams who came at the time, Blackburn were prepared to have a go back. Such undisturbed scrapping inside a ground is unthinkable now, but the late seventies and early eighties saw some of the wildest City games, as the pre-casuals learned their trade. Most of the City involved were teenagers, many still at school.

Our early optimism that we would soon escape Division Three proved ill-founded. After a decent first season, we spent the next two years battling to avoid the drop into the basement, and in 1981, having won only eight games from a possible 46, Hull City were relegated to Division Four for the first time in history.

By August 1981, we were lining up to play mighty Torquay United. Our average crowds had suffered terribly, going from 6,000-plus (1978) to a paltry 3,000 (1980). Yet out of this gloom there was, for us, one shard of light: more and more 'lads' were attending home games, fuelled by the success of the city's two rugby firms and the reputation gained by the founding fathers of the City Psychos. Lads began to look for their thrills once again on the terraces of Boothferry Park.

Yet it is true that many still stayed away, as they refused to integrate with their neighbours from either side of the river divide. Years of inter-area rivalry had put paid to reconciliation even for the good of the football team, and this continued to rob us of many lads who preferred to go to Old Trafford, Elland Road, Anfield, and even White Hart Lane and Stamford Bridge. Lads didn't support the national team in the way they do today, so many of the less successful provincial clubs had lads who divided time and loyalties between their hometown team and their First Division favourites. At least our younger element were intent on showing that Hull as a city and as a club were not to be dismissed as easy prey. As we entered the eighties, they marched forward to do battle.

At the same time you could see a change in attitudes and dress. Joining a mob became fashionable again. By 1978/79, different areas of the UK had begun to evolve a new style of terrace wear. In London, teams like Arsenal had flirted with a resurgence of the skinhead fashion but soon progressed to a more Mod appearance. The Manchester lads favoured Fred Perry shirts while the Scousers had a look which encompassed shirts with thin collars, buttoned down, and tight-leg jeans. For the first time since perhaps the skinhead era, football lads became recognisable by their clothing. As many Hull lads frequented these bigger clubs, the new styles developed in the city in conjunction with their evolvement elsewhere.

The lads at all-nighters also glimpsed how their peers from other towns were dressing. A lot of the Hull lads were into Northern Soul at that time, while others, myself included, preferred George Clinton and Parliament ('If you hear any noise, it's just me and the boys'), Ohio Players, Fatback Band, People's Choice and MFSB, among others.

During the punk period I had found myself drifting more into reggae and was lucky enough to get records sent direct from Jamaica. Some that spring to mind are Justin Hines and the Dominoes, Junior Murvin for the excellent 'Police And Thieves', Trinity, U Roy and Burning Spear. These groups were old hat by the start of the eighties – I had been collecting their singles and LPs since 1975 – yet the sounds stand the test of time. Groups like Talking Heads and Maze got a lot of airplay during Saturday nights at the legendary Henry's. But 'Soul' was still a big puller among the lads. Who can forget the sounds of Atlantic Starr, Wizzards of Ooze, Curtis Mayfield, Leroy Hutson and others?

My personal memories of the seventies close with yet another game against Sheffield Wednesday, this time in the old League Cup, first round. It was played on a Tuesday night, August 14, four days before I was due to be married. The Owls brought the usual amount, approximately 2,000 fans. They took a few slaps before the game; we were mobbed up, while the Wednesday fans were arriving in small groups. The after-match hostilities looked promising as they had plenty of lads. Wednesday seemed to have a much older firm than the Blades, yet the United boys were more organised and brought it to you.

I had been warned to be on my best behaviour, and I couldn't have done any better. We were following a large group of Sheffield lads down Boothferry Road towards Fiveways. Three of their group moved across to the grassy island running the length of the road and began taunting us. They were much older than our lads, well into their thirties, and thought they could intimidate us, playing up to their colleagues on the other side of the road. We were straining at the leash, but knew it would have to wait, wait, until we'd got further away from North Road and the eyes of the police. These three took our lack of response as weakness and pinpointed my mate Jimmy BS for a bit of fun. Jimmy responded with a flurry of insults directly at a more portly member of their little group. This was too much for the tubby Owl, who launched himself onto Jimmy, knocking him backwards. His two mates quickly moved in for the kill. I looked round but no one moved to help Jimmy. I couldn't believe it. The other Sheffield lads were coming across. If we didn't act fast we'd be on the floor or on our toes. Fuck that.

Jimmy was on the deck with kicks thudding into him. I ran straight into the three of them, probably stomping over Jimmy in my eagerness. A solid punch to the head of the fat one and all three panicked. They must have thought we were all running at them, and they turned and fled. The rest of our lot now bounced over to the larger group of Wednesday fans, but they didn't interest me, I wanted the Three Stooges and set off in pursuit. I caught the first with a sidewards punch to his head. He tripped on the side of the kerb and a boot from Jimmy coming in behind knocked his head back. His mate ran into a garden and hammered on the front door to escape. Never mind him, it was the big bastard I wanted. I caught up with him and ran alongside. He took a swipe and caught me on the bridge of my nose. Still running, I grabbed his hair, swung him round and brought his head down onto my knee.

I didn't have time to gloat. As he knelt wiping the blood off his face, one of the lads shouted, 'Look out, there's a copper.' I turned and felt cold, sure I was nicked, but the shouting stirred me into action. I ran just out of arms' length of the officer and nipped between some oncoming cars, which stopped him from reaching me. I sprinted down the road, slipped down a 'ten-foot' (access road to garages and back gardens) and hid in a back garden for over half an hour. I wasn't about to take any more chances; a cut nose would be enough to explain. Bang go the wedding photos.

* * *

MANNIX: I don't know how the name City Psychos started, but at the back end of the seventies I became aware of a bunch of older lads who could be relied on to organise transport to away matches. Although the name Psychos would seem to indicate a bunch of off-their-heads nutters, when I got to know those who ran the trips, they were just decent lads who would take the trouble to book coaches, rather than being the gamest or handiest lads in City's mob. They used to print the 'Psychos newsletter' as well, and hand them out every few months. I had one during my last year at school and tried to drum up support from the lads in my year, few of whom had an interest in City. This issue stated that for the first time in years we were to meet

Grimsby and Barnsley that season, and that we wanted at least four double-deckers of lads travelling to each match. The language was quite colourful but would nowadays be considered juvenile and innocent: 'Lets smash their heads in, stamp on their guts, and puke all over them,' etc.

These lads had a deep love of football in general and City in particular. Once in the early eighties, when a match at Barnsley was postponed, a lot of the lads drifted off to do whatever, but 60 of us went on one of the double-deckers to Doncaster, who were at home to Bournemouth. We stood with the few Bournemouth and tried to get an off with the Donny lads. A police sergeant was heard saying over the radio, 'I don't know why they're here, but we have a coach of mad Hull City fans here.' For those who ran the trips, the name Psychos seemed a misnomer, like a five-foot lad calling himself 'Killer' and gaining a rep without actually doing anything. For a lot of the lads who went on the buses however, now that was a different story.

By the beginning of the eighties I was attending Northern Soul all-nighters, was no stranger to drugs, and was going to Manchester and Liverpool shopping for clothes that no-one in Hull was wearing. We quite arrogantly considered ourselves a cut above the rest; we were fighting and sharply dressed all the time. I imagine that's how the original Mods felt around 1964.

Around this time, there was a split amongst the fans who stood together singing on the terraces. I remember standing at a match wearing a burgundy leather box jacket, Kio shoes, straight-legged jeans and sporting a wedge haircut. The lads who I had looked up to were still dressing as if they were going to a Status Quo concert. They had led the charges into a ruck regularly, you tended to look up to them and, to a certain extent, 'follow' them, but now it would be embarrassing to stand near them. Still good lads, supporting the same team, but there were differences creeping in.

Later on, as we became known as 'casuals,' I don't think people steered clear of us as such, but we were different from the then-stereotype football hooligan, and we were different from the older lads, who still had a West–East Hull rivalry going on. We tried to overcome this, with younger lads mixing more readily with their neighbours from across the River Hull. This gave us a tighter unit who could rely on each other when needed. There were definitely pubs that were known as 'West Hull' pubs and vice versa, and we didn't mix that much during the week, but Saturdays were different.

For me, being different was more of a north-south thing. I remember talking to a Londoner at a match in 1981. He had a short haircut and was wearing a flight jacket and some Pod shoes with jeans. He stated that he and his mates were 'trendies'. I asked what he would call us, at that time in Lyle & Scott or Pringle and sporting electric blue jumbo cords, strap trainers, and wedge haircuts. He said, 'New Romantics'! We tended to copy the Scousers and Mancs, and it was clear the Londoners, although smart, were a year or so off the cutting edge.

More and more lads wanted to be part of this casual scene, as the transition was made from the old hooligan style. Also around this time, the wearing of colours among the lads stopped suddenly. In the mid-seventies I would often have a scarf round my neck, a silk scarf trailing from my waistband, and another tied around my wrist. What a difference a few years make.

As we separated from those that still wore the team's colours, the entering of opposing ends became much easier. The downside was that I have lost count of the number of lads who have dished out, or taken, a bat from their own boys accidentally as a result of this, especially as new members were joining the ranks each week and hadn't yet become faces.

Rugby league was big in Hull and all our monsters, the dockers and fishermen, used to stand at Hull FC, meaning our mob at football was predominantly young lads. When mobs of men came fighting us, we quite often came off worst, and I used to hate the fact that Hull, a very rough city, did not give as good an account of itself. I used to hate rugby for that. Rugby league took all our mature support. I am convinced that if all the dockers and seamen had been attending City, we would have gained the notoriety Millwall did, as Hull is a rough place, and when some of these blokes came home from sea they had only a few days to enjoy themselves before their next trip. They were lawless bastards. It didn't occur to me at that time that if my age group stayed tight and kept attending, we would eventually be like some of the other teams' mobs I envied. Both the Hull and Hull KR rugby league teams were more successful than City, each had their own firm of boys, and this rivalry affected the football scene.

To us it was excellent, although it divided Hull and fights with different gangs were still weekly occurrences around the town centre. On a Sunday we would go up East Hull if Rovers were playing Warrington, Salford, Widnes or St Helens. They were perceived as being football lads from the Manchester and Merseyside teams, and some of the fights were as memorable as any at football. On a lot of weekends, representing your city became a two-day job.

This also helped bond us younger lads together; instead of just being 'that twat from Boothferry', or wherever, you had drunk, laughed and fought together and it had given you an identity, making it that bit more difficult for lads from other estates to hate/want to batter you. For the older lads who were steeped in it, there was probably too much history to contemplate doing what we did. They could or would not let bygones be bygones, but my age group didn't have that problem.

Certain teams gave us a testing time, Warrington without a doubt at rugby. They had numbers and were as game as I have EVER seen. Football-wise it was Sheff U, Middlesbrough, Stoke, clubs of that ilk. As we became more organised, we started to meet all over Hull and leave at different times to away games, to avoid detection. We were never that clued up, or flush with money to stay overnight, so matches like Bristol City, Torquay, Portsmouth and even some London clubs saw a mob of lads leave a pub at midnight and go down on a coach through the night. We must have looked like a set of tramps roaming cities with thin jumpers on at 6am, looking for a cafe to keep warm as much as out of hunger. It made for long days but days like these are what legends are made of.

To prove how naive I was at that time, in the early eighties we played at Oxford. I had visions of their supporters being students wearing college scarves. Had it been a few years later after I'd seen the Blackbird Leys Estate riots on the news, I would have been forewarned. Two coaches of lads went, had a drink in Headington and then went in the ground thinking we owned the town. Wrong.

We were fronted by an equal number of lads, many of them blacks, who stood their ground behind the stand to the right of the large, open away end. They were game and neither side gave way, the OB interrupting it after a couple of minutes. We were put in with the City fans, and a little later we saw Oxford's end erupt as a handful of lads swung out at anybody. Oxford ran at them and they were dragged out by plod and put in with us. They weren't Hull, but a group with a big Cockney lad called A–, whose parents used to run a hotel/pub up in Hull. He was West Ham, and had 'ICF' tattooed on his arm, but had a soft spot for Hull, and quite a few of us knew him from his time up north.

Later on in the eighties, some Hull lads got very friendly with C–, an Oxford lad, at England games, and he came away with us for a while. He was a good, game lad who never took a backward step. Goes to show you should never underestimate any team.

BURY

Bury live in the shadow of much larger Manchester/Lancashire teams, and while I wouldn't pretend anybody rates them,

EVERY team has a couple of dozen lads at home, and the attempted taking of ends was a weekly affair. The first time I went to Bury was in the late seventies, as evidenced by the fact that some of the City lads had shirts and scarves on underneath their Harringtons. This occasion was effortless, City didn't even bother going in twos and threes, just all together, stood there and started singing as the Bury end parted like the Red Sea. Getting paraded out by the plod 40-handed while the rest of the Bury supporters were still paying in gave me a great sense of pride, especially at my age.

The second occasion was a night match when we beat them 3-2, coming from behind to win courtesy of a great goal from Andy Flounders. This time we paid in the Bury end in singles and there was only ten of us. Bury had a few lads singing insults at the City end, and I went to the hot dog stall. When I came back I could see that City had kicked it off and been dragged out. They were being put in the away end opposite. I'll leave it up to you to decide whether I bottled it or discretion won the day, but I was in my late teens and could see that even ordinary blokes were pissed off that we had been in their end, kids were crying, so I walked up to a plod and said, 'I'm Hull mate. I think I've paid in the wrong end.'

When Bury heard that, they ran towards me and the plod dragged me out, with me making a few token kicks as they tried to drag me back. I got marched round the pitch to the Hull fans, to a thunderous ovation, as they thought I had kicked it off by myself. I said fuck all at the time, revelling in the unwarranted applause.

READING

Apart from the famous Hull v Hull KR Rugby League Challenge Cup final, Rovers reached Wembley again, in 1981. Obviously there were many travelling down, while only seven of us were up for taking the train to see Hull City at Reading on the same day: the Simmo brothers (Paul and Tony), a lad called Dill,

Gareth, Jack, myself and some other whose name I can't recall. A lot of good lads from all over Hull were going down for a weekend at the rugby on the early morning train, so we decided we would join them, changing in London for our trip to Berkshire. It was the weekend of my 17th birthday and to celebrate I had bought a bottle of whisky and some cans, which somehow got polished off before we reached Doncaster.

We got off the train to wait for our connection to London, and bumped into four local lads who announced they followed Sheffield Wednesday. In the course of discussing the merits of our respective teams, three of them and two Hull lads were laid out, with a mate of mine called Gav (R.I.P.) battering one of them over the head with a menu board from outside the buffet.

Next thing I knew, I was handcuffed to the banister leading up to the main station entrance, while the plod fucked off to make more arrests. In my thick, drunken state, I could not believe they had left me there, reasoning that all I had to do was run to the top of the stairs and the cuffs would slip off the banister. Of course I hadn't realised that the said banister must be bracketed onto the wall. This was brought home to me when I ran at top speed, only to be lifted off my feet and bounced headfirst down the stone steps like something out of a *Tom and Jerry* cartoon.

The rugby lads had carried on to The Smoke, with six of us City lads nicked, together with a Leeds-supporting skinhead from Selby in Yorkshire, who kept me awake all night in the next cell singing about Leeds 'saying goodbye to the Third', so they must have been promoted that year. We were charged and then released at about 9am, so it was touch and go if we would make the game. We had to run alongside a moving, London-bound train trying to get on, with British Rail staff and Transport Police chasing us. We were lucky not to get nicked less than half an hour after being released.

We got to Reading's old ground just before kick-off. I remember little about the match, except that in a stand next to us was a reasonable mob of lads, mostly skinheads, some wearing West Ham shirts. I realised lads in London sometimes shared loyalties, but my clueless geography told me Berkshire was too far away for this to happen. After the match we were nervous and very wary at what might occur, there being only seven of us, but got to the train station unthreatened.

Next time I bumped into Reading was at Hampden with England in 1999-2000 and they had managed to fill a coach of lads to take up there. They are currently doing well, get decent home gates, so must have some good lads. Maybe they felt sorry for us that day. Not as sorry as I did!

GILLINGHAM

In the mid-eighties we took the Hull City 'war wagon' to Gillingham, leaving at midnight but not getting far before the plod swooped and searched the coach, finding a number of weapons, including an air rifle. Amazingly they allowed the coach to carry on once all the weapons were confiscated. But the away match at Gillingham I remember best was earlier in that decade when we set off in the back of a van at 6am. There were about 20 of us, and as I looked around at some of the good lads we had in it, a lot older than me, I felt confident we would at least hold our own. That was until we dropped four of them off down the Fulham Palace Road. They were going to watch Chelsea!

We parked up near the ground, had a beer and then paid in. City had maybe 200 supporters there and only us that would stand our ground. A group of Gillingham fans nearby started to bait us, and I retaliated, taking the piss out of a kid who looked like Bernie Winters. After a while he walked over to me and I thought we were going to start fighting under the noses of OB, and both get nicked. Instead he tried to calm things down, stating there weren't many of us, so let's just talk. I was naive at that age and must have been brought up too trusting, as I accepted this on face value and spent the rest of the first half talking to him.

After the match we walked the 500 yards or so to our van, turned the corner, and there it was, surrounded by 40 Gillingham lads, some with milk bottles and pieces of wood.

'Fucking hell, how did they know we were parked here?' said George, an older lad.

I said nothing, realising now why my mate from Gillingham had seemed so interested in our day out! We had no option but to run into them, get the driver in the van, try and get the doors open and drive through them. We managed this, which leads me to believe they didn't want to give us more than a kicking, as we had neither the numbers nor quality to make a getaway if they had really wanted to stop us.

Apart from a cut head and some black eyes/bruises, we got away unscathed, but against a nastier mob we would have been wasted. I lost some of my innocence that day, perhaps not before time.

Of course, other mobs down in the lower divisions were developing their own notoriety. This was the era when lots of the new casual firms were making their mark, and their names were becoming known for the first time.

NICK: Hull City versus Blackpool, 7 February 1981. With the Tigers struggling in the basement of Division Three, the game at Boothferry with fellow strugglers Blackpool was keenly anticipated, not least because Blackpool had a group who were not shy about publicising themselves. The name 'Benny's Mob' was painted in white all along the railway line from Preston to Blackpool, and all around the outside of their Bloomfield Road ground, in extremely large letters, letting visitors know who the local boys were. No undercover police operations needed here then. Blackpool in March '78 had had a mob which seemed to consist mainly of sharp-dressed punks in mohair jumpers and combat gear, and who used to come round to the visitors' section at the end of the game challenging you to have a go. As

Blackpool's slow decline mirrored City's, the two teams continued to play each other every season, lower and lower down the league, and Blackpool's mob seemed to shrink as City's continued to grow. Maybe because Blackpool had been in Division One at the beginning of the seventies, their decline had been going on for even longer than City's.

How many were in Benny's Mob? Which one was Benny and how naughty was his firm? Would they put on a decent show at Boothferry? These were some of the questions being asked in the run-up to this relegation battle.

Plenty of City were in the ground early in the North Stand, where the Blackpool were almost certain to enter: punks, soulboys, normals, old heads, pre-casuals all discreetly positioned to observe the arrival of any new faces. No dramatic entrances or 'here we are in your seats!' tricks but a slow trickle of Blackpool who took up position directly behind the North Stand goal. Dressed down for the occasion in combat jackets and jeans, subdued but definitely Blackpool. Slowly, as City were sure no large mob of Blackpool latecomers was hanging around on the car park, attention turned to the 50-100 who stood behind the goal. Already the net was closing as the game was underway, and attention turned to the match. As the first half passed, the Blackpool were no doubt aware that they were surrounded, with only a few police separating everyone. (This same thing had happened to City at Blackpool in the mid-seventies, an unpleasant way to watch a match).

The away support became quieter and quieter as any shouts for their team were met with stares and abuse. As the first half was drawing to a close, a scrap started and quickly spread. At the same time, City attacked from the other side, from behind and from in front. This assault from all sides at once overwhelmed Blackpool, who tried to protect themselves from the blows raining down. The coppers flapped around and eventually got enough in to stop it all. As the first half finished, the police tried to lead Blackpool to a safe haven. With no fences between the North Stand and Kempton, and Bunkers reserved for home fans, the police escorted the Blackpool onto the track round the pitch and towards Kempton as 100 or so City shadowed them on the terraces ready to repeat the dose. The police twigged that they couldn't put them back on the terraces so escorted them into the centre circle on the pitch, where they surrounded them and thought what to do. This brought the house down — away fans penned in like sheep on *One Man and His Dog*, while the coppers scratched their chins.

Eventually it was decided to put them in the Well next to the players' tunnel, having first cleared a gap for them. Here they remained unmolested for the second half. A dramatic late winner from King Edwards sent everyone home happy.

But Blackpool were not finished yet. Parked up near Fiveways in various cars, they came out aggressively, as most of the crowd had drifted away. However most of them got yet another lesson in a long day as they became hunted again, and this time with no police to rescue them. A comprehensive kicking was administered to about 20 Blackpool who didn't stick together and help each other when faced with modest numbers. No sign of Benny though.

CHAPTER SIX

The Rugby League Wars

AS THE CITY Psychos name spread, so the numbers grew. But our unity, fragile as ever, was soon cracking again, due largely to the success of the city's two rugby league outfits. Traditionally the lads living east of the River Hull were Hull Kingston Rovers fans, while West Hull and the majority of the North Hull estates were Hull FC supporters. This drove a wedge between both sets of lads and the city centre became a battleground each weekend. Though this confirmed Hull's reputation for 'hardness', it meant that to some extent two firms existed within the Psychos' mob and we were not as organised as others.

We also never managed to get a good FA Cup run going in this period and so never attracted back lads who had put their slippers on for a while. At the same time, the RL scene was resurgent, with both rugby teams doing well and attracting bigger crowds than at Boothferry Park. This led to intense rivalry, much fighting between lads from either side of the river – and some raucous away matches. In the late seventies it was not uncommon for Hull FC to take 50 coaches away, an amazing support even though there were no long journeys to consider outside Yorks/Lancs/Cumbria.

One attraction of rugby matches was the lack of policing at places like Widnes, St Helens and Warrington ('the Wires'). The latter, in particular, drawing on the Liverpool-Manchester overspill, were something else, and that fixture, along with derby games between Hull and KR, was a must-go game. The Wires crew were very much like us, lads who divided their weekends between football and rugby league. Their boys ran with all of the big north west mobs, and because of this they often came across quite cocky. Outings to Warrington saw Hull lads from east and west joining up, something rare indeed for trips away from football.

A Friday night game was attended by two coaches and a double-decker full of lads. Our coach was the first to arrive and, as the driver was finding his way to the ground, a few lads on board spotted a group of Wires going into a pub. The driver was ordered to stop, but he argued the toss, saying, 'Look lads, I'm not stopping here, I'm going straight to the ground.'

He was persuaded otherwise and the coach emptied. We headed straight for the pub and trashed the outside, along with a few of their lads who were caught napping. We strolled about looking for more victims but all we found were the police. During the course of the game, an inspector began asking for the coach organiser, and informed him that the driver had decided to return home after feeling threatened, leaving us stranded. He had left with half of the lads' jackets still on board, and the Warrington police weren't too happy either. A few managed to sneak onto the other coach and decker, but the police threatened their drivers with arrest for overloading. It left forty of us with nowhere to go, a contingent of police beside us and an angry mob of locals after tearing us apart.

We were taken to the railway station and more or less told to fuck off by the Old Bill; once we were on board a train we would be out of their hair. A few of us decided to hitch home and jumped in a taxi for Burtonwood service station on the M62. Four of us paired up to hopefully make it easier to gain a lift. It wasn't too long before we got a chance. The lad I'd paired up with was an avid Liverpool supporter and he nudged me under the table.

'Fucking hell, that's Craig Johnston, he might give us a lift to the A1.'

Apparently Craig had just signed for Liverpool that night, while they were at home to Stoke City, and we hoped he was going back home to Middlesbrough.

'Let's go and ask him.'

As we stood up so did Craig, and headed straight to the toilet. Both Glen and myself stood either side of him, and he must have been a bit wary.

Glen nodded to him. 'Alright Craig?'

'Err, alright lads.'

Glen spun him a yarn about us being Liverpool fans from Hull who were hitching it back after watching the game; he kept congratulating Johnston on signing for the Scousers. I thought, *fucking hell Glen, don't overdo it*. Craig began to explain in great detail that he was only going as far as a hotel in Manchester and, as much as he would like to help us, the car was full. He left. All Glen could do was repeat, 'Craig Johnston, I've had a piss next to FUCKING CRAIG JOHNSTON. He would have helped us you know, if he could have.' Personally, I thought he couldn't wait to finish and get away from two weirdoes.

H of OPE can take up the story of another meeting with Warrington where we went mobbed up:

H of OPE: I missed out on the mid-seventies scene, spending three-and-a-half years inside for various offences, but when I came out rugby league was massive in Hull. The rivalry was just as intense as at football. Hull city centre on a weekend was not the place for the faint-hearted. The normal estate gang wars had escalated to such an extent that it was now east against west, with the River Hull the traditional dividing line.

The weekly rugby league paper carried stories of people intimidated by the atmosphere and rowdy behaviour of both the Hull clubs; many hated them. Games played at Warrington,

Widnes and the like brought out the locals eager for a pop at the Hull lads. Add low policing levels and you have the perfect setting. I began to organise coaches and got together a good mix of old Orchard lads together with the up and coming City lads. This coachload was as good as anything I'd been involved with before and we had many Sunday outings following the Airlie Birds.

An away game to Warrington was top of the list. My favourite moment there was when Hull FC played them in the Challenge Cup. This time the driver wasn't too bothered about dropping us off near the town centre. No sooner than getting dropped off, we met up with an equal number of Wires; not young scallies this time but their more experienced lads. We ran at them and vice versa till we again clashed at the base of a bridge, which straddled a canal. This time we were really backing them off; their confidence had all but disappeared as we pursued them. A few Wires lads went down and were left by their mates. One of these quickly got to his feet and began lashing out even though he was surrounded, but the poor cunt was lifted off his feet and thrown over the bridge. Luckily for him he landed on the towpath.

They couldn't match our numbers that day. We hunted them down after the match and attacked from all angles; even the Hull FC shirters were joining in. This was the last time we went to Warrington mobbed up. I don't think we had anything else to prove, so we left it on a high note.

* * *

At a semi-final against Widnes, ten of us found ourselves confronted by 30 or 40 Widnes lads. They stood at the top of a steep bank of terracing, calling it on, and stupidly we went for it. Running up the terracing before me were two good mates, James BS and Tony S. Tony was the first to reach them. A few moved to one side, revealing a lad with a massive stave in his hands. Tony hesitated, then flew back down the embankment, off balance as the wood connected with his head. James went berserk, and ran right at the Widnes lad with the wooden club. He was on top of him before he had chance to swing it, but the clubber was rescued by his mates, who came at the rest of us from all sides. They pushed us back, past Tony, who was well out of it, but they didn't go in for the kill. They moved back to their original positions, leaving us at the bottom of the stand, regrouping for another try.

That was the difference between us and most other rugby lads – they would front anyone but they weren't as vicious as the likes of us, HKR, Warrington, Leigh and Salford. If any of these teams had you on the run, they would stomp all over you. No mercy would have been shown and that's why these lads were feared throughout the rugby world.

Each week in the letters column of the *Rugby Leaguer* you could read accounts of violence as Mr Deeply Upset from Dewsbury bemoaned the fact that football-style hooliganism was rife. Yet the picture painted to the country at large was of fans who mingled together, drank together and all got on famously. That was the official view, spouted every year by the BBC commentators as they reported on that great Wembley showcase, the Rugby League Challenge Cup Final. They never saw us lot, getting shitfaced before a game and brawling with anyone we could find.

Only once can I remember anyone trying to discuss the issue, and that was Harry Gration, the *Look North* anchorman. He slagged off (on air) people who were causing trouble at matches and made a point of mentioning both Hull clubs as the main culprits. A little while later, Hull FC were at Thrum Hall, Halifax, and as usual there was a couple of thousand black and whites there, including us. We began to infiltrate the home stand and aimed for a set of Halifax lads abusing the Hull to their left. As we pushed through the crowd, J***o came face to face with Mr Gration.

'Hey Harry, watch this,' he shouted.

He turned and whacked a Halifax lad in front of him, as the rest of us piled in from all sides.

Other teams tried mixing it. Wigan, St Helens, Bradford, Castleford and Featherstone always showed resistance when we came to town, but our numbers (both Hull FC and KR had upwards of 300 'lads') were usually too much. The period from 1978/82 was probably the golden era for rugby league in Hull. Average attendances shot up, with Hull FC commanding gates each Sunday of 12-13,000 whilst Hull KR managed 8-9,000. Away trips saw anything from 2-5,000 fans from both clubs leaving Hull on a Sunday morning. During this renaissance, Hull City were doing what they do best – struggle.

For any lads not *au fait* with rugby league who may be thinking I am referring to a minibus of lads on each side, please don't be fooled. Sometimes you would be talking about a couple of hundred on each side, and some of our best fighters in the town were involved. Even small mining towns like Castleford and Featherstone generated fervent support from people who had little focus for local pride except their team. With sometimes only one or two policemen in the ground, it was pure terrace warfare, akin to football a decade earlier.

MANNIX: With rugby league being a phenomenon of Yorkshire, Lancashire and Cumbria, to envisage mass fighting at a match may be difficult for any southerners reading this book and trying to picture Stanley knives at, for instance, Bath v Harlequins. No upper class twits or twats up here though boys, just plenty of the same you may have met on Saturdays at football grounds up and down the country.

For lads a few years older than me, steeped in the gang rivalry between East and West Hull, the very idea of some lads from west of the river going to back up Rovers boys would be

Thousands form orderly queues outside Boothferry Park to watch Manchester United in the flat cap and raincoat days of 1949 – and not a hint of trouble.

The Orchard Park Estate Mob in the mid 1970s. How football and fashion had changed over the course of a generation.

Surging across the pitch to attack our deadly Sheffield United rivals as a pissed-off goalie stands, hands on hips, in October 1983 (for story see page 137).

The boot on the other foot: this time it's the Hull casuals who are in retreat across the pitch when Middlesbrough came and shocked us in a pre-season game that same year.

Toe-to-toe combat on the terraces versus Bolton in March 1984. This was the heyday of hooliganism in Britain, and scenes like this were commonplace around the country.

Two fans from the same Hull-Bolton game battle it out on the pitch. But by the mid-eighties improved segregation and policing would shift the focus of violence from inside to outside grounds.

A Hull minibus in Middlesbrough in March 1986, with the police closing in (see p170). Our van squad brawled in the street with the Boro, which led to 22 Hull lads ending up in court.

Travelling thugs left 'calling card'

by Angus Young

THIS IS the sick face of soccer as presented by Hull City supporters.

These weapons of hate were captured by police before Saturday's match at Middlesbrough.

Included in the haul is a fireman's axe, a weighted cosh and a Stanley knife blade belonging to City fans.

The pre-match swoops by police saw three rented mini-buses from Hull packed with fans being ordered out of town.

But the action failed to prevent some of the worst football violence seen in Middlesbrough this season, with 22 Hull youths arrested.

Chief Supt. Alan Bruce, who led the police operation, said: "On this occasion the blame must be put firmly on the shoulders of the travelling supporters from Hull who came looking for trouble.

During this season things

A series of tip-offs and intelligence reports from Hull police helped identify the soccer thugs left copycat calling cards "congratulating" their honligans arriving in Middlesbrough.

"We got very good pre-match reports that a number of troublemakers were coming here with the expected intention of violence," said Chief Supt. Bruce.

"As it was, we had sporadic, premeditated violence throughout the town centre from a minority of youngsters.

But the police operation could not prevent several street battles where Hull victims on having met Hull City.

In one incident, 26-year-old 'Boro fan Brian Williams suffered a broken arm after three bricks were thrown into a pub.

"The pub was full of people, including women and pensioners, so anyone could have been hit. It was totally

CONGRATULATIONS!
YOU HAVE JUST MET
Hull City
Hull City Football Club

One of the calling cards left by those who slipped through police cordons.

The 22 Hull youths arrested, along with four 'Boro fans, will face charges in Teesside at a date to be fixed.

Four juveniles from the Middlesbrough area bound for Ayresome Park were also arrested in the town centre for the alleged theft of Stanley knives.

Saturday's events were a repeat of violence in Hull last September when the two

Headlines from the same game: calling cards, weapons hauls and arrests - the usual.

A coachload of Bradford City's Ointment mob find themselves tracked and trapped near Boothferry Park (see p156).

Birmingham boss feared for safety as coach attacked

FRY-TENED

BIRMINGHAM City manager Barry Fry described the ambush by Hull City supporters on his team coach as the most frightening experience of his life".

Fry was slightly cut in his neck after debris from missiles thrown y a gang now believed to be about 20 youths, stoned the bus.

Broken bottles, bricks, rocks and a for sale sign were thrown at the Birmingham coach as it passed the group outside the Griffin pub in Anlaby Road, bout half a mile from Boothferry Park on Saturday.

Fry was the only person injured, although his players were said to be very aken up and three windows on the coach were smashed.

Earlier he had tried to play the incident down, saying one man had hrown a brick three times and I headed it back three times" but after the me he said he and the players had been terrified.

Fry, who was playing cards at the time, said: "We were stuck in traffic and about 20 fans were gesturing at us on the coach, but it was all good natured.

"Then all of a sudden loads of people came from nowhere and started throwing things like rocks, boulders, broken bottles and even a for sale sign.

"They smashed three windows and suddenly glass came down in front of me.

"We couldn't do anything because we were stuck in traffic and all the lads ducked down in the aisle of the coach.

"It was the most frightening experience I've ever known and not something I think any of us would like to go through again.

Hull City chairman Martin Fish surveys the damage caused to the visitors' bus before Saturday's game at Boothferry Park

"It was the most **Fish vows**

Newspaper headlines after an attack on the Birmingham City team coach. Manager Barry Fry was among those frantically trying to hold the doors closed (see p.204-5).

Clashes with the police in Italia 90, one of many tournaments disrupted by England supporters. International games always see a big Hull following.

Italy again, years later, and a Hull contingent fly the flag for the firm.

The French police mount a charge in the Old Port area of Marseilles during the infamous riot at the 1998 World Cup.

Hull fans gather outside the Silver Cod pub to watch police manoeuvres before our game with Cardiff City. The Soul Crew are a challenge for any firm.

A 'team photo' of some of the lads in the beer garden of the Prince Regent, a well-known hostelry on the edge of Hull city centre.

The author in 1980 (left), sporting a Le Coq Sportif T-shirt, and now, probably wiser and definitely older.

anathema. However, my age group were on the cusp of a 'gathering of the clans', when the fighters from the traditional fishing areas of West Hull would join with those from industrial East Hull for the common good, i.e. the reputation of the town, and Hull City.

Hull KR v Salford: I had no idea at the time where Salford was, or that Man U drew a lot of their support from there. I only knew that some of the football lads had stated it was a guaranteed 'off', with the bonus of lax policing. T, a mate from my estate, and I caught a bus to town, had a pint in the Green Gingerman pub in Hull station, then got a bus to the ground. It was early, but we were in bandit country and paid into the ground straight away. After five minutes on the near-deserted terraces, a group of ten lads started walking by a few rows down, singing out loud, 'UNITED . . .SHIT, UNITED . . .SHIT.' We stood there more bemused than worried, and after a minute the biggest lad walked up and tried the old 'Got the time mate?' sketch. When we answered in broad Hull, he said, 'Fucking hell, we thought you were Salford, they dress like that.' By way of explanation, these particular Rovers lads were still into jeans and Harringtons, whereas T and myself were sporting wedge hairstyles, Kios and strap trainers, yellow or electric blue jumbo cords, and Lyle & Scott jumpers and cardigans in bright colours. After a minute's chat to establish what we were doing there, and a bit of name-dropping of some of Rovers' better-known lads, they left, and we stood waiting for the ground to fill up.

Kick-off came and went. By that time there were about 150 good lads in there, 80 per cent East Hull but with a fair number of City lads. We were all stating what a letdown it had been when a cry went up, 'They're here!' We ran to the fence and looked outside, where a double-decker was emptying its cargo of decent-looking Mancs, mostly dressers. The rugby fans were brushed aside as we scaled the fence and started shouting abuse at each other. I remember Dave B, a very smart Hull lad in Lois jeans and a deerstalker, gesticulating at the Salford lads, one of whom shouted, 'Hey dickhead, Lonsdale went out with the Beatles,' in reference to Dave's sweatshirt.

We managed to get the message to them to stay outside, and started to leave the ground in droves. The stewards probably thought, We've got your entrance money, so who gives a fuck? Outside we charged onto Holderness Road and chased them near to their decker, when one of them, a small lad with a black wedge and a silver bubble coat on, shouted, 'Blades out lads.' With this they stopped running, turned as one and started throwing sharp metal objects at us. There is debate in Hull to this day as to what they threw, with some of the lads claiming it was kung fu-style 'shuriken' stars, but what nearly hit me was nothing of the sort. It looked like they had been cutting squares out of the top of food cans with tin snips. Whatever, I'm just pleased I don't see the result of one hitting me every day when I slap on the shaving foam.

When their ammo was gone, a few of them ran, but most were dead game and stood their ground against our bigger numbers. A lad from East Hull, a tidy dresser whose head is now shot and who did a stretch not long after for manslaughter, was on the floor across the road taking a hiding, so I ran across and dropped the lad fighting him.

Salford had been driven back onto East Park by then, and the East Hull lads, knowing the area, were splitting up and going down side streets that could access the park and get behind them. I have to give it to the Mancs, they were organised and knew what they were doing. I chased a lad who ran and thought I was Superman, then realised he had disappeared. He then came round the corner with a house brick in his hand and proceeded to batter me senseless over the bonnet of a car. I can't remember who saved me, but I felt he had cheated by not sticking to fists, feet and head. We were behind the times then in strategy: you just fronted someone and fought a straightener until someone dropped or ran, and he had not adhered to that code. Maybe my pride was hurt as much as my skull.

We ran them onto East Park once more and there was a lot of toe-to-toe. A lot of the lads on both sides were wearing smart expensive gear which was getting ripped and trashed, but we were still running into each other and brawling. Sometimes nowadays I feel too much emphasis is placed on clothing. I hate to hear, 'They had 150 lads Burberry'd up to fuck.' There isn't half as much fighting nowadays, and some lads are like peacocks preening their feathers at each other without wanting to get their hands dirty. It's similar to the 'bellboy' syndrome in *Quadrophenia*, where we take off our smart togs and go back to boring grey jobs in overalls, uniform or shirt and tie, but on the weekend, well, that's different.

Suffice to say this went on for at least another half hour, with the greater numbers of Rovers eventually prevailing on East Park bowling green. If there are any Mancs reading this who were on that decker, I hope it brings a wry, nostalgic smile. And if you were the bastard with the brick . . . well, let's just say cheers for the education.

Any football lads who bumped into Rovers in services or train stations will bear testimony to the fact that, number for number, they were as good as ANY football lads, though it galls me as a West Hull lad to admit it. But the biggest offs by far were between Hull FC and Rovers, not necessarily at the match but in the days or weeks before round the town centre, with threats backed up and revenge sought for previous matches.

The match that gained national press publicity was the Good Friday game at Hull FC's Boulevard ground in 1981. There are not many clubs that can say they have had pages one-to-three of a national newspaper like the *Daily Mirror* devoted to trouble at one of their matches, but Hull can. On this day, Hull FC played host to their rivals across the river and before the game the usual scuffles occurred in the city centre and en route to the match. Once inside, the Hull FC fans massed in the Threepenny Stand whilst the Rovers boys favoured the terracing behind the goalposts. All the main Rovers boys were positioned at the top of the stand, but mixed in were small groups of Hull FC in a central position among the away supporters.

The trouble began just after Rovers had scored a try. A couple of our lads moved across the terracing to have a piss/ get some food, and in full view of the rest of us a small group of Rovers lads bundled our mates down the steps and began hitting them. This sparked us into action and a few of us moved in towards where the crowd had parted to aid our mates. Our movement had a knock-on effect in the crowd as the Rovers boys at the top of the stand thought it had kicked off and began to rain down bricks and lumps of concrete left over from terrace renovations. Many innocent fans were caught up in this barrage and, as the casualties mounted on the pitch, the rest of us fought up and down the stand. This continued for ages as both sets of lads piled into each other.

The match was halted and the teams withdrawn as the police tried to stop the fighting and organise fleets of ambulances to take away the injured. Huge numbers of police reinforcements arrived, order was finally restored and the game recommenced after a 20-minute delay, but the trouble continued after the match in the streets around the ground, and all over the weekend around the city centre.

City were playing Huddersfield on the Easter Monday and both sets of lads met up in the town centre. It seemed everything that had happened two days before was put to one side. We were now Hull City and Huddersfield were in town; they were tracked down and found in a pub, the Centre Bar. The Hull lads ran in and dished out a hiding. Huddersfield offered very little resistance, which has normally been the case in encounters between the two teams. (I remember going there in 1973. Some of their lads came into the side stand and one, wearing a sheepskin, pulled out a knife. Everyone backed off for a few seconds, then somebody shouted, 'Get Andy Cu*****s.' He was a main player at City at the time, built like a brick shithouse and game as fuck. He came through the crowd and knocked out the lad with the knife as if he was holding nothing more offensive than a banana.)

That long Good Friday was a watershed. After it, the east-west hatred began to decline. An entire weekend of disorder had somehow relieved the pressure; we could now look at each other and laugh about the whole thing. This was a distinct advantage as new firms were coming to test us, with the likes of Leeds, Middlesborough, Derby, Stoke, Birmingham and Man City visiting Hull along with old rivals like Sheffield United and Barnsley. City had a growing rep within the M62 corridor, but had not ventured much further in numbers. We were getting high-profile policing up north, not solely due to football but also from the experiences and incidents other forces had with the rugby lads.

Violent scenes in Britain in the early eighties were not just reserved for the football terraces; many firms resorted to attacking their counterparts in their own boozers. Lads now saw these places as legitimate targets and to 'do' the opposition's pub was a big scalp. But this wasn't the only violence witnessed in our inner- cities. Massive riots broke out in Brixton, Toxteth and Moss Side. These were the actions of a disenchanted population fed up of being treated like second-class citizens. For the first time in decades, mainland Britain was engulfed in a form of anarchy.

The riots were well documented by the media, and the summer of 1981 saw copycat rioting erupt up and down the country. All these later troubles did was to dilute the real issues and problems that the Brixton and Toxteth youth were experiencing. The looting, vandalism and fighting that took place elsewhere was either opportunist or probably instigated by criminal elements who saw it as a way to make a quick buck and to settle old scores with the police. Hull was no different. The local newspapers headlined with stories of rioting youths battling with police in the city. Shops were trashed and their contents shared out.

Similar scenes were played out in Leeds, Bradford, Sheffield and most other major cities; the local television news reports showed community leaders in Yorkshire meeting with police to try to prevent further trouble. In Hull we had no excuses, no community leaders and virtually no ethnic minorities. The Chief Constable was interviewed and stated he couldn't understand what all the fuss was about; it was just like any other Saturday night patrolling the streets of Hull for his officers. Looking back, I think he was right. The city centre on a Saturday evening in the eighties was not for the weak. The area was ruled by gangs intent on causing as much damage to each other as they could. The weekend pub culture was something you aspired too; it was traditional. People from Hull were brought up with it. We were from a different environment, a different stock; our ancestors were hard-working, hard-drinking fishermen or dockworkers. Fighting was a way of life. This part of our persona was never shown more clearly than in the intense rivalry between our rugby league teams and the lads who flocked to the cause.

CHAPTER SEVEN

Babylon by Bus

AT THIS TIME an enterprising coach driver entered the scene, and before long hordes of Hull lads were enjoying day trips on Mad Eddie's Battle Wagon. Eddie must have coined it in as he took City boys, Hull FC and Rovers lads to away games every weekend during the football and rugby seasons. It wasn't unusual to see upwards of 80 lads crammed onto the coach as it travelled down the motorways, nor to see Eddie himself leading the charge into rival fans as we all piled off.

One memorable trip was to Spurs in 1981 in the FA Cup. A lot of older lads, some of whom hadn't been seen for ten years, turned out and after the match we had a ding-dong with some Spurs fans who ambushed our coaches opposite Tottenham Hale Tube station. If they had bricked the first coaches in the convoy, they would have inflicted damage and got away, but they waited until the end, and the last three coaches were full of lads. We charged off and into them. I targeted a tall, ginger-haired lad and we went for each other, but he hesitated while I carried on and sort of ran into him, jumped and hit him at the same time. Now I'm not the tallest of people, 5ft 6in and stocky (some call it fat), and I thought he would just bowl me over, but instead he turned and ran – it might have had something to do with the half dozen Hull lads running up behind, though I like to think otherwise.

Fighting continued as we moved back and forth up the high street. Each time the coach moved forward in the heavy traffic, we would run back to it in case it drove off. That was until Eddie must have got pissed off stop-starting the coach. He turned off the engine, jumped out and ran into the Spurs lads brandishing an African tribal club! Feedback is always useful, and it was nice to hear through a few Hull lads who followed Tottenham that we had gained a bit of respect for getting off the coaches and standing.

The lads on the coach were always looking for opportunities to earn some extras and once, in the middle of a ruck, a couple of the lads took time out and loaded a moped onto the back of the coach for a quick sale back home. This was fine but the traditional sacking of service stations often meant we got pulled over by the O.B. and had to sit it out whilst the shop staff pointed out the perpetrators.

This came to a head on the way down to Chelsea, again in the FA Cup, in January 1982. On this occasion the full coach was escorted to a Nottinghamshire police station. We parked outside and an inspector informed us that we would be interviewed about thefts, and if the people involved gave themselves up, the rest would be allowed to carry on to the match. His offer changed as soon as the empty cider bottle glanced off the top of his head.

It was stand-off time as we refused to get off the coach and the O.B. were wary about coming on. It was comical to see the police hanging out of the station windows watching events unfold and we sat there for ages while the inspector decided what to do. They eventually used snatch squad tactics, with two padded officers grabbing one off at a time. It took them over an hour to empty the coach. They jammed us into two cells and left us there until the identifying of the suspects took place. Five lads were charged with various offences and the rest of us were told we would be escorted home. We had the undivided attention of several police forces, ensuring we had a trouble-free homeward journey, and as we arrived in Hull we were met by a homecoming committee of at least 50 officers, who despatched us off home in small groups.

Policing had changed – it had to. Football hooliganism nationally was about to undergo perhaps its most active and notorious phase. And though we were now in Division Four, there was no way we were going to miss out.

NICK: 15 August 1981. The first game after the 1981 July riots (with Hull featuring high in the arrests league table and being one of the first places after Toxteth to kick off) was Bradford City away in the pre-season Football League Group Cup. A low turnout might have been expected for this friendly game, but two full coachloads of City boys went, with a similar number of Supporters' Club coaches.

Bradford was yet another trip into the unknown. They were a Fourth Division team at the time but from a far bigger city than most in the Fourth, bigger even than Hull, so they might have a few naughty tricks up their sleeve. Undoubtedly they would be keen to 'welcome' City as a Yorkshire rival coming down from a higher division. With this in mind, the two coaches approached Bradford around two o'clock on an overcast and humid afternoon. As usual, the drivers didn't have a clue where they were going and soon got separated. After touring the suburbs of Bradford, one bus arrived behind the Main Stand (the old Victorian one that got burnt down in 1985) half an hour before kick-off, followed by a large group of Bradford who watched the bus turn down the narrow, sloping, dead-end street which led to the turnstiles. As City got off they were met with bottles, stones and bricks and were sitting ducks at the bottom of the slope, with no space to spread out. The police slowly moved the laughing Bradford away. Not a promising start – outnumbered and outmanoeuvred.

The bus somehow managed to get out of this tight cul-de-sac and travelled down the Victorian terraced streets of mill workers' houses now occupied exclusively by Asians, many of whom were out in the streets, squatting on the kerbs chatting. Not coming from a 'multicultural' city, many on the buses had never seen such scenes. So it was true what they said about Bradford . . . no white faces in sight down these streets.

As this busload got into the ground, they found themselves in one half of a large, roofless kop with 100 or so Supporters' Club. No sign of the other busload – or Bradford. But hang on . . . at the other side of the fence, in the Bradford bit, were several familiar faces, spaced out in small groups, giving sly nods and winks to the City through the fence. Further away near the turnstiles and the Main Stand were Bradford, keeping their distance and presumably waiting to get their numbers up to have a go at the City intruders. By five to three this was still the situation, and slowly the coppers understood what was going on and rounded up the City, who were now occupying the spot at the top behind the goal. The coppers opened up a gate in the fence and 50 or so HCFC casuals were put back in the visitors' section. Bradford suddenly hurried to take up their places, causing much amusement among the City, who wondered why they hadn't challenged the intruders.

At the end of the game, City were kept back, and a hail of stones and half-bricks came without warning over the wall of the kop from waste ground behind it. City were in the mood for war as the gates finally opened, and as they made their way down Midland Road towards the coaches, a small group of Bradford skinheads in green flight jackets appeared, only to leg it almost immediately as City spotted them and gave chase. One skin stood his ground and launched a spectacular chest-high drop kick which found its target and knocked a Bransholme kid to the ground. The skin paid a high price for this, as he was being leathered before he hit the ground and was rapidly submerged beneath flailing arms and legs. He was left alone after a bit, still in one piece and just about conscious, but probably regretting his Jackie Pallo antics. No more Bradford were found and the buses headed back to Hull.

Wigan v City, Division Four, 6 March 1982. The first-ever football visit to Wigan. Done the rugby and the Casino. . .now for the football. The Battle Bus conked out somewhere in West Yorkshire and we pulled off the M62 to try to get it fixed, blue smoke in the bus not being a good sign. A long drink with the friendly locals in some WMC before we set off again, late as usual. By the time we got to Wigan the game had started. Some firms try to show off by arriving after kick-off, but to City it just came naturally. A police officer boarded the bus, called us all cunts and threatened to nick everyone if there was any trouble. As it was the first time City had ever played Wigan, this seemed a bit prejudiced. Right you are, cuntstable.

We had a job getting in, as all the turnstiles seemed closed. We eventually found one and entered the home terracing, where the coppers were waiting for us and very kindly directed us towards the away section via the Main Stand. A human crocodile of 60 of us slowly walked across the empty terracing in front of the Main Stand, causing the Wigan in the far corner to spot us and start acting up . The City already in the away end (about five buses) also started acting up and invaded the track round the pitch (led by a bus from Cottingham, apparently), trying to get at the Wigan in the corner. The coppers soon had it under control and we took our places on the muddy mound with tin shed that was the away end.

We lost 2-1 against a promotion-chasing side in front of 6,000. As usual near Mancland, it pissed down all afternoon. As we stood near the gates after the whistle, waiting to be let out and back onto the buses, a volley of missiles came over from the Wigan grouped in the car park behind the Main Stand. This caused a surge down the sloping terracing to avoid the rocks. The coppers had already opened the lock on the gate, though no one knew at the time. With the surge, it opened enough for City to realise what was on. Another quick push, the gates swung wide and the Wigan were right in front of us with their gobs open.

Angry normals and scarfers joined in the charge while the coppers stood aside, powerless. In no time Wigan were retreating with City after them. The normals and scarfers gave up after about 50 yards and got back on their buses, but about 100 City kept going at Wigan and chased them through streets of terraced houses. This mob didn't get back to the coach park till half five, having legged Wigan all over their own town. Wigan just kept running and running and running. . . and City kept chasing and chasing and chasing. Lots of lads were shagged out on the bus back but were also angry that Wigan had not stood and had it out after all the brick throwing.

We had three memorable matches in the eighties against Wigan. The final one was in the mid-eighties in the cup, when we took thousands, all the old boys, and kicked off that much they had to bring police horses on the open away end. But the one I remember best is the away match around '82-83. We had gone on two coaches and got split up on the motorway. Our coach arrived first and drove into the town past the rugby ground. We saw a mob of young casual dressers who gestured at the coach as we went past. This was my type of match, as we seemed evenly matched. We were predominantly in our late teens and early twenties, rugby league having cornered the older market. The Wigan lads seemed of the same age. We got in a pub out of sight of plod and started to have a game of pool and a laugh.

Just then, R- beckoned us to the door, where he had spied the same mob of Wigan coming up the street, totally unaware we were in the pub. Most of the lads were for running out straight away and fronting them, but an older lad with some tactical nous told everyone to tool up with pool cues and balls and wait until they were right upon us. We took his advice and held tight until they were 20 yards away, then ran out screaming. I'm sure they must have had some decent lads but after a token resistance they all ran, straight into the other Hull coachfull who were coming out of a side street. They took a hiding, and I'm sure the element of surprise had a great deal to do with it. They had no time to gee each other up and gain confidence before 50 tooled-up Yorkshiremen were on them like dervishes

* * *

By 1983, clothes labels like Le Coq Sportif and the craze for wearing cycle shirts were well worn out. They were surpassed by the classier French designs of Lacoste and the like. Everyone had their own personal favourites: Pringle, Lyle & Scott, Tacchini, Armani, Fila, Hugo Boss, Valentino, etc. I preferred to seek out the more obscure Italian clobber, and one of my favourites was a label by the name of Nanni Bonn. I had half a dozen of their jumpers, they were all one-offs and that gave you the exclusivity of knowing nobody else had that jumper.

Everyone was wearing Farah slacks. A number of shops in Hull must have shipped them in thinking the trend would last, and their storerooms are probably still floor to ceiling with boxes of Farahs, hoping they will one day be *de rigeur* again. The main shops in Hull for designer gear were Leonard Silver and James Wright, but for the really serious gear a lot of the lads had to travel to Manchester, London and other cities. I had shopped in Manchester since the mid-seventies. My favourite haunt at one time was a shop called The Last Picture Show. There you could buy clothes which no one else in Hull was wearing and that was half the battle.

The eighties casual scene was aided by an unlikely source, Persil, whose cheap travel offer in conjunction with British Rail helped to mobilise firms all over England. Wives and mothers up and down the country must have wondered what was going on as their partners or offspring started taking a great interest in which soap powder they were using. The Psychos were riding high.

It came against a backdrop of high drama in the boardroom

and dressing room. Our first season in Division Three had seen us flounder near the bottom and gates were some of the lowest ever. The club was leaking money due to expensive signings and big wages, and finally suffered the ignominy of having to call in the receivers. Hull City's very survival was threatened and the manager and his team were sacked, but suddenly things on the pitch began to gel. By the spring of 1983, we were hot on the scent of promotion.

Local derbies against Grimsby and Lincoln during this period always provided us with an extra stimulus, especially against the Codheads. Grimsby always turned out for us and had a good solid bunch of lads, yet apart from a few skirmishes on the seafront at theirs and a couple of minor incidents at home, the games between us were usually kept quiet by a heavy police presence. They once turned up in Hull on a normal Humberlink double-decker and caused a few heart attacks among the Old Bill.

A funny incident at Lincoln in the early eighties occurred during a League Cup tie at Sincil Bank. After the game, four Hull lads found themselves separated from the main firm. They were spotted and chased by a large mob of Lincoln boys who ran them into the fire station behind the ground. Once inside, they had nowhere to run and a couple of the lads fronted the oncoming Lincoln youths, to no avail. One of them, Darren, told us that although he was getting booted and punched up and down the station, he couldn't stop laughing at the sight of his mate Melvin who, in blind panic, with several locals at his heels, tried to climb up the fire pole!

★ ★ ★

Infiltrating the opposition was a dangerous operation, especially at that vulnerable stage as you entered the ground in ones and twos. You ran the risk of being sussed while your numbers were still low, but when it worked the results could look very impressive.

A game against Sheffield United saw over 50 of us mingle with the visiting Blades. Small groups of us stood in the old North Stand and just to the right on the edge of Kempton. We were waiting for the right moment to run in from two different angles. Then we saw it kick off in the South Stand – the Blades had beaten us to it and were fighting with a mob of Psychos in the corner.

The intense fighting and numbers bearing down on them forced some of the Blades onto the small track adjacent to the pitch. Play continued until a couple of our boys abandoned the planned attack and entered the field of play. This was the signal for the rest of us, and we all made for the Blades still fighting tooth and nail in the corner. Those watching from the South Stand must have dreaded the sight; it looked as though we were Blades ready to bolster their attack on our end. Nobody was left in any doubt who we were after the first wave of lads reached the corner of the pitch. The Sheffield lads didn't wait for the rest of us to reach them either, as they quickly retreated to the safety of their own supporters in the East Stand.

An FA Cup replay versus Chelsea in 1982 gave us the opportunity to mix it with the Headhunters. Our attempts at reaching Stamford Bridge had resulted in the full coachload being taken into a Nottinghamshire cop shop for questioning (see page 130). For the replay, we didn't expect many to travel up with it being a night match, but nevertheless we had to show them we weren't the same set of mugs from five years earlier. With this in mind, we paid into the away end 20-handed. We expected the Chelsea fans to be positioned midway or further down the terracing, clearly visible and partaking in the usual pleasantries of abusing all and sundry. But no, they weren't having any of it; they'd firmly positioned themselves in the dark recesses at the top of the stand. It

ruined our element of surprise; all we could do now was stand
before them and challenge them. They only outnumbered us
two to one, yet both sets of lads hesitated for a few seconds,
then the Chelsea came crashing down. The fight was fast and
furious. Neither side came out on top and I think we probably
surprised them by not leaping the barrier. A line of police
separated us until other officers arrived to pull us out and lead
us to the usual heroes' welcome in the South Stand.

It was common years ago for hooligans to be spurred on by
almost everyone in the ground. We represented them, and if
we came away with a victory you could hear the 'normals'
praising our efforts. When we used to enter from the railway
platform, eyeing up the away fans at the back of Kempton,
arms folded and legs outstretched 'kung fu bad boy style', the
South Stand used to erupt with cheers and applause, letting
the world know that we were their lads and we'd save the day.
Now the hooligans are reviled, especially by the middle classes
that have invaded our beloved game. These people haven't a
clue.

The Chelsea game finished with a 2-0 victory for the Blues
and the fun and games began. Some Chelsea were pointed
out in the South Stand seats and were pummelled from all
sides. The lads baying for blood were rewarded with one of
the Londoners being unceremoniously thrown from the seats
to the terraces below. North Road became the next battleground. Chelsea rounded the corner and began walking
through the home fans looking for revenge. The Chelsea
grunt was audible as the pace quickened and the Blues found
their prey. They tore into the Hull fans, causing panic and
confusion in the dark street. They had the upper hand and
attacked us while most were still leaving the ground. I realised
what was going on only when I saw lads rushing past me –
going the wrong way. A few of us got together and dodged
through the crowd, making our way towards the Chelsea.

Another group of City lads had already clashed with them,

stopping them from moving further down the road. They'd run in armed with broken staves ripped from garden fences. An isolated policeman was hit by a lump of concrete and knocked to the ground as he tried to separate fighting fans. James BS, Derek P, John L, Ian T and myself moved between two parked buses and came face to face with an equal number of Londoners detached from their mates. Derek headbutted the nearest, hitting him square on the bridge of the nose, and down he went. A brief scuffle with his mates ensued and then it was all over as police moved in.

After many lads had at first let us down, we had managed to quell the oncoming Chelsea, but not before they had spread confusion. Another valuable lesson had been learnt. The night was rounded off with some Hull fans following the Chelsea team bus and, as the trailing car drew level, an empty sherry bottle was hurled through a side window, damaging the eye of a young Chelsea reserve team player – a cowardly act which did nothing to enhance our reputation.

Sometimes just a couple of lads would infiltrate an enemy section in an act of pure bravado. Normally these lads would set themselves in such a way that the opposing crew didn't realise they where there, while the lads watching could make out the small hand gestures of acknowledgement made towards them.

On one occasion, James BS and I decided we'd take this a step further. I'd met him down St. Georges Road and we set off towards Boothferry Park. We were late and could hear that the game had started as we entered East Stand. We were two lads on a suicide mission. Neither of us talked. We had both agreed to enter the Millwall section no matter what, and we were true to our word. We knew we couldn't achieve much except maybe a moral victory, but we still intended to front them. We were unaware of the numbers they'd brought up for the game but that was unimportant. We had to be seen.

As we approached them, I could see the odd nudge as they realised we were there. Most stared in disbelief, unable to comprehend that anyone would be stupid enough to confront them, never mind that there was only two of us. As one, they bounded down the steps. We stood, arms outstretched, ready to strike. Yet they stopped and began to hurl abuse instead of moving in for the kill. We didn't back off. Instead we walked alongside them, letting them know who we were.

'C'mon, we're Hull.'

The expected rush never came. Police and stewards alike swamped us and quickly moved the two of us away. The lads back in the South Stand went mental, and envious mates who couldn't believe our audacity mobbed us. From such actions, names are made.

★ ★ ★

All firms have a ground or area they love to visit, some for the test it puts on them, some for the liberties they take each time they visit, some because previous visits have always produced confrontation. I would put the matches between us and Wigan in the middle bracket. Every time we've gone there, it has resulted in incident and I believe it is one of those games where one firm has the Indian sign over the other.

The first time I went was on the train and we took a good 140 lads. After the game, I got separated from my mates and wandered down a back street. Trying to double back towards the ground, I turned a corner and found myself looking onto a scene of utter chaos. All around me, people were running from a massive set-to. The actual fight was further up the street, where a mob of 50 Hull lads was battling with some very game locals. I ran towards the scene and managed to spin a Wigan lad round and let him have one. He didn't stand a chance and dropped to the floor. More of our lads piled in and put the locals to flight.

A police inspector came racing over to me and shouted, 'You, stop there,' much like a schoolteacher lambasting a delinquent pupil. It was obvious he'd seen me attacking the Wigan lad. As he lunged at me, I side-stepped and pushed him in the face, handing him off in classic rugby league style. He overbalanced and fell into a privet hedge. I didn't hang around waiting for applause; instead I darted round the corner and handed my distinctively coloured jumper to one of the approaching Hull lads.

I now had two choices: stay well away from the football crowd and make my own way home, or walk back round the corner minus my jumper and hope the inspector didn't recognise me. I didn't fancy hitching, especially in a tee-shirt, so chanced my arm and casually walked back towards my mates. We were rounded up and escorted to the station. The inspector was in charge of the escort and kept walking up and down, glaring. I avoided eye contact with him and was relieved when the train finally left the platform. I'd got away with it again.

My next visit to Wigan was in the FA Cup. We went in a minibus and, as we arrived in the area, we took the wrong road and began driving back towards the town centre. Two vans were coming towards us and as they levelled with us they told us to turn round as, in their words, 'There's two hundred of the cunts coming this way!'

Our driver put his foot down and in seconds we were in the middle of the Wigan mob. All doors opened and we piled out straight into them (twelve of us). This course of action took them by surprise and, I think, unnerved them, given our numbers. Apart from the lads actually fighting with us, the rest turned and legged it back up the road. We heard later that something similar had happened outside a pub but the Hull van didn't stop to let out its occupants, it just ploughed into a mob of Wigan, leaving one with a broken leg. Another set of lads decided to stay on after the game and kicked off in the town centre, mixing it with locals and bouncers, alike but came unstuck as they were attacked from all sides. Some people never know when to finish in front.

In May 1983 we finished second in Division Four, accumulating 90 points, a club record, and were promoted. New challenges beckoned, and with them, new methods.

CHAPTER EIGHT

Van Damned

POLICE PRESSURE AND the risk of losing his licence eventually killed off Mad Eddie's coach trips, and so we adopted a new routine for away games: meet in town by the YEB, empty the nearest off licence and wait bleary-eyed for the driver to turn up. Our mode of transport needed constant changing to keep one step ahead of plod. Many trips saw us travelling by Luton van, three in the front and 20-plus in the back. Newport County and Swindon Town are two that spring into mind. At Newport, the locals were rightfully unhappy when some of the Hull contingent sang sarcastically, 'There's only one Johnny Owen,' days after the little Welsh boxer had tragically died from injuries suffered in the ring. The police threw out some of the offending Psychos but they still managed to watch the game and shout abuse – they drove the van up to the wall of the ground, climbed on the roof and continued as before.

The Swindon trip in April 1983 was an all-round good day. We didn't actually meet up with any Swindon fans, in fact they probably weren't even aware we were there, but the laughs we had on the journey there and back were enough. Our driver confidently told us he knew the way, so when we stopped at a country pub we happily sat drinking the local brew with the intention of leaving at 2.30pm for the ten-minute drive into Swindon. As luck would have it, just after 2pm an RAC mechanic came in and struck up conversation with a couple of the lads.

'Where are you lot from?'

'Hull.'

'Hull? What are you doing round here?'

On informing him we were on our way to watch the Tigers play at Swindon, he looked at his watch and shook his head.

'Swindon, that's miles away. You're only ten minutes from Oxford!'

We quickly drank up and left, leaving the bemused mechanic alone in the bar. The abuse the driver took as we raced up country lanes was well deserved. We arrived on half-time and it took some persuading to let us in. We still managed to see a Brian Marwood goal, which gave us an important away win in our quest for promotion to the old Third Division. Our visit, which lasted 65 minutes in total, was over when the police bundled us all back into the Luton van. We were stopped twice and told to pull the shutters down – we'd hoped to have a drive round and jump out at any unsuspecting home fans, but the cops were wise to our plans and escorted us out of town.

Well away from the area we were again left to our own devices. The shutters went back up and as we passed through a small village, one of the lads was pushed out and had to run for all he was worth to keep up with the van. Everyone was laughing as he pleaded for us to stop and it was only the fact that we slowed down at a roundabout that let him scramble back aboard.

By the time we hit the M1 we could see coachloads of dejected Wednesday fans returning from Highbury, where they'd just lost in an FA Cup semi-final. They were fair game for a bit of abuse. We stopped off at services just outside Derby, figuring maybe some disgruntled Owls would seek solace by trying to rearrange our faces. Instead we were met by the motorway police, who'd been informed of our antics hanging out the back of the van screaming at the Sheffield. After refreshments and the threat of arrest, we set off on the final leg. I had managed to claim a seat in the cab, as I didn't fancy the prospect of a bumpy journey home in the dark. Within ten minutes of driving we could hear banging and shouting coming from the 27 occupants behind us. The three of us in the front laughed as we assumed they'd managed to get the shutter back up and were continuing their abusive remarks towards any passing Wednesday fans.

Two minutes later, the van's engine coughed, spluttered and died. We coasted onto the hard shoulder and got out to investigate. Surprisingly, as we rounded the back of the van the shutter was still down, so why where they banging? On opening, it became apparent: they stumbled out like refugees, coughing and spewing. The inside was filled with the smell of carbon monoxide. What we'd taken for noisy abuse were in fact desperate shouts for us to stop, as the back was filling up with smoke and fumes. I shudder to think what scenes we'd have encountered if the van had limped along for a further five minutes. The lads in the back had luck on their side that night.

It didn't finish there. A call to the emergency services provided us with an undignified drive back to the service station behind a pick-up truck, with many V-signs flicked at us from smug Wednesdayites. One of the lads, Greg, was hanging out the back when he slipped and fell off, landing in a heap on the inside lane of the southbound M1. He disappeared in the distance as the truck continued back to the garage. We didn't see him again till the next home game. He was lucky twice that night, escaping poisoning and being run over. None of us would forget this trip in a hurry.

★ ★ ★

Vans featured heavily in other trips. One of our key challenges in the 1983/84 season was Sheffield United away. Everyone discussed the plan. Normally a day there meant a heavy police reception committee as we alighted the train, followed by an escorted march to the ground, trailed by a token force of Blades on the opposite side of the road. They rarely bothered seeking us out in large numbers, as they knew better then anyone how their police reacted to our visits. If we arrived early enough you'd think it would be reasonable for us to be put into a pub once we'd all been rounded up at the station, but not here. We were East Yorkshire scum and not afforded the luxury of choice; if we arrived early it meant we had longer to wait outside the ground with a small army of police stuck to us like limpets.

Coach and double-decker journeys had in the past resulted in us being picked up on the motorway and brought in by convoy. Although these methods had prevented any big disturbances, you always had to be on your guard, as much from the police as the locals. South Yorkshire's boys in blue were one of the worst bunches you could meet; they didn't give you an inch and any lip was dealt with swiftly. They were total twats.

A previous train journey to Sheffield typified this. We set off from Paragon Station with over 300 lads on board, and decided to piss off the hordes of police waiting with their dogs and horses. We got off at Rotherham and walked across the road to the first pub, making the landlord's day as he stood rubbing his hands, mentally working out his profit margin from this 300-customer windfall. Apparently the train arrived on time in Sheffield, with the embarrassed Hull Transport Police on the empty platform shrugging their shoulders and trying to explain to an irate senior officer what had happened. Within the hour we had a visit from said police and we were ordered out of the pub; this was met by the usual answers. The police proceeded to baton-charge the pub and began clearing the place with the aid of a few canine accomplices. The landlord was livid; his profits were going up in smoke. He remonstrated with the police, saying how he'd had no trouble from us and they were out of order, but it fell on deaf ears.

The scene outside was one that thousands of lads from firms up and down the country will be familiar with: police cars and vans blocking the roads, their sirens silent but blue lights flashing, dogs barking constantly as they strained on the leash. We were pushed from pillar to post. Eventually someone made a decision and we were put onto the waiting train and sent down the line to more pissed-off plod, who had been waiting for over two hours. This could only happen to football fans.

So in 1983, while the usual train and coach crews were making their way to Sheffield, some tried Bedford vans. These were ideal, as you could see only the driver and front passengers from the outside. We dismissed Lutons, as they were emblazoned with the hire firm's logo and location, and instead borrowed a number of builders' vans and crammed them full of bodies. We got to Sheffield undetected and parked on the housing estate overlooking Bramall Lane. Forty good lads had managed to evade detection and were now walking up towards the Shoreham on the lookout for known faces.

As we entered John Street, we confronted some surprised Blades who either ran or took a beating. Among them was one of their top boys, T****r, who was pushed against a wall by one Hull lad and was hit without retaliation. He was then allowed to move on. He skulked off down the road, pissed off that we'd got a result and probably furious that he'd been left by his mates. Luckily for him we weren't bullies and all that was hurt was his pride.

Our trip to Oxford that same season was one of those where everyone seemed to turn up without any pre-planning. We parked our vans down a quiet, leafy lane filled with grand houses and walked to the ground. We tried to gain access at the front of the stadium but an old growler of a sergeant ordered his officers to ensure we paid into the away section down a small alleyway.

The atmosphere crackled as each side baited the other in the small, compact ground. We had a contingent of around 20 lads in the seats to our right who noisily declared themselves: they were younger members of the casual scene who had grown up together hanging around Hull city centre. They formed a formidable team and were gaining recognition as a tight little unit willing to front anyone, and often took it upon themselves to start trouble rather then wait for numbers to arrive (as Boro will testify in their city centre).

On this occasion they hadn't reckoned on finding a resistant mob of local youths in the same stand. They were soon outnumbered as the Oxford casuals clambered over the seats to reach them. One Hull youth threw a cup of hot chocolate over an approaching black lad and managed to bang him as he put his hands up to his scalded face. The Hull lads were being backed off down the walkway as the leering home fans took swings at them. All the while we stood screaming abuse and encouragement yet were unable to do any more. The stewards and police moved in and brought the bruised lads back to the Hull fans massed behind the goal.

Almost immediately, a roar went up from the packed stand full of Oxford fans. A gap appeared on the terracing and you could just make out a group of lads, arms flailing like windmills, as they pushed through the crowd. They then turned with their backs to the fence and prepared to repel all boarders. Eventually they too were removed and brought over to our section, where an appreciative applauding audience welcomed their arrival.

The newly-arrived warriors stood a few yards away from myself and a few mates and it turned out that there was only a few Hull lads amongst them. These were the West Ham lads who had teamed up for the day with some Hull mates they had met on holiday (see page 110). It didn't matter to us that they weren't Hull lads, their actions would be seen as a small victory for Hull City. They said they enjoyed travelling to watch and socialise with us Hull lads as something interesting always happened.

After a hard-fought 1-1 draw, we couldn't wait to get out and hopefully meet the Oxford lads who'd caused the damage in the seats. The gates stayed shut, we were penned in and this suited the home fans, some of whom crossed the field of play and began gesticulating to us from the safety of the pitch. In the corner, a pile of debris including masonry and bricks was picked over by the Oxford lads and they began to shower us with lumps of concrete and half-chockers (bricks). I caught one just above my right eye; blood oozed down my face and the pain was intense.

We pushed to get out and take it to them, but to be honest my heart wasn't in it. My head was sticky with blood and I felt sick. A mate of mine, George (a headcase who once jumped off a moving train just to have a pint), suggested I get it seen to. We went one way and begged a lift on a coach while the lads in the vans went looking for the offending brick-throwers. They met up with them and scattered them about the affluent avenues surrounding the ground.

With honour restored and five stitches in my head back at Hull Royal Infirmary, I reflected on a long day's outing. Not too bad: now home to face the wife.

★ ★ ★

In May 1984, we needed to win at Turf Moor by three goals to go up to Division Two. In the event, we won by only two, and our arch-rivals Sheffield United went up instead. There were three coaches of lads in the group we travelled with, not just football faces but lads with big reputations in Hull. We got off the coaches and ran through the Old Bill, some of who panicked and let their dogs off the leash, causing a fair bit of chaos in the ranks. I can remember one lad, who still turns out, ending up on the floor as an Alsatian ripped into his leg; he managed to limp away only to end up with a copper on a horse bowling him over. He got up fuming, ran over to the horse and punched it right on the button; I suppose he felt better after that.

A number of Blades lads were at the match anticipating their own promotion, and both Burnley fans and police must have wondered what the fuck was happening as mobs from three teams were battling with each other. After the game we were in no humour. If you weren't from Hull you were seen as fair game; we dished out some punishment that night.

★ ★ ★

Most city lads who attended in the eighties regard the '84/85 season as one of the best. We had memorable games against the likes of Derby, Bradford, Wigan, Doncaster and Brentford, unforgettable cup games against Tranmere, Brighton and Southampton, and the season reached a nail-biting climax as we battled for promotion to Division Two.

Our numbers were at their highest. With hundreds of Hull youths and twentysomethings riding on the back of a promotion-chasing team, we were doing the business on and off the pitch. The team and lads were in 'harmony' for the first time in over a decade. Away games became must-see occasions, coaches were filled with ease and rail excursions saw hundreds filing onto the platform.

Lincoln at the start of the 1984/85 season saw the usual good first-game turnout, with everyone confident that this year we would finally get our just rewards after previous disappointment. It was still hard to believe that we had missed out on promotion by a single goal in 1983/84 and to make matters worse it was Sheffield United who had benefited that night in Burnley. I had the choice of coach, van or car, chose the latter and set off to Lincoln with nine mates in two vehicles. We arrived for opening time and pulled into the car park of a pub called the Lincoln Imp, which seemed to be situated on the edge of a housing estate on the outskirts of the city.

We received the traditional stare from the locals as we entered the bar, but nothing seemed untoward and we settled down for a quiet drink to await the coaches and vans. At first we didn't notice the amount of curiosity we'd caused as we sat chatting in a corner, looking out towards the main road, but on a visit to the toilet it was evident that word had spread and extra faces had arrived in the bar area. We felt wary rather than threatened; after all, the locals were hardly casual types, they had more of the previous era's stereotypical bootboy/Status Quo headbanger look. I for one shouldn't have been so blasé, as I was the oldest of our group at 26 and had seen blokes like these do plenty of damage over the years, but surely they knew the rules of engagement had changed? Casuals only attacked other casuals.

Nope, afraid not. They'd not made a move on us but the atmosphere was getting ugly and stares changed to knocks as you made your way to the bar. It was time to get out. We reached the outer door and they rushed us, spilling us out onto the car park. We purposely moved away from our own cars, as we didn't want them trashing. All we could do was shout, psyche ourselves up and front them. It took some guts, as they were older, bigger and more numerous, and we knew they'd probably run right through us. They did. Our united front was breached at the first onslaught and we were picked off as individual scuffles filled the car park. I was being pounded by two of them.

But as in all good Hollywood movies, help was at hand. A passing removal van stopped and emptied 50 City Psychos onto a verge next to the pub car park. These lads had paid the driver £1 each for a one-way trip to Lincoln and gleefully joined the fray. Within seconds the tables had turned. Now the locals tried to muster up some courage as the Psychos charged into them. Aided by some 'borrowed' scaffolding poles from a lorry, the lads began to rearrange and refurbish the front of the pub, along with any cars unfortunately parked nearby – except ours.

The locals retreated behind closed doors and we knew it was time to move on before the O.B. arrived. The furniture van had already departed the scene and our two car drivers decided to carry on towards the ground, while the rest of us continued to walk with the main mob. We managed to reach the outer area of the town centre before the police rounded us up and held us without moving. It soon became apparent why: the pub landlord arrived in a squad car. He walked over to the senior officer and stood talking, glancing over towards us and eyeing us up and down. I began to feel uneasy. Only a short while before, I'd been buying drinks at his bar, and would be one of the favourites for the accusing finger. So I and a couple of the other lads made a conscious effort to distance ourselves from each other and not trigger any recognition by the landlord.

After half an hour, we were allowed to continue our march into Lincoln in the company of the local plod. A few minutes down the road and we were again stopped; this time the police had decided to split us into more manageable groups of ten or less and set each one off in different directions with equal numbers of O.B. as our tour guides. Our own personal escorts informed us they were putting us in a pub two roads off the main high street. It was a typical, Victorian, working man's boozer with a dozen or so Saturday afternoon customers and the landlord told us we'd be allowed in as long as we behaved.

The police, who had been right on our case, disappeared. This made us edgy and we sat pondering what to do: stay for a drink, then order taxis to the match, or chance it and wander through the centre, hoping we didn't meet up with the locals. The decision was made for us when two blokes from the Lincoln Imp popped their heads through the door and sussed us.

'Fucking hell, not twice in an hour.'

Doubts flashed through my mind. I knew only a couple of the lads I was now with and didn't know if they were up to it. How many were outside and could we hold them off? We didn't have to find out, as the landlord was the first to react. He bolted the main and side doors, preventing a vengeful mob from entering and wiping us out. He'd read the situation and saved us from a beating. The mob outside was eventually moved on and our favourite landlord sorted us out with a ride to the ground.

It makes me wonder if our little group was set up. At the time it seemed strange that the police had put us into this back street pub rather than walk us to the ground and even stranger that they then left. Were their tactics to dilute the threat of the mob by splitting us up and allowing the locals revenge on our small group. Who knows? But thank fuck for a greedy removals driver and an on-the-ball landlord.

The Derby County fixture had been eagerly awaited since news of their relegation. This once-proud team, who ten years earlier had been pitting their skills against the might of Europe, now had to contemplate travelling to places like Newport and Cambridge. Hopefully we would give them something to think about. We planned to arrive in Derby as late as possible, hoping to pay into the home end without being stopped. The idea was that by arriving so late, the police would assume everyone was already inside and would wind up their operations until full-time. These were the days before proper intelligence was used against the hooligan firms, so the plan wasn't too far-fetched.

Many Hull fans had made the trip and were already in the ground, but our main firm, which consisted of three full coaches, was yet to arrive. Twenty Derby lads prevented a certain ginger-haired 'lad about town' from entering the ground at 3.05pm. They began to push him around and started to slag us off for not showing; apparently we were all the wankers and spineless bastards. The complete works were hurled at the Hull youth and one of the Derby lads poked him, saying, 'Where's your fucking boys then?'

The Hull chap looked over the Derby lad's shoulder and pointed. 'I think these are 'em.'

The locals turned and saw 150 boys, with wedges and mullet haircuts bouncing in the breeze, trotting towards them. Exit 20 DLF (Derby Lunatic Fringe – the name of their mob).

We thought our plan had worked, but the police were onto us. They steered us towards the away end, where we burst into the seating area and rushed towards the Derby fans on our left. Our late arrival and sudden appearance made many of them recoil in shock, but enough realised what was happening and tried to reach us. The atmosphere was highly-charged as both sets of fans taunted each other. On the field, Derby provided us with a lesson in taking chances and beat us convincingly 3-1. The home fans took great delight in abusing our teak-tough centre-forward Billy Whitehurst's every move (but he'd have his revenge). We just wanted to get out and get into them.

At the final whistle, we jostled forward and spilled out onto the street. The police started to get very physical, and forcibly held us back. They were desperate to stop us reaching the parking area and the inevitable clash with the DLF but were finding it hard to contain us. Horses were drafted in, and one over-zealous officer began backing his steed into a group of Hull fans crushed in a corner. These fans weren't there for the trouble, just 'normals' caught up in the pushing and shoving, but they began to react accordingly. This was a sight to see: Mr Average Supporter attacking the police. The mounted copper bore the brunt; he was dragged off his horse and set upon. The horse began to panic and many of us took this opportunity to break the police lines and head for the car park.

It was hard to say how many got through, but we had a decent amount dodging through the parked cars and on up the road. We were met by a mob of Derby lads and fought up and down the street heading towards a housing estate. Their gamest lads were a small group of blacks who stood their ground longer then the rest, but in the end our extra numbers coming up behind ensured we had them running all over the estate.

The corresponding fixture saw Derby apply similar tactics to ours. Forty of us were halfway down North Road when we heard a commotion behind us. Derby had appeared from Pickering Road and attacked some younger Hull casuals at the corner of Boothferry Road. They scattered the Hull lads, who ran toward us with the DLF in full pursuit: 'It's Derby, it's Derby.' We spread across the road and waited, and the Derby mob suddenly stepped down in gear. At the front, a black lad who was obviously the leader desperately tried to egg on his troops but they didn't have the stomach for it. We made our move but they turned and shot back up the road.

In the ground they were surrounded on three sides in a very intimidating atmosphere. Derby were 2-0 up but goals from Whitehurst (two) and Flounders ensured we snatched the points. This fixture had everything: fun and games in the street, a comeback of immense proportions and a mass pitch invasion to boot. Afterwards we hunted down the DLF, with hundreds of marauding Psychos seeking out the shell-shocked and deflated visitors, who by now had seen enough and weren't up to the task.

★ ★ ★

A coachload of Bradford City casuals had the misfortune of arriving just as a large group of Psychos left the Silver Cod. The coach was bearing right on the main roundabout (near Three Tuns) through the football traffic, but turned into the path of 200 Hull. The driver frantically sounded his horn and his passengers dived for cover while we rocked the bus and banged on the windows. The police saved them but a lot of lads continued to harass the occupants, while 50 broke away and stood waiting in the car park.

The wary visitors stepped off the coach, with a line of officers on either side preventing the baying Psychos from reaching them. They had just got onto the car park when they were attacked from all sides and fled towards the visitors' enclosure taking kicks and punches as they ran. For us older lads it was payback time, as Bradford weren't averse to bricking you from above as you left your coach outside their ground.

After a crap display, we began to drift out of the ground. We had lost 2-0 and none of us was going to leave the area without gaining some form of revenge on the arrogant, piss-taking West Yorkshire bastards. Small pockets of Psychos milled around watching and waiting, the cold, dark, February evening masking our presence. These were ideal ambush conditions; we just had to be patient. We knew the coach of Bradford casuals would claim sanctuary and stay on the car park under the eyes of the Old Bill, so they were out of the equation, but they had more than one coach of lads at the game.

A group of thirtysomethings were set upon by a pack of young Hull fans halfway down Boothferry Road. These older, larger Bradford fans at first put up a fight, but the weight of numbers from the eager, younger, fitter Psychos began to take its toll. In the end, they clambered over fences and hedges, banged on doors and hid behind local residents. Vans were also targeted, with one terrified driver mounting the kerb and driving the wrong way up the highway to escape the onrushing mob.

Heading home after another day at the office, we heard that a couple of Bradford lads had been slashed. That was unlucky for them, but each and every one of us knew the risks involved. One day it's them, and then another match would result in a Hull lad receiving 100 stitches up his back after being involved in a ruck (Doncaster, the same season). I'm not saying it's right, but shit happens. The backlash from the slashing incident was fairly intense: the local Press and police combined to heavily condemn the actions of the hooligans and the police presence increased two-fold for the rest of the season.

The FA draw had us playing away at Tranmere in the second round. This game would provide us with the chance of revenge for a painful visit endured by the early Psychos in August 1978 (see Chapter Five). This time we would be better prepared: upwards of 2,000 City made the journey over to the Wirral and a quarter of these were lads.

A vicious fight broke out in one of the many pubs overrun by Hull fans. Tables, chairs and glasses flew through the air as both sets of lads clashed. One Hull youth was dragged away unconscious after a perfectly-aimed glass ashtray connected with his skull. Neither side gave an inch and both were probably relieved when the screaming sirens could be heard approaching in the distance.

Inside the ground, a thin piece of yellow barrier tape separated the warring factions in the seats. It didn't need Einstein to calculate that the frolics would continue. City fans poured over the seating and before long were occupying the area reserved for home fans. Tranmere gave as good as they got and the fighting went on for a good 20 minutes, with the police screaming for back up; they apparently had to draft in coppers from all over the Wirral and beyond. The Hull lads of 1978 felt that the present day Psychos had done them proud.

A 3-0 victory set up a match against Brighton. Buoyed by

the previous round's incidents, many lads planned to make the journey down to the South Coast. But not everyone would finish the trip. I arrived with a small group of mates just over two hours before kick-off. We expected to find more than the couple of vanloads of Psychos who we spotted in a public house near the ground. We couldn't understand where the main body of lads had got too; after all, an over-filled coach had left Hull after last orders on the Friday night and should have arrived hours earlier. Our crew of just over 30 sat in the away section, freezing in the open stand, while the Brighton lads vented their spleen. *Wait while the rest arrive*, I thought, *we'll be more of a match for these tossers*. We waited and waited, but no show. After the game, we went our separate ways. My group of five quietly got on the coach. We were gutted.

All became clear the next day. The coach had stopped at a service station on the way down and the lads had got up to the usual tricks, thieving from the café and shopping area. The coach was pulled up and taken to the local nick, where it was agreed that a whipround would make up the money owed and they would then be allowed to continue. It all went into a hat and was about to be presented to the officers waiting patiently by the coach, but just before it could be handed over a certain person managed to let off the handbrake and the coach began to career down the sloping road towards two parked squad cars. Officers ran alongside the coach trying to board and stop the advancing vehicle before it crashed into the cars. They failed.

In the confusion, the handbrake puller jumped off the coach and escaped through the grounds of the nick. On reaching a bus stop, he casually boarded a bus and sat next to an old lady. The bus had only managed a couple of hundred yards when it was stopped by a police car. An officer got on and proceeded to drag off a protesting punk who was sat in front of the escapee. A couple of stops later and he decided to get off. His next step was to hitchhike to London, where he stayed the weekend with some good mates from Catford. He could afford to live it up; after all, he had £70 in his back pocket, along with a new hat.

* * *

Doncaster away, 14 games to go and we were just off top slot in Division Three. This was the cue for thousands of Hull fans to make the short journey to the Bell Vue ground. As mentioned earlier, one Hull lad was cut during a fight with some local youths but most of us didn't come across any opposition. The attendance must have been 70:30 in our favour and it was the crowd that made this game memorable: the sight of Hull lads filling the road all the way back to the town centre will stay with me forever.

As the season came to a close, a 1-0 win at Walsall ensured City were promoted. All talk was now of our last game of the season at Brentford, and the chance to celebrate in London. If we could win our last home game against York City, it was still in our reach to be crowned champions. But it wasn't to be: York spoiled the party in front of 16,000 fans. This defeat at the hands of our Yorkshire neighbours put a dampener on the celebrations and many lads who had been up for the trip elected to give Brentford a miss.

We still managed to set off with two coaches and a couple of vans, all looking forward to sampling the bright lights. A few of us commented that we could meet up with Leeds fans as they travelled to Birmingham. If we were lucky we might get to slap a few. Our coach stopped at Leicester Forest Services, and the younger lads were warned not to fuck up the trip by pilfering. The vans were already there. As we passed by the younger element in the amusement arcade, they were quick to inform us that the empty coach to our right was Leeds. We took note.

We sat idling the time away as our driver slid his greasy

breakfast down his throat, when young Alex came bounding up the stairs. 'They've started, fucking Leeds have started. They're on the coach nicking our beer.'

Everyone rose and moved quickly and quietly down the stairs. I could see that the Leeds boys stood between both coaches and our back exit door was open. We spread out and met them head-on. The Leeds thief who'd been on our coach was desperately trying to move well away from the action – still carrying a crate of beer.

Br****ie casually walked up to the Leeds coach. The smirking driver's face soon altered when the window exploded as a full cider bottle sort of slipped out of Br****ie's hand. He winked at the terrified driver, then moved on to find another victim. The Leeds lad with the crate was soon the centre of attention. A couple of Psychos moved in for the kill and seconds later the crate was nearly wrapped round his head. They were screaming to each other for help and all trying to get back onto their coach at the same time. Kicks and punches pummelled them as we taunted them continuously with 'Who are yer?'

Some were pulled back and hit with the beer bottles they'd taken. I had a Leeds lad up against the side of their coach. He stood there with a sharpened screwdriver in one hand (doing nothing with it) while trying to shield his face from my blows with the other. They thought three choruses of 'We are Leeds' would have us shaking; it did, with laughter.

Time to leave. We were soon speeding down the M1 and distancing ourselves from the blitzed coach and its shell-shocked occupants. On arrival it was straight into the boozer at the side of the ground. For most, the usual pre-match drinking ensued but a few of us decided to have a mooch about. There was obviously no need for mob tactics here; our scouting mission, which bore no results, was testament to that. The turnout wasn't too bad after all, and we had 130 proper lads. *Let's get the game over with so we can enjoy the delights of the capital.*

To our left in the seats were about 20 Brentford, constantly shouting abuse. They were young lads and presented no threat at all, just an irritation. The game itself was a non-event, both teams going through the motions after a very long and hard season. At the final whistle, we invaded the pitch to salute our conquering heroes; a few shouts of derision could be heard coming from the home terracing and about 30 lads moved away from their backslapping colleagues and raced towards the Brentford end, which emptied in seconds before they'd gone past the six-yard box. There was no need for them to hand out any slaps, as Brentford aren't that sort of club.

The policing had been relaxed all day and we didn't even get an escort from the ground. We were aiming for the bars and pubs of the West End, time for proper celebrations to begin and see what the evening had in store. During the early part of the night we met up with small groups of fans from Chelsea and Portsmouth, all quite chatty, no mouthing off from anyone, just plenty of info shared from lads in the know. As is normal (with us anyway) during much consuming of alcohol, the night began with conversations about family, work, mortgages, holidays booked, then later the mood began to change; the decibel levels increased, every other word was 'fucking' this or that, and everyone around us suddenly became Cockney bastards. It was bound to end in tears.

Our numbers decreased as we moved from place to place, and round about 10pm the trouble started. Some Hull lads had nipped down a side street for a piss; secretly they were being monitored by a vanload of police who were keeping their distance. As they stood there relieving themselves, they didn't notice an officer coming up behind. A certain resident of Orchard Park was grabbed; he instinctively turned and lashed out, laying out cold the officer, who unfortunately was female.

'Officer down.'

The police moved swiftly. Their first action was to block off all exits. Back-up arrived and the rounding up of suspects began. Hull lads were dragged away, some kicking and punching, and thrown into the cell van. Twenty-three lads were charged with a number of offences and many ended up with custodial sentences, which at the time were not un-expected, coming as it did after the furore of the infamous Millwall pitch invasion at Luton that same season. For the rest of us, who hadn't been involved, it meant spending the rest of the night under the watchful eye of the boys in blue. As we boarded our coaches on the corner of Hyde Park, both they and us gave a sigh of relief. At least there was plenty of space to stretch out on the way home.

A year or so later, we had another jaunt down to London, a trip to the Old Den. Millwall, mid-eighties: a daunting place in daunting times. We set off by double-decker. Apprehensive wasn't the word for how we felt but it was something we had to experience, something we had to do. On arrival, 80 of us went walkabout, looking for action . . . but encountered nothing. We entered the ground expecting hassle . . . nothing. We got on our bus and headed for home, thinking we'd got a right result, walking around their manor giving it the big one. The Sunday papers told a different story: 5-600 Millwall had been waiting in ambush for West Ham en route to Crystal Palace. Talk about bigger fish to fry.

CHAPTER NINE

Yorkshire Rivals

OUR FIRST AWAY game back in Division Two was a magical pairing against our neighbours Leeds United. What a comeback game . . . but on the day it didn't really live up to expectations. Plenty of lads made the 60-mile journey, with many letting the train take the strain. There were at least 300 lads on board as we sped out of Hull; we'd be on the streets of Leeds by 11am and hopefully up to all sorts of mischief. In fact this was never really on the cards – the Leeds Police saw to that. They were well versed in dealing with football crowds and knew us from old, as they'd come across us on many occasions on our rugby league travels. We knew the area well and had filled the city centre pubs to overflowing during outings to Headingley and Elland Road, where we often played RL finals and semis. (At one of these showcase events, a trainload of Hull Kingston Rovers fans disembarking at Leeds train station met up with a mob of Leeds United off to Forest. East Hull's finest promptly ran them off the station concourse – that's right, the mighty Leeds were run out of their own station by a mob of rugby supporters.)

The escort took us straight to the ground: 300 very frustrated lads outside the turnstiles at the Lowfields Road away section. We hadn't had a chance of meeting up with the locals. One of the lads had a different perspective on our situation: he argued that the tactics used by the West Yorkshire

Constabulary was testament to our reputation and we should class it as a compliment. I was just pissed off.

We filled our terracing area and had a further 200 lads in the Lowfields seats. The Gelderd End was to our right but all eyes were on the Service Crew filing into the seats behind the other goal. Looking back, the Leeds fans were strangely quiet; it was us who provided the entire atmosphere among the 16,731 crowd. A respectable 1-1 draw saw us leave the ground expectant, but well-disciplined officers cordoned off the street corner and directed us with a bit of persuasion away from the locals. They force-marched us through an industrial estate to the station without a hint of trouble, and pushed straight through onto the platform where we waited for our connecting train. Our numbers had increased as we made our way back to the station and the sound of 500 voices bounced off the station walls.

The police ushered us onto the train, with lads hanging out of every window shouting abuse and chanting, 'We all hate Leeds and Leeds and Leeds.' As the police began to move off, 20 of us jumped off the train just before it started. We quickly moved down the platform and came to a mesh gate that led to the street. Three Leeds casuals stood opposite and moved across the road to abuse us. One of them ran to the gate and jumped up, feigning to climb over it but as he hung there it slowly swung open; the fear in his face was a picture as he realised the barrier between us was no more. We couldn't do anything for laughing, and he darted up the road trying to catch the mates who had left him to his fate.

After this comical interlude, we focused our attentions on the Leeds fans now filing onto the platform. All we passed were white-shirted fans with their heads down but it wasn't them we were interested in. It was apparent nothing was going to occur unless we went outside, but the police were still around the concourse in large numbers. We doubled back to the open gate but two parked police vans further up the street changed our minds for us.

'Fuck it, we'll get the next train out.'

Our party boarded the train and made ourselves comfortable. A group of Selby Whites walked by our compartment giving it the 'Leeds, Leeds, Leeds' cry, and got on further down. They were mostly 'shirters' but there was a sprinkling of lads amongst them. We sat and waited for the train to start. As soon as it left Leeds station we went for a walk. Now we didn't have any intention of hitting them but they didn't know that. We moved through the seated Leeds fans who sat very quietly, most staring out of the window. We didn't say anything but you could see they were feeling very uneasy. I know this all sounds like bullying, but we needed some form of sport; we'd had a long, frustrating day. The outskirts of Selby appeared and these apprehensive locals must have been wondering when we'd make our move. True to form, as soon as they were off they started giving it the big one, loads of slavver and bravado. We just winked at them.

Home fixtures never lived up to expectations when we played Leeds United: for some reason all matches played against them at Boothferry Park were pretty low-profile and they never seemed to bring the numbers of Sheffield United or Middlesbrough. They would probably argue it was because they didn't rate us. I always found that weird, after all the publicity that abounded about the Service Crew. I can remember only one occasion where they had lads who looked as if they wanted an 'off' before a game at Boothferry Park.

We approached the green bridge near the ground 15-strong. We weren't youngsters (I was the youngest at 30) overawed by the Leeds fans who could be seen ahead, milling round the car park. A shout was heard from their ranks: 'Come on Leeds, they're here.' They came together and moved quickly towards our group. We emerged from the shadows, out from under the bridge, ready for them. The oncoming Leeds suddenly thought better of confronting our crew. They about-turned and assumed their previous positions, choosing to ignore us completely rather than face us.

No change there, then.

★ ★ ★

The Second Division also saw us pitted against two of our bitterest rivals: Sheffield United and Middlesbrough. Any action with these teams had an added edge due to the associations some of their boys had with the Hull lads who frequented all-nighters around the North. One of the Blades lads had a girlfriend in Hull so he got to know all the 'Town' lads very well.

Sheffield always came on the train, so we would to try to organise the lads up town early, but not always early enough. They often headed for the Manchester pub, known locally as the Trogg Bar. It was frequented at weekends by bikers, Hells Angels and suchlike; the decor inside made it look like a cave. This was a good ploy by United, as it was deep in the city centre, so when they marched to the ground they had to go through town and pass many pubs where Hull lads would be drinking.

At one game, myself and four mates turned into a side street in Hull city centre and saw a mob of boys coming towards us. In front was a Hull lad (his sister was seeing Mu***y, one of the Blades' top boys), so we assumed they were our boys – but we soon found out they weren't. Our only course of action was to move sharpish as they came at us. We ran towards Paragon Station, where we knew a mob of Hull were drinking in the pubs. Anyone who has been in this position knows that all you can do is hope to keep on your feet and stay one step ahead of the pack giving chase; it doesn't help when one of your own mates thinks it's funny to try to leg you up as you are running.

As we reached the safety of The Stonehouse, all our boys piled out ready for a go back, but as so often happens the wailing sirens soon became louder as the O.B. arrived. The two sets of fans met near the Cenotaph, with lads coming out of pubs and running across roads to get involved. Honours were even. To give Sheffield their due, they knew they would get a lot of attention in Hull but were always up for it and stood their ground.

Sheffield United lad Steve Cowens, in his book *Blades Business Crew,* mentions an incident at Hull when some Blades had their car smashed. The accusing finger was pointed at a handful of our younger lads who frequented the all-nighters. They had nothing to do with the attack but they suffered the consequences later. The attack occurred before a night meeting between the two clubs. Eight Hull were travelling down Anlaby Road by bus when Mu****y was spotted in one of the two cars. They were seen turning down Walton Street, which wasn't what you'd call part of the normal route to the ground. Intrigued by this, the Hull lads got off and walked back to see what was going on. Now, these lads weren't your run-of-the-mill hooligans; a few of them had pedigrees which ran a bit deeper (so to speak) and were not the sort you'd want to bump into unless the odds were heavily stacked in your favour.

One car was found on a derelict car park but it was empty. As the Hull lads looked about, Mu***y and his pals turned the corner and came face to face with them. Straight away the Sheffield boys bounded over and tried to get in front of the car, shouting, 'Leave the car, leave the car.' Attacking the car hadn't been on the agenda until they harped on about it. If they'd fronted us as they turned the corner, we'd have gone for them there and then and the car would never have come into the equation. But they didn't, so it did. One of the Hull lads, Blakey, ran up to the car armed with a house brick, and with a smile shouted, 'Happy Christmas.' He proceeded to stove in the windscreen. The Blades were chased off and had to endure the sight of their car being totalled by the locals.

Inside the ground, word spread through both sets of lads about the incident with the car. Taunting and threats from lads pressed up against the chicken-wire fence increased and were aimed at a personal level, especially from within the Sheffield camp. To us it was hilarious; they were taunted throughout the match with 'Mu***y, Mu***y, where's your car?' He had to endure further suffering as hundreds of Hull lads mimicked the Madness dance and sang, 'I've been driving in my car.'

Another meeting ended up with both sets of lads facing each other under the bridge near Boothferry Park. Both sides casually walked towards each other, ready to mix it, but the police noticed and were on their way to break us up when one of the Hull lads lunged at a Blade and slapped a raw egg down his face. Both groups started laughing and this defused the situation. Afterwards it seemed every man and his dog from Hull was mobbed up after the lads from South Yorkshire, and it appeared they were splitting into ones and twos to get past us under the green bridge. A few of their lads were seen heading towards Boothferry Road, although they had come on the train and the town centre was in the opposite direction. As stated before though, the Blades were always game, and had the Indian sign over us for a number of seasons.

* * *

Middlesbrough were another good, solid firm who stuck together. Some used to come to Hull and were often seen at our games watching our boys in action. We knew a few of their lads from the Rotherham Clifton Hall all-nighters, and at that time neither side saw the other as a threat, as we were in different divisions. I can remember Hull lads being invited up to Boro to help them when they faced some tasty opposition.

This all changed when we played them in a pre-season friendly and Boro brought a good crew down and caught us by surprise. We thought there would be no show, and the few City were in the small standing area in front of our best seats when a coachload of them arrived. They suddenly came charging down on us, and I don't know if it was the element of surprise but there was some panic, with some City lads jumping on the pitch to get away, leaving about even numbers on each side.

The fact that they had caught us on the hop stuck in the craw. They tried this tactic again during an early season game in September 1985, when they arrived in vans, parked down Beverley Road and walked towards the city centre. The Hull boys were drinking in Bass House and Cheese and word got round that Boro had been spotted. Rumours had been flying around all day that Boro would do this, do that, arrive in vans, come on the train, etcetera, so a small crew of 20 went to check out the latest sighting.

As we reached Prospect Street, we could see the Boro lads in the middle of the road, bouncing towards us. We piled into them, causing panic among the Saturday shoppers. I targeted a half-caste lad and decked him with a beauty. I then went to hit another and fell over the lad I'd just cracked. BOOM, I was kicked in the head (by a misguided Hull foot) which opened up a nasty gash under my eye, and was dragged away by a mate as the mounted police moved in.

Because of these actions, we decided to play them at their own game and have a day out to Teesside. We had six vanloads as well as two coaches turning out for the match. Three vans drove to the town centre whilst the other three parked near the ground. Both sets of lads found the opposition, with the town vans jumping out and battling with equal numbers of Boro lads all over the bus station.

The rest of us positioned ourselves outside a known Boro pub and a Hull lad casually walked in and invited them outside. As the first rush came out, they were met by a hail of bricks and were beaten back in. They had a couple more attempts at coming out but we had too much ammunition and they didn't fancy their chances. We didn't want to be picked up outside the pub by the Old Bill so we moved on, looking for other targets. This enabled the ambushed locals to muster a counter attack. They must have rung for reinforcements, as the side streets were soon swarming with Boro. A few skirmishes took place but Boro kept on coming at us (we must have really pissed them off) and, although we were game, it was a relief when we approached the ground and the welcoming arms of the police.

One of the lads in the town centre fracas, Ian, can explain what happened to them:

IAN: Boro away, by far our biggest game of the year and we had a point to prove. The first time Boro had come down to us I was a 16-year-old novice, but now as we travelled up the A1 I considered myself a veteran of three years standing. We had the added incentive of knowing a good few Boro lads personally, among them were A**o and De****k who frequented the same all-nighter scene as ourselves. They'd given us some stick after the 'friendly' and we'd promised them that we would we go to theirs and return the compliment.

These lads knew we had a capable mob but we weren't what you'd call a named outfit. Our exploits only hit the local newspapers and we felt it was time our lads received more credit. We wanted maximum publicity and decided to reintroduce the 'calling card.' One of the lads came up trumps and handed out a block of these cards. To us it gave the plan a professional edge and at the time this seemed important. What we didn't realise was that these cards would come back to haunt us.

As the vans loaded up, we split into the usual groups: a

vanload from Boothferry, another from East Hull, three vanloads
of the older lads, and ours filled by the younger elements of the
firm, mostly around 18-19. All told, we had 60 lads, no runners
and everyone was up for the challenge – and we'd need to be.
We reached Redcar and stopped off for a pint, but our van was
itching to crack on. The consensus among us younger lads was
that it was pointless sitting in a pub in Redcar when we could
be having fun in Middlesbrough. An argument ensued, with
everyone joining in; we wanted to hit the town centre whilst the
older lads were intent on hitting a pub. This is the last thing you
need, especially when travelling to somewhere as dangerous as
Middlesbrough, but we do things the hard way. In the end we
agreed to disagree, and set off for our respective targets.

We now numbered 22 lads in three Bedford vans. We drove
in unnoticed, followed the signs for the city centre, came to a
busy junction on Corporation Road and pulled up at the lights.
That's when we saw them. It was only a dozen or so at first,
coming up an escalator at the main bus station. We signalled for
the other vans to follow us and pulled up round the corner. We
jumped out and ran towards them. Our presence startled them
but, as the shouting started, we realised there was more of
them. Boro poured out of the station, and as they ran they
shouted 'Howay Boro' and 'Come on then, you Yorkshire bastards,'
which was ironic, as they were Yorkshire-born themselves.

The odds were slightly in their favour but we gave it a good
go for a bunch of young kids. Neither side gave in, nor did
anyone run; we were too psyched up for this one. We carried
on brawling till the police cars arrived. The Boro lads scrambled
over railings to the station while we ran back to our abandoned
vehicles. We wanted to be off before the police could round us
up. Unfortunately for us, as we rounded the corner the police
had surrounded our abandoned vans. We were told we'd have
to go with them; I thought they were taking us to the ground
but they took the keys to the vans and drove us straight to the
local nick.

We kept on asking them if we would get out for the game but our questions fell on deaf ears. An officer came over, laughed and told us we were going nowhere. They'd found a few items hidden in one of the vans: a fireman's axe, a weighted cosh, some Stanley blades and, worst of all, the calling cards. They charged us with a Section 5 and affray and we were bailed to appear back in Middlesbrough on my 19th birthday. Nice present.

We received the publicity we'd been craving – our exploits were splashed all over the newspapers of Hull and Middlesbrough as well as being mentioned on the regional TV news stations, and there was talk of us needing to be made an example of.

On the day of the court case, five of us went up in a car and the other 17 in a van. We arrived first and parked up in the courthouse car park. I'd just got out when I noticed three blokes coming over. They were plain clothes detectives. They said they knew who we were and they had information that our vehicles were going to get trashed; a welcome committee was waiting.

We opened the doors of the courthouse and there in front of us was a small mob of Boro. A few came over but were pushed back by the police. I nodded to A**o and we went over to see him. 'Alright lads,' he said. 'Ignore some of these, they're just wankers.'

He asked where the rest of our lads were, then said, 'That was a good show. We'll have to do it again some time.'

Within minutes, the doors burst open and in came the other 17. They'd arrived under escort and walked in flanked by the Old Bill. It looked impressive. We all went into court. The Boro lads sat smiling and waving in the public gallery, surrounded by police. The proceedings got under way, the evidence was presented and, to be honest, it didn't look too good for us.

Then our brief homed in on a statement made by one of the arresting officers:

'Are you telling me that two police officers signed the charge sheets for all twenty-two youths?'

'Yes, that is correct.'

'So you two must be supermen. How can two officers witness what twenty-two individuals are doing at the same time?'

They'd fucked up big time. The judge called a halt and asked to see both the prosecution and defence lawyers in chambers. The Section 5 and affray charges were thrown out but we had to answer to a lesser charge and were all bound over for a year and fined £200. As we were led out, we waved to the Boro lads. A**o and a couple of his mates gave us the thumbs-up. The police held them in the gallery and we were given an escort out of Middlesbrough.

Later, we met Boro at home in the meaningless Zenith Data or some such competition, and again they turned up, 20 or so strong, on a cold wintry Tuesday night and caught us by surprise. A couple of our lads were caught outside Silver Cod early doors and took a right pasting. One of the lads, Jamie, was hurt pretty badly and Ian T was spitting blood and gunning for revenge, so about ten of us went looking for the assailants.

We headed up towards the ground and spotted them across the club car park, near to the away seating entrance. Outnumbered but undaunted we went for it. Ian T ran in amongst them going absolutely ballistic. The rest of us were pushing and shoving each other as we moved forward and piled into them, trying to reach Ian. He needed no help as he dished out a bit of retribution for the earlier fracas. It was evident that this wasn't Boro's top boys, yet a few faces were known to us and they were the ones we were after. We were backing them off towards the corner, with Ian's fists working overtime, when suddenly the Old Bill appeared through the melee and rushed straight at Ian. He was hit with full force and you could hear the 'pop' as his shoulder hung loosely by his side. Ian was arrested yet tried suing the police for damages. His case fell down in court when the officers stated that they needed to use such heavy force as he was behaving like a 'raving lunatic,' and they were right.

★ ★ ★

We would have six seasons in the old Division Two, a period which, apart from the events just described, saw few highlights, on or off the pitch. The club ran through a bewildering succession of managers, including three in under a year. Despite trying out everyone in the hotseat from Stan Ternent to Eddie Gray, breaking the club transfer record and installing a new chairman, the Tigers were, by 1991, staring relegation in the face.

Perhaps our most memorable off-the-pitch success came in 1987 when we were drawn against mighty Manchester United in the League Cup, or whatever guise it was under then, and played them over two legs, with the first at Old Trafford. Over 5,000 fans made the journey over the Pennines to witness a 5–0 thrashing by the Reds, but the mood was ugly even before a ball had been kicked. The lads had a great time around Old Trafford, leading plod a merry dance, and for about ten minutes were over United like a rash, battering them around the streets and the warehouses on Sir Matt Busby Way. I think they underestimated us that night.

The policing left much to be desired as nearly a 1,000 Hull fans were prevented from entering the ground until nearly half-time because not enough turnstiles were operating at the designated away end. Two coachloads of lads weren't even allowed off because they were deemed too rowdy by a police force struggling to cope and were escorted via Rochdale police station back to Hull. Inside the ground, the City fans in K Stand surged towards their counterparts but were pushed back by police and stewards, but once outside the Man United lads bouncing about next to the bridge soon turned and ran through the small industrial estate in blind panic as hordes of pissed-off Hull fans ran amok.

As the eighties came to a close, performances and results on the pitch indicated we would soon be plying our trade in the lower reaches of the Football League. The team's fortune seemed to change after a close 3–2 defeat by Liverpool in the FA Cup, and for the rest of the 1990/91 season it was downhill. Goodbye Division Two, hello Division Three. Although the Liverpool result went against us on the pitch, off the pitch we had a result against the normally cocky Scousers, who were subdued due to several incidents prior to kick-off. This included a pub full of Liverpool lads being attacked and refusing to come out to play, and all other groups met were run by a serious mob of Hull lads walking down Anlaby Road.

The final big game of this era saw us playing Millwall, who were on a promotion run to Division One. They brought a massive following, but the atmosphere around the ground was carnival-like, much to the relief of local residents and police. As usual, most lads met in town before making their way towards the ground, but I and a dozen mates headed off to a pub were we met some Millwall fans who were known to us. In the bar at the same time were a tidy firm of 'faces', all Armanied up and looking the part. They stood away from the Millwall lads we were talking to. There wasn't a hint of trouble until a small group of Hull lads entered the pub. They saw us and assumed everyone was Hull but one of the incoming lads heard a Cockney accent and proceeded to whack the speaker over the head with a bottle. With this the full pub erupted and beer glasses and bottles rained down on everyone. I ended up on the floor after a departing Londoner 'Pearl Harboured' me across my back with a barstool. They ran out the pub and separated, making it harder to spot them through the Saturday shoppers and leaving us in the street dripping wet with beer!

As the fortunes of the club had declined – in 1992 we escaped relegation to the bottom division only by a late season rally – a change occurred on the terraces too. People like myself who loved the football would still travel to Wimbledon, Carlisle, Exeter and so on, but many of the lads would now only turn out for big home matches, or an away one that was guaranteed to go off. I understood this to an extent. One of my friend's older brothers had stopped going to City in the mid-seventies. When he told me I would be more discerning with my money when I was older, I laughed and told him I would be at every City match. When you get debts, mortgage and kids, though, if the team are not performing you do weigh up the cost of travelling, beer money, match entrance and peripherals. You only have to look at the gates Leeds and Newcastle were getting during their bad times over the past 20 years to see that a poor team can decrease hooliganism far more than the judicial system ever can.

CHAPTER TEN

National Service

TRIPS ABROAD WITH England gave us our only chance to experience supporting your team on the Continent. Hull City could never give us this opportunity, but we could still enhance the name of our firm through our willingness to travel and 'mix it' when required. It became a source of pride for any lad to witness his team's flag on display. Sometimes in far-flung corners of the world you would only get a few lads travelling, but once they'd arrived and unfurled the flag, we were all there in spirit.

We didn't always come out on top. It wasn't all plundering and pillaging, as the media like to portray. On a number of occasions we were on the receiving end of vicious beatings dished out by foreign police officers. These law-enforcers often attacked without us even lifting a finger, and sometimes on trips like these the England reputation was a heavy cross to bear.

Gary T from West Hull, an England veteran, gave me a detailed account of what occurred on many of these forays into enemy territory:

A match played in Santander, Spain, saw approximately 300 England fans attacked on the terracing by the Spanish police. They clubbed people mercilessly without discrimination. This 'old bird' from the FA got leathered all over just like the rest of us; they didn't give a fuck who they were hitting. I expected a furore in the morning papers as we arrived home the next day, national outrage over what we had to endure – nothing. Not one mention. If we'd turned over a bar or battered some Spaniard senseless, there'd have been countless reports and photos depicting the shocking events. They only report what they want you to see or hear.

The first proper organised trip was to Luxembourg in 1983. Puss and Jacko booked 38 of us onto North Sea Ferries and then sorted out the itinerary onto our destination. It was full-on mayhem from start to finish. At the main station we came out to a reception committee of Luxembourg's finest riot squad, a section of paratroopers who'd been deployed around the central area. The sight of these crack troops was a red rag to the England fans pouring out of the station. Led by the Hull contingent, they ran at the paratroopers, who proceeded to drop their shields and batons and leg it up the road. The more opportunist members of the England party took maximum advantage and began pilfering in the local shops, while those fixed on a wrecking mission obliterated all before them. A Hull lad had a photo taken with him and his mates stood atop a turned-over car, with the occupants still strapped inside, upside down. The trouble carried on throughout the day, with the Hull lads never far from the centre of things.

One of the Hull lads got lifted and spent the rest of the day in cells. He had his camera confiscated on arrival at the police station and much to his annoyance had to endure the piss-taking of the local bobbies, who used up all his film on him as he sat sulking. He had the last laugh though. He gave his name as Mr John Player of 10 Park Drive, Clegghuddersfax, Yorkshire, and after a couple of hours cooling off he was released without a blemish on his character.

After the game, the train journey out provided another source of amusement. The Hull lads were in a carriage next to the buffet car and began abusing and threatening anyone trying to wander through. As far as they were concerned the match was over and everyone was now fair game. They defended this carriage as though it was a section of terracing at Boothferry Park and found no one willing to take them on.

My first real scary moment following England was at Hampden Park in March 1985. Richard Gough scored in a 1-0 win. We'd travelled up on a coach from Hull (50 of us), joined up with the rest of the England party just outside Glasgow and came in under escort. Inside the ground I took stock of our numbers and was totally dismayed when I realised we only numbered around 200 fans: 200 amongst 72,000 hostile Jocks. We stood at the bottom of Section M and after about 30 minutes it went off. The Scots surged down, hitting out at any England fans in their path. We were pressed up against the fence and it was all we could do to fight them off. We punched, pushed, pulled and kicked ourselves into exhaustion; my whole body ached yet they still came down at us. This pummelling lasted till just after the half-time whistle, when the police finally arrived on the scene (nearly 20 minutes after the trouble began). They made a wedge between both sets of supporters and then opened a gate onto the pitch, which we tumbled through. We were then told the police were taking us to a secure section, so off we set past hordes of screaming, spitting Jocks. We were their half-time entertainment. The police led us through the section, opened a gate at the back and booted us out, with 'Fuck off you English scum' ringing in our ears. At first I was seething, but in hindsight they did us a favour.

My second visit north of the border gave us a chance to redeem ourselves for years of domination by the Scots. We had all witnessed the two-yearly invasion of the capital and a group of pissed off England fans (including Hull lads) decided to do something about it. A sortie into enemy territory was required. By the mid-eighties England fans ruled the roost on the Continent; it was now the Jocks' turn to experience fear in their backyard.

As match day neared we found out that our allocation of

tickets was ludicrously small. A campaign was kick-started by a Hull fan, Mark Jackson (Cockney Jacko), to allow more England fans to travel to the game. Mark sent scores of letters highlighting the unfair distribution for this high-profile Home Countries match. The most galling part was that the English F.A. was always so accommodating to Scottish fans yet this was never reciprocated. Many of the high-profile faces chose to ignore the letters, including both the English and Scottish F.A.s and the then-Sports Minister, Mr Moynihan. The campaign, though, suddenly gained momentum when it was taken up by the *Daily Sport* and before long the Scottish F.A. relented and made many more tickets available. This campaign played a significant part in allowing fans to travel up for the game, where they would finally explode the myth of Scottish invincibility.

On the morning, trouble broke out at Glasgow's main train station. A small group of English, including several Hull, were inside the station, waiting for the main support to arrive. They stood out against the backdrop of feathered Tams, kilts and curly wigs, and were kept on their toes as sporadic fighting broke out. It looked as though it was going to 'go off' proper as the Jocks began grouping up on the edge of the main concourse, and the English casuals came together ready for the expected rush. Luckily for them it never came, as a train packed to the rafters with England lads pulled into the station. The small group waiting on the other side of the barrier decided to take the initiative and waded into the twitchy Jocks, who scattered in seconds.

I and 15 other Hull lads had come up by car and stupidly drove too close to the ground looking for a parking spot. It was obvious by our code of dress that we were English and our small convoy was attacked several times by brick-throwing locals. I turned into one road and found myself trying to drive through hordes of Jocks, who rocked the cars back and forth and banged and bounced off the sides and roof. I couldn't decide what to do for best: do we sit it out or move off fast? Not for the first time in Glasgow, I was happy to see the police, who intervened and escorted us well away from the crowd. We parked up miles away from the ground and hung about waiting for the train crew to show.

Soon the other Hull lads were regaling us with their experiences on their march to Hampden. They told of how the Scots were 'steamed' time and again and this news was greeted with immense relief by our small group, who were in need of a confidence boost after the mental torture we'd endured in the cars. We just wanted to get at them and hand out a few slaps of our own.

The ground approached and we let them know we'd arrived. I've never sung or shouted so fervently as when we walked down that road leading directly to the stadium. We were trying to mingle in with the Jocks but the police weren't having any of it, they were pushing us towards the turnstiles and trying to get us inside. Most Jocks in the vicinity were now giving us a wide berth and it felt good, especially compared to my last visit, when we'd more or less sneaked in trying to look as inconspicuous as possible.

We stood behind the goal, a good 600 lads amongst the England party. This time they stayed well away. We got plenty of verbal but they weren't so keen on mixing it now. The ghost was definitely laid to rest. Nice one Jacko.

Italia 90. Abroad, I always felt superior. The locals often seemed naïve whilst we were more streetwise and cocksure, but a journey through Naples en route to Sardinia brought a few of us down a peg. We began the trip on North Sea Ferries and managed to stop off in Amsterdam for our goody bags (to help us through the tournament). We continued on the train to Naples, where we commandeered four taxis to take us from the main station to the Ferry-port. Off we set, rumbling through small squares and narrow streets, taking the piss out of the driver and hurling abuse at the Neapolitans as we drove by. Twenty minutes later we arrived at the Ferry-port. The driver wanted £40 a taxi, so we paid up and gave him a two-fingered wave goodbye. I moved my belongings off the side of the road and looked around.

'Why, the Italian cunt . . .'

From were we stood, I could see the main entrance to the train station up the road. We had moved about 200 yards. He'd definitely seen us coming.

After enduring a 14-hour ferry crossing in gale force seas, we finally docked in Sardinia a bit green around the gills. We made Alghero our base and booked into a fairly decent hotel. The people seemed friendly and the nightlife wasn't bad either. I suppose I was completely taken in by the friendliness of the place. One night I was walking back to the hotel, slightly worse for wear. I'd split up from the main bunch and decided to call it a night. I heard a shout and turned to see a scooter whizz up to me. Before I knew what was happening, I'd had my legs whipped from under me and this cunt was sat on top of me while his mate went through my pockets. After a bit of a struggle, in which I took a few digs, they were off down the road on this white Vespa.

I'd had only a bit of change on me but my pride had been hurt. Fuming, I went back towards the bars and met up with the lads. 'I know what they look like,' I kept on saying. 'They were riding a white Vespa.' We went out looking for this pair but our mission was doomed from the off – everyone in Alghero seemed to be bombing about on a white Vespa.

A trip to North America to watch England play in an indoor tournament showed us what we would miss in 1994. Three Hull lads saw all the games whilst three of us flew into Toronto for the last game in Detroit. Straight away we were spotballed as we walked into a few bars in downtown Detroit. A few refused us entry and once we'd settled down for a drink we found out why. Apparently they thought we were local neo-Nazis because of our short haircuts. The barman told us of recent troubles between these right-wing extremists and the local black youth and warned us to be on our guard at all times.

The match was played in a part of Detroit called Pontiac and we'd heard it was scheduled there because it was a relatively 'safe' area. Yet on the day of the match, nine killings were reported to have occurred in the Pontiac area the day before! The warning from the barman would definitely be heeded. We found a bar near the stadium which was full of England fans, and were enjoying ourselves when it suddenly kicked off between a few of our lads and a group of Leeds fans from Bridlington. Stood in a bar in Detroit thousands of miles from home and you end up fighting with a set of idiots who live 35 miles up the road.

The bar closed its shutters, so the only option was to make our way towards the ground. On the massive car park we came across one of those carriages you see at Disneyworld, the type with a golf buggy pulling it along. We decided to have a spin in it – 30 of us. We wound our way through the parked cars, doing 'figure eights' and even tried a couple of handbrake turns, while the stadium security gave chase. We were eventually stopped when a police car pulled in front of us and it got a bit hairy for a few minutes, with drawn guns and much screaming. Luckily they were happy enough seeing us off it and away into the ground.

We soon realised that certain rules had to be adhered to. The reported murders were testament to the fact that you can't go swanning off wherever you liked on a whim. You had to make sure you stuck to safe touristy areas, but the question was, what constitutes a safe area in Detroit?

One night we were stood in a nightclub queue when a black lad came over. He stood in front of us, shaking his head and waving his arms frantically.

'You can't go in there. You'll end up dead.'

We were lucky we had met someone decent, as the other black geezers in the queue had said nothing to us.

It wasn't just Detroit where you had to watch yourself. We stayed a few nights in Niagara Falls (on the Canadian side) and because the bars closed at 1am, we walked across the bridge and carried on drinking on the American side. These bars stayed open till 4am and were a bit livelier then their Canadian neighbours. On our last night there, we ended up running for our lives with a pub full of 'Micks' after us, just because one of the lads walked in wearing a Rangers shirt. And I thought they knew nothing about football.

There were other kinds of dangers encountered by some of the lads on jaunts abroad. In Australia a few of the lads decided to give white water rafting a go; after all, it can't be that hard, you just paddle like mad and bump around a bit. Before embarking, they were given instructions by their guide, a cross between Grizzly Adams and Crocodile Dundee. He emphasised the importance of keeping cool and ensuring that, whatever happened, they kept hold of their paddles. Afterwards, he was screaming and shouting that they were the worst bunch of cunts he'd ever set eyes on. Apparently as soon as they hit the first rapid most of them shouted, 'Fuck this,' then hoyed their paddles over the side and clung on for all they were worth.

We went to the vital World Cup qualifier in Rome in 1997 on a Northern Holidays trip (two nights hotel and coach travel) for the ridiculously low price of £160. After paying the money you try to put to the back of your mind the two mind-numbing days there and back. This was a big game so was deemed worth it.

The holiday company was bringing three coachloads over and we were to be billeted in three different hotels just outside Rome. There were 40-plus from Hull on our coach and we made up the largest contingent. The trip down was fairly quiet until we stopped off at a service station where one of the Hull lads, Gav, was seen talking to two Italian youths. We watched from the coach as hands were shaken, then the Italians shot off fast. Gav came on board, beaming from cheek to cheek, having obviously just completed some sort of purchase.

'Hey lads, we'll have this full trip on camera.'

He whipped open his jacket and produced a camcorder case. Everyone cheered him, then the cheers turn to howls of laughter; the Eyeties had done a switch on him and left him holding a case complete with a bag full of salt, which had cost him £150. He was slated for the rest of the trip and reminded at every opportunity. In cafes and restaurants lads were constantly offering him pots of salt for a good deal. Gutted.

Once in our hotel, which was good considering what we'd paid, it was shower then out on the town. We met up with a lot of the lads off the other coaches and settled down for a session. They were all Nationwide teams on this trip: some Man City, Plymouth, Exeter, Swindon, Oxford and a couple of good lads from Birmingham. We had a good drink, sang a few songs and basically let the locals know we were there.

They started gathering on the edge of the square, watching and waiting, as did the police. A couple of Hull lads, along with myself, walked through the line of Old Bill and wandered in amongst the locals. We weren't being demonstrative but goaded the Italians in hushed tones: 'Come on, we're here, lets have it.'

All we got back was, 'No, no, in the stadium, it will fight in the stadium.'

'Fuck the stadium, let's have it now.'

They weren't interested, but it would all change later.

I don't know what sparked it off, maybe a chance remark or someone had strayed too close to the other side; no matter, it was what we were waiting for. Bottles, stools and tables rained down on the Italians and our lads were soon in amongst them, chasing them back to the edge of the square. We didn't know it but a couple of undercover police were in with us and one of them made a grab for a Hull lad called Jason just as he let fly with a bottle. He stood there, hitting Jason with this truncheon with no back-up to help him. He must have been crazy. A couple of lads realised what was happening and went for him. He was lashing out at them and didn't see one of the Brummies running up with a chair – mind you, he felt it. Jason was hurried away and in time-honoured tradition was given a different top to hide his identity.

The police by now were pretty angry and started pushing us back to the far corner of the square. Someone shouted, 'They're trying to detain us.' The police were forming a pincer movement to get right round us. We charged, breaking the line, and ran across the square where only moments earlier the Italians had stood. The local youth had all but disappeared and it was time for us to do the same.

Around an hour later, Glen (one of East Hull's finest) approached me and asked if I fancied a walk to see what was going on. The two of us went on a tour of the back streets adjacent to the hotel. On a street corner five minutes into our stroll, we came across a bunch of Eyeties. Over we went and Glen moved in, aiming for this one.

'I think you . . . are a right wanker,' said Glen, gesticulating as he spoke.

I stood next to him, clenching my fists waiting for it to go, then the Italian said, 'Hey English, you lose your hotel?'

Glen had more or less spat venom in his face, we were both bouncing up and down ready to mix it with the lot of them, and this guy was trying to give us directions back to the hotel. We gave up and walked away, shaking our heads. Yet the next day over breakfast, we heard a few English lads from another hotel had been picked off and one ended up in hospital with a broken arm. In the cold light of day, two sober Hull lads realised they'd been lucky.

It was time to board the coach for Rome. Within 20 minutes we'd been pulled over by the police, who emptied the coaches of all our beer. They gave us an option of staying with the mini mountain of cans and bottles or continuing to Rome on a dry bus, so we continued. Our worst fear was that they'd be on top all day. We trundled through the outskirts of Rome with our escort, up to a coach park on top of a hill, where they left us.

We were anxious to move in case they changed their minds and came back, and began walking down the hill, through the steep-sided street, not knowing where we were going but down looked the best bet. A few started drifting away, probably not wanting anything to do with us, especially after last night's events in the square, but it left us with a good 90. Our presence seemed to be noticed immediately as countless Italians on scooters drove by giving us the old cutthroat sign. It didn't take us long to find bits of rubble and debris and hurl them down the road at the departing Vespas. We aimed to knock them off but stopped if they had a girl on the back – true English decorum!

As the street turned a bend, we could see where the riders had been heading: a square with ornate fountains was heaving with people as well as the Vespa boys. We didn't need an invite. A roar went up and we steamed down the narrow street to meet the Italians head-on. Panic ensued as we encountered the first few; they were pushing and pulling each other to get away as we motored on through. A few of ours got carried away and were called back; experience told you not to drift too far when you are up against ambushing blade merchants.

Our little rampage had left us with the need for liquid refreshment, so the Italians were forgotten as we headed for two small bars opposite each other down a street just off the square. The party was more or less equally divided, with us Hull lads in one bar and our new acquaintances on the other side of the road. Yet again the scooter boys came down for a closer look but this time we had bottles to throw at them. You could see they wanted it but didn't have a clue how to go about it.

The bottle-throwing lasted 15 minutes at most, until the police cordoned off the top of the street and access from the square. They'd stopped the scooter boys from coming down but now the square was filling up with more and more Italians. We stood outside the bars singing England songs, 'No Surrender' and the like. The Italians now easily numbered 400 and were pressing against the cordon making a hell of a noise.

We saw a commotion behind the police line, fists flying, and a few officers waded in and dragged out three England fans, who hurried towards us puffing and panting. They'd taken a few punches but apart from grazes to the face were none the worse for their ordeal. Word went round that the Italians in the square were Lazio Ultras. Things had been bubbling for a while and the appearance of these three lads proclaiming some of Italy's best were waiting for us was enough to light the spark.

Both bars emptied and we charged up to the cordon. A roar came from the square and the Italians were likewise straining at the leash, with many pressed up tight against the police vehicles. Yet as soon as we were within spitting distance, the Italians again turned and bolted. We carried on and ran into the police. Lads were ripping the shields off them and throwing them beyond into the square until the police baton-charged us. It was every man for himself as we fled back to the relative safety of the bars. The bar to our left quickly filled and down came the shutters. We Hull lads weren't so lucky, as the police followed us inside before we could get the shutters down. They waded in cracking skulls.

'Do 'em, do the Old Bill,' someone shouted.

We bombarded the doorway with empty wine bottles lined up on a ledge behind the bar. Now armed with bottles, stools and anything we could lay our hands on, we blitzed the cops and forced them back into the street. We were ecstatic.

'As soon as they come back in, give it them again.'

We waited and waited. Minutes passed by . . . nothing. Glen slowly made for the door and timidly looked out, then laughed. 'They've fucked off back to the top of the street.'

We piled out full of bravado, shouting abuse. The shutters came up and the rest joined us in the street. We headed away from the police line, our quickened pace turned into a jog and before we knew it we were running down back streets, smashing windows and kicking over parked scooters (like watching dominoes fall), bellowing the England war cry.

We soon hit a main road and slowed down. We didn't know our whereabouts and expected the police or an ambush at any moment. We'd just scattered 400 locals and had it with the Old Bill, yet here we were left on our own. I thought, *aye, aye, surely they must be planning something*. A few lads began flagging down taxis, but I and a couple of other England fans rounded on them and more or less threatened them. The last thing we could afford now was smaller numbers and we spelled out what would happen to them later if they didn't get out of the cabs. They sheepishly rejoined the ranks.

We marched on, ever wary. We had bottles stuffed down trousers, up jumpers and in our hands, imagining every corner would have hundreds of Italians laying in wait. The streets seemed quieter, shop windows were shuttered, bars were closed. It was obvious we were heading the right way yet we still hadn't seen any other England supporters. A bar was found and we all piled in. I was gagging for a drink: I'd listened to some idiot who said the day's forecast was poor, so I'd spent the day sweating in a heavy coat.

The bar owner confirmed we were on the right road and the ground was only a steady 20 minutes walk further on. I relaxed and settled in for a few drinks. By the time we reached the stadium it was 5pm. We'd left our coaches just under four hours ago. We sat by a bridge for over an hour, totally exhausted. Slowly more and more England fans arrived and our numbers swelled to 500. Beers again flowed as the stallholders did a roaring trade, the singing began, and expectancy was high.

The outer perimeter of the stadium was filling up with fans from both sides, and from our vantage point on the bridge we could see wave upon wave of Italians being directed over the busy road beneath us. The traffic would start up till the next group was ready and they then crossed, moving down the concourse. Whispers spread: the next wave of fans was their boys (Lazio Ultras) and as they came over, we steamed into them. I don't know if it was their boys, but no matter, anyone will do.

The Italians once again couldn't handle this full-frontal assault. They were knocked from pillar to post, then the stalls lining the main boulevard were ransacked as the lads moved through. A police car was attacked. I could see three England fans dragging the Old Bill out and leathering them by the side of the road. Another clothes-lined a motorbike cop whose bike swerved dangerously before coming to a halt in the middle of an upturned stall.

It was obvious what was coming next. Within minutes, the riot squad arrived. Tear gas canisters rained down on us. We all tried to cover our faces (luckily I had my coat) and lads were shouting for us to stand and hurling back canisters at the approaching line of police. The gas kept on coming, as did the police. Our mob was now spread very thinly and many lads began to drift away; they'd had their five minutes of fun and it was time to get in line. I heard someone calling me and realised Glen and a few more Hull lads were moving back as resistance was futile. I sprinted over and joined them. We melted into the crowd and made for the official England section.

All our tickets were for the other end but we didn't fancy entering an Italian section in small numbers, especially after the pummelling we'd just handed out, so we bunked into the England section. Once inside, we were hit with a barrage of plastic seats, bottles and stones. The police stood by as young Ultras ran up and let fly with all manner of weaponry over the so-called safety screen; it didn't surprise me, as these actions are par for the course in such places. We could see it going off at the other end, with England fans battling with the baton-wielding police, but it wasn't till I got home and watched a re-run that I realised what they actually had to put up with throughout the match.

The players did us proud. A heroic draw saw us through and the feeling was euphoric. Unfortunately the police put a dampener on our celebrations by keeping us inside for four hours after the match had finished. When at last allowed out, we were escorted to a coach park near the stadium. Our three coaches were surrounded and we had a massive escort all the way back to the hotels, where they made us go straight in. Police outside each hotel wouldn't let anyone leave the area; it was obvious they didn't want a repeat performance in the town square tonight. Anyway, we were all dead on our feet. We'd had our result; now we had the two-day trip back home to think about.

France 98. Our many European trips saw us forging long time friendships with lads from other firms: Manchester City, Bury and more recently Sunderland, for example. At times, we purposely stayed away from the bulk of England supporters, who always headed for the main squares to 'perform' in front of the cameras. To us, it made more sense to drink in bars away from all the attention. Not only were you clear of prying eyes but you weren't paying inflated prices for your drinks. You were far more likely to end up in a ruck without worrying that the police would be breathing down your neck in seconds.

Marseilles was no different. We stayed away from the Marina – the scene of the televised rioting – and sat drinking in an Algerian area, about 50 of us: Hull, Bury, Man City and Man United. We could hear a band playing in the distance. It seemed the locals were celebrating, as we could see people dancing round this band as it made its way towards us. Initially we were wary, but dropped our guard and began to relax again. It was just a brass band.

Wrong. The band got 50 yards away when out of the marching ranks appeared a mob of North Africans armed with bricks and bottles, which flew through the air towards us. We quickly closed ranks and ran at the ones nearest. For the next 15 minutes we were toe-to-toe with the fuckers. Pockets of fighting broke out up and down the street as they started to stretch us. You just had to look out for each other; if a few were caught or looked in trouble we'd hurtle back into the fray and either back off the locals or drag our lads out. The police arrived and the street quickly quietened. For once we weren't looked on as the aggressors. Racial tension and trouble often raises its head in these areas as these first/second/third generation North African migrants no longer bow down to their French hosts after years of oppression. It was scary but, for us, enjoyable. *C'est la vie.*

Over the years I've clocked up some miles watching England, I'd been to three World Cups and was hoping to go to Japan. I had never been charged with any sort of offence while following my country. Yet this didn't stop the authorities from preventing me from travelling to Holland for the arranged friendly a few months before the 2002 World Cup.

I'd decided to check out the cheapest flights around and found one to Belgium from Stansted, £20 each way. It would be simple enough to hop on a train to Amsterdam, meet up with mates who work and live in Holland, stay with them and go to the game together. This was a much cheaper alternative to most packages on offer and I couldn't foresee any problems; that was until I got to Passport Control.

A uniformed officer from Southend and a member of Special Branch pulled me to one side. I was asked to produce my passport, which they deliberated over for a few minutes, then shocked me with the news that I wouldn't be allowed to leave the country. They took me to one side and explained that I wasn't under arrest but I was being detained. I stood there for 30 minutes quietly fuming, then thought, *fuck this, I'm off home.*

I went up to the Southend Old Bill and said, 'Look, you've got my passport, I can't go anywhere, so I'm off home.'

With this, the copper jumped me and we started scuffling on the airport floor. I was aware of bodies flying by as I continued struggling out of his grasp – a good few England fans had run through without being checked, using my misfortune to their advantage. I was eventually dragged to a secure area and left for over two hours in a dingy little room. The Special Branch officer came in and told me they'd been onto the Hull police, who'd said they were surprised I wasn't on the 'Battle Wagon' with the other Hull lads. He then came out with a load of bollocks about me being deported from France in '98. Talk about fabricated; I'd left France of my own accord after the first game in Marseilles because my daughter had been involved in an accident and broken both her arms.

All my protests and counter arguments fell on deaf ears. A paper was produced of some football-related Act and I was told I had to be at Harlow Magistrates that afternoon.

So off I set and arrived to find two other lads (Plymouth and Bristol City) in the same boat as me. There was no duty solicitor, so I demanded one, who eventually arrived and saw to us all. The Plymouth lad was up first. He was already banned from all domestic games and even had a case pending; he was knocked back. The Bristol City fan went in and, even though he had a month left on a domestic ban, he was allowed to go. So I walked into court thinking, *I've no football-related convictions (in the past ten years), all I've been done for in recent years is a fight over a traffic incident.* Within ten minutes I was back out, completely numbed, along with a two-year domestic and international ban. They had done me up proper. Oh well, there's always cricket.

CHAPTER ELEVEN

Return of the Minority

AS THE NINETIES began, the decline in football-related incidents in and around many grounds continued. The reasons argued for this are as diverse as heavy policing, undercover operations, the rave scene love-in and the Hillsborough Disaster. These may have been factors at the fashionable clubs, but I believe the decline had to do with the formation of the Premier League, the alienation of those left in the Nationwide League, and the rise in admission prices as much as anything.

In Hull we continued to meet before a game but the opposition was nearly always lacking and this, coupled with poor results on the pitch, saw lads drift away. They still turned out if an off was expected, which at the beginning of the decade usually meant cup games. In the early nineties the only team we played of any real pedigree was Chelsea in the FA Cup third round. Plenty of Chelsea turned up but they seemed like student types compared to their formidable forebears of the seventies and eighties. A mob of City outside The Eagle pub called it on to a decent-sized group of Chelsea inside but they didn't want to know; they sat staring at their glasses of lager.

To us, these Premiership fans had no backbone. Subsequent games against opposition like Newcastle United, Aston Villa, Bolton Wanderers, Derby County and then-Premier League Crystal Palace proved the point further. We craved the opportunity to mix it with the so-called elite, yet all of these teams made only a token show against our travelling army. We certainly expected a lot more from Newcastle, Villa, Derby and Bolton. All four matches saw upwards of 400 lads travelling to take on the might of the Premiership but all we came across was hordes of shirt-wearers too frightened to even stand up inside the ground for fear of incurring the wrath of the dreaded stewards. If that's the Premiership, you can keep it.

The young lads who had been willing disciples in the mid-eighties were now seasoned veterans but hooliganism on the English club scene was at its lowest ebb. These lads were the backbone of the firm and had never needed any encouragement; the danger now was that some were beginning to drift away. What was needed was a couple of morale-boosting results. Luckily for us, a couple of games against Midland opposition and the Hammers ensured the momentum carried on for a while longer.

I will introduce you to a main 'player' of this period, Paul from the Orchard Park Estate, to continue the story:

PAUL: I'll never forget my first encounter with an away fan; we were playing Preston North End and as usual I was tagging along. I'd been on the periphery for over a year and you always knew who to follow. It's funny thinking back, but these lads were looked up to and for me they were on a par with the players. In some respects I was awestruck by the whole hooligan experience.

These Preston lads came out of the away section just as we poured out of the new North Stand. It was going off all round the coaches, and there in front of me was this lad, probably around 17 or 18 years old. I don't know what made me do it but I ran up, banged him and ran off again. It probably didn't even mark his face but all the next week at school we were talking about it.

The school grapevine was working its magic; by the end of the week I'd not only hit him, I'd sparked him clean out. My reputation and popularity knew no bounds (well, would you have said owt?). I'd crossed the line. It was as though I now had something to prove, not just to myself but to my mates. From now on we'd be there, spurring each other on and daring to do that little bit more. I was a Psycho now.

I started attending away games and often sat on the coach listening to the older lads talking about the seventies. They always talked about the Sheffield teams, especially United and how they were seen as our biggest rivals. I had experienced matches against them; they always seemed game and came in big numbers but to me 'the team' to watch out for was Boro. Games against Boro were always edgy, they came at you with a viciousness that I've rarely witnessed with other teams, and it was often scary, especially for a 16-year-old.

During a game against them at Boothferry Park, I remember standing near Three Tuns with five mates; we were hanging around after the game waiting to see the Boro escort go by. The bulk of City's mob had moved up Anlaby Road, thinking it was all over and the police were in control.

These two Hull lads came over to us. I didn't know who they were and I still don't. They just came up and said, 'Get ready lads, it's gonna go.'

We didn't know what was going on until we saw four lads hurtling towards us from over the road. They came straight at us, carrying the little brollies that a lot of lads used.

'Come on then City!' they shouted as they piled into us, cracking us about the heads and arms with the brollies. The two Hull lads were right into them, and there was the rest of us, doing fuck-all but watch, open-mouthed. Sure, I bounced around, lashing out with my foot but it was a token gesture; inside I was screaming. I wished I was somewhere else, and that feeling was compounded when Boro's main firm came straight off the car park and charged at us. We were off. I always had a thing about Boro after that, very wary of them.

Years later, I was coming home on the ferry after watching England play in Holland. Again there was just a few of us, drinking, when in walked this mob of lads. They were Boro, around 30 of them. One came up and asked us where we were from.

'Hull.'

'City fans?' (*Here we go*, I thought)

'Yeah, mate, yeah.'

'Nice one, I used to love coming to your place, you were always guaranteed an off there.'

'Yeah mate, I know'

'What are you drinking?'

'Cheers, mate, I'll have a . . . (*thank fuck for that*)

Such introductions to hardened rivals were a necessary part of the hooligan experience. They either put you off for life, or whetted your appetite for more. It wasn't long before the younger lads were well into the swing of things and organising trips.

PAUL: I was conned into organising a coach to Coventry City; I'd never done it before and saw it as a way of getting there without having to pay. It was mostly filled with lads off our estate, Orchard Park, with a sprinkling of lads off Newland and a few Town lads; a good-quality bus. The ride down was fairly civilised, with a few playing cards, drinking and smoking. There wasn't a hint of trouble; it seemed like money for old rope.

As we approached the outskirts of Coventry, the Old Bill picked us up. We knew where some of our lads were drinking and that's where we wanted to be. We passed the pub and piled off. One lad was stopped and searched; he'd only pushed by this copper but they ended up arresting him after finding some 'gear.'

The pub was packed to the rafters. I couldn't believe the

turnout; already there was around 200 lads singing. I was buzzing; you can't beat days like this. After a few pints, we marched to the ground. As we came around to the away end, you could see that one of the turnstiles was unmanned. Loads just steamed in, including myself. We made our way down and sat as near to the home section as we could. We could see a group of 40-50 lads and began mouthing off to each other.

City seemed to be holding their own, then up popped a Coventry player, bang, 1-0. A few seats were smashed and thrown about, nothing drastic, just the usual frustration. We all started to move; we left our seats and stood in a walkway that separated the upper and lower sections. I must admit we looked impressive; there were hundreds of us.

Five minutes left on the clock, time to go. The police were really lax: as we came out, someone realised that the home section gates were also open. We steamed straight in and it went off at the bottom of the stairwell. Coventry had a good few lads and stood their ground, with both sets of lads trading blows, but in the end they broke ranks and scattered. I was at the front and gave chase. I remember looking over the ground from inside Coventry's own end and thinking, *we've taken their end.* This was more or less unheard of in the nineties.

I came bouncing back down the steps towards the exit, full of confidence. I thought we were all over the stand, loads of Hull in Coventry's end. As I reached the bottom, I moved through the crowd.

'Fuck, the exit's been closed.'

I was oblivious to those around me, then it began to dawn on me that these lads were Coventry. I went cold. Keep your head down and your mouth shut. A couple of lads nodded and winked at me. At least I wasn't alone.

A few of the Coventry lads were getting impatient and started booting and pushing the metal doors. A lad near us shouted, 'Let's do the Hull cunts.'

One of the Hull lads turned and banged him. *Oh no, not now.*

'Whoa,' said his victim, 'I'm Coventry.'

Luckily with all the noise and commotion, nobody twigged what was happening; the gates opened slightly and that was my cue to move. The police moved in and began lashing at the Coventry fans trying to pile out. Behind them stood another line of coppers pushing and whacking City fans. Somehow I got out, ran over to the Hull lads, turned and began mouthing off to all and sundry.

The police pushed Coventry further back inside and concentrated their efforts and attentions on us. Time to move on again. More police were arriving as we walked from the ground, yet they ignored us and carried on towards the exit gates; that suited us as we made our way down a street alongside the ground. I don't know who started throwing or why, but in seconds everyone was caught up in this mad rush down the street. Cars and house windows were going in, it was stupid and pointless but we carried on. A car was stuck; inside were four Rastas. One lad dived on the bonnet, obscuring the driver's view, so they tried reversing but their way was blocked. The car was trashed and they were trying to drag the occupants out of the windows but they were saved as the police arrived. Yet again, though, we weren't stopped; everyone just ambled on, slowly making our way back to the coaches. Our driver was sound, he was willing to stay back a while so we could pick up a couple of the lads who'd been arrested and an hour later we were on the motorway heading for home.

We stopped off at Trowell Services, as the driver was adamant he wanted a half-hour break. Now most of the lads were speeding and I didn't think stopping was such a good idea – I knew what they'd get up too. Sure enough, the usual pilfering began. Anything not nailed down was taken, members of the staff were threatened when they asked for payment and a massive food fight broke out on the concourse. It was obvious what was going to happen next: the coach would be searched as soon as the Old Bill arrived.

Most of the lads were on the coach when the inevitable officers arrived but the driver was still inside finishing his break. One of the Orchard lads was in the driver's seat, completely off his trolley. Two officers approached the bus and began talking to him as though he were the driver.

'I'm just waiting for the rest of them officer and I'll be off.'

The copper was shaking his head. 'No, no, you'll have to stay put, there's been a spot of bother.'

'Really? They've been good as gold, if you ask me.'

The real driver walked up. 'What's going on?' he asked.

The officers were fairly reasonable, especially after being taken for a ride by the bogus driver. They went on to explain in great detail what the consequence would be if we refused to pay for the damaged goods.

'Look lads, if you pay up £150, you can be on your way.'

All they received was a torrent of abuse. The lads swore blind they'd done nothing wrong, yet all around the floor was debris, bits of strawberry flans and torn porno magazines.

'I'll give you five minutes to make your minds up,' stated the older of the two officers.

They got off and stood by their squad car talking to the driver. Inside we were punching the windows and hurling abuse.

'What they gonna do, nick the full fucking coach?'

Fat *** piped up and in his dulcet tones (like Les Dawson with a sore throat) said, 'I've been nicked here before, Chelsea '81. They'll take us to Nottingham, they're bad cells there.'

True to form, everyone still refused to cooperate. More police arrived and the driver was informed he had to follow an escort. Everyone began stashing their drugs. Pot and whizz was flying about under the seats.

Lines of white vans flanked the coach and others covered the front and back as we travelled down the motorway. They were stopping traffic and sealing off roundabouts until we reach our destination. We pulled into a courtyard filled to overspill with police and dog handlers, a definite case of *déjà vu* for the lads who were on the Chelsea trip in 1981.

'Right lads, file off the coach.'

No one moved.

The officer lost it and screamed, 'GET OFF NOW.'

It started going loopy. They tried to open the back exit and throw on the dogs to flush us out but our legs kicked out, preventing the rabid German shepherds from getting near enough. A group of officers stormed the front but were pulled onto the seats and roughed up. Lads were running up and down the aisle ready to repel any further invasions. Outside, the police nursed their wounds and helmets were strewn over the gravel floor. It was stalemate. The whole scene seemed surreal.

A spokesperson came across and stood at the bottom of the steps. 'Look lads, you're coming off one way or another, just think about it.'

Typically, those furthest back began shouting him down: 'Nobody fucking move.' It was all right for them, they wouldn't get it first.

A group of officers were given instructions by the side of the coach: 'Bring them off two at a time.' The first two lads who the police stood over were given an option. They refused to move. This time the police had positioned officers behind the seated lads with batons drawn. The lads struggled and fought but were dragged off. The next six lads took the same option and had to be carried off but then more and more took the option to walk off. Yet it still took half of the Nottinghamshire Constabulary two-and-a-half hours to empty the coach.

We were put into huge cells and split into groups of ten or twelve. After a couple of hours they tried to make out that everyone else had gone and we were taking the rap for it but we could hear lads shouting and singing from other cells. I'd been banged up for around 18 hours before I was even spoken to; they waited for the Hull Football Liaison Officer to turn up so he could point out known troublemakers. I was taken into an interview room, where the officer leading the questioning looked at me, and the first thing he said, was, 'What's with the jacket?'

It was a scruffy green jacket that I'd worn to work in the morning. I couldn't follow his drift.

'What do you mean? It's a jacket.'

He moved in close and nodded towards the jacket. 'That's a British National Party jacket.'

I laughed out loud. 'Fucking British Home Stores more like.'

I was thrown back in the cell. I could hear some movement and recognised the voices outside. Something was happening at last. Eventually we were all taken into a large room; it was our turn for the dreaded I.D. Parade. We had to stand holding cards with a designated number and the workers from the service station were walking back and forth pondering who to pick. The room was full of police, many with their truncheons across their chests. They must have thought we were mental.

The I.D. thing was pretty unjust. A couple of the lads who were fingered by the workers actually paid for their food. Yes, they were known hooligans but in this instance they'd done nothing wrong, nothing that the staff had seen anyway, but they were main players in the disturbance afterwards on the coach. Let's just say it was payback time.

One of these lads didn't take to kindly on being pointed out. He tore up his card and had to be restrained from attacking his accuser. The room was chaotic, with Old Bill running round blocking doorways and shielding the witnesses. The rest of us were quickly ushered into a side room where we all stood looking at each other. Talk about laugh. . .

We were kept in custody for 24 hours. When the police started throwing us out onto the streets of Nottingham it was 11pm on a Thursday night. We had to leave twelve lads behind, with the words of a senior officer ringing in our ears:

'If you ever play here, then by God we'll be waiting for you.'

We met up outside a McDonalds. Someone said, 'Let's have it with all these cunts round here then.' I couldn't believe what I was hearing; we'd been released only 30 minutes earlier. Luckily common sense prevailed. I shared a taxi with four mates and arrived home 41 hours after setting off. It was a good while before I organised another trip.

A game against Birmingham City had been talked up for a good month before we played them. To us there was no doubt, Birmingham would come, they always showed. There was also a lot at stake. Birmingham were going for promotion and for once we'd found ourselves just off a play-off place. It had the makings of something big.

We were on our usual march to the ground when a coach was spotted, stuck in the match-day traffic a couple of hundred yards in front. A group of 50 City fans broke away and charged towards it. They were joined by others who ran out of Griffin pub. Emblazoned on the back of the coach were the words 'Birmingham Executive Travel.' Maybe some of their lads were travelling up in style. As we drew level, it was apparent we'd chased after the team bus. People had armed themselves with bricks and rubble and were gutted that it wasn't full of Zulus.

One lad shouted at a few who hadn't caught up, 'Relax, it's not them, it's the players' coach.'

An oncoming Hull lad replied, 'Well do them, then.'

A barrage of bricks, bottles and pint glasses hit the coach. I'll never forget the look of horror on the players' faces. Kevin Francis was mouthing warnings to his team-mates, some of whom hit the deck as we let fly. Some of the lads were nearly foaming at the mouth, like frenzied animals: 'Let's do 'em properly.' Some even tried to force their way on; one lunatic ran at the door pummelling it in with a large For Sale sign. Birmingham manager Barry Fry helped hold the door shut while the driver sat there continuously sounding his horn. Saturday shoppers stood open-mouthed. I dread to think what would have happened if the door had been breached. It took over five minutes before you could hear the approaching squad cars, and when they did arrive it was to move away the battered bus and its shocked occupants. We were left to our own devices.

The main firm had now joined up with our renegade group and everyone was buzzing. It had set the tone for the day. We knew Birmingham were in Silver Cod and that would be our next stop. We made out as though the main section was going straight on to the ground but as we approached Cod from the opposite side of the road we all bolted across and barged through the doors. City pressed on and steamed right in; there wasn't any time for posturing outside. It was now or never. The Birmingham lads didn't fuck about either; we were met with full resistance as they hurled stools and glasses and all manner of fixtures and fittings. It wasn't just a few lads kicking and punching, the full bar was in uproar. People were thrown to the floor, jumped on and battered. The Zulus took a few casualties but they were game lads right up to the police arrival. The Old Bill had followed us in and were scuffling with the lads at the back while the Birmingham fans were up against the fire exit trying to get out.

Satisfied that they'd taken care of business, City swarmed out of Cod. It was going off down the road with another group of Birmingham and we all aimed for the action. I could see that a couple of their boys were Rastas and one was being dragged around by his dreadlocks. A couple of his mates came to his aid and managed to get him away before the arrival of our main firm. They retreated to the car park, where they had larger numbers. A group of around 30 Zulus, many hooded up, stood apart to the left. These looked the part. They waited until Hull followed the retreating Brummies onto the car park and then came at us from the side.

One of their lads fronted me. I could see he had a beer bottle hidden up each sleeve. We were a few feet away from each other and they backed off as far as the turnstiles. We hadn't even thrown a punch. The lad who'd fronted me was off and to say that I was relieved would be an understatement. I can only presume that they expected us to do a runner and when we didn't, their bottle went (forgive the pun).

At the most I would say they had 100 willing lads at the game. Now a crew of this size had probably done the business all season, but they were foolish to think they could get away with it here. On the day, they hampered their chances by fragmenting the firm and trying to take us on in small groups. It's dangerous to think that you can turn up in Hull with a few vans parked here and there, because you'll pay the price.

This wasn't the end of hostilities. After the game, Hull broke through the police lines and again attacked the Birmingham fans. They were stunned but it didn't stop them fronting us as we battled it out under the bridge. You could always rely on the Zulus to make things interesting.

MANNIX: I wasn't at the match, as I was travelling up from London, where I was working at the time, but I include this if only for a sense of perspective. My brother's best mate had lived in Birmingham for nearly 18 years but was an avid Hull fan. He brought a van full of Brummies up with him for the match. They stayed the night and had a beer with our kid and myself in a boozer (Mermaid, Boothferry Estate) not a million miles from the ground. Many of them were sporting black eyes, cuts and bruises and were stating they hadn't seen the Zulus backed off like that for an age.

As my brother was in his mid-forties and not into the scene, I had my respectable head on and was sympathising when J- and G- came in the pub, greeted me and without realising who my company was, launched into comments like, 'You should have seen them Brummie bastards on their toes today.' They went into graphic details about their part in the day's proceedings. My cover totally blown, the Birmingham lads didn't seem so keen on me after that. Can't understand why! Does show, however, that the Midlanders admitted Hull came out on top.

The other game against equally notorious opposition during the early nineties was at home to West Ham United.

MANNIX: We had drawn them at Boothferry Park very early in the season, and the town was buzzing with old lads' expectations and younger ones keen to prove themselves against some of the best. I got a taxi at 10.30am and picked up two of my mates, W- and D-, and was in the town centre before opening time. We had thought there would be a large presence of West Ham on the train but there was no evidence of this, and at 11am we settled for a drink in the Bass House, a pub as central as you can get in the town. By midday, our numbers had grown to a respectable 150 when word came through that there was another mob of City drinking in the Green Gingerman, which was in the bus station adjoining the train arrivals.

With everyone getting restless, we marched from the pub and picked up the other lads in the station, taking a back route to avoid the O.B., who were amazingly nowhere to be seen. We walked through St Stephens Square and over Park Street bridge, well over 200-handed by this time. As the front two emerged on Anlaby Road (myself and G-, one of a family of good lads from East Hull), we saw three carloads of West Ham at the traffic lights, all lads.

'Excuse me mate, where's the football ground from . . .'

He didn't even complete the sentence before mutual recognition set in and he saw the rest of City's lads coming round the corner. G- and I ran across the road to drag them out of the car but the front one accelerated through the red light and drove at us. Good job there was only a few of us there at the time, otherwise it would have been carnage. I jumped out of the way and kicked the car on the way past, pointless I know, but a token gesture of intent. The other two cars were reversing at high speed back up Anlaby Road towards the town centre, pursued by a rabid mob of City. I realise there was little more than a dozen of them, but Hull at that time adhered to few rules of engagement, and the beer-fuelled disappointment of their no-show made the lads eager for anyone to take out their frustration on.

Four blokes came out of Steam Tavern public house. They were definitely Cockneys, walking 20 yards in front of a mob of around 300 Hull, yet they didn't look back once. These were proper 'geezers'. A few lads at the front were itching to get in amongst them but this wasn't my bag. Several lads bounced up to them and these Hammers just turned and went for it. It was all so pointless; after all, the police were there in numbers and parted the two groups in seconds. I believe that it would have made no difference at all to these blokes, as they were prepared to stand no matter what, and for that I salute them.

Little else happened before the match, but afterwards was a different story. We were coming out of the ground from under the Best Stand seats; we had a tidy mob of around 60 lads. We positioned ourselves in the open-air section, just inside the perimeter of the ground; we knew they were in the seats and they soon came out to face us. The gap between us soon filled with bodies as lads from each side pounced. A mate of mine wrapped himself around this Cockney; he was too small to confront him, so instead he hung there like a limpet while I banged away at his head. The poor fucker didn't know what to do, in the end we got him down and he took some punishment. A lot of their lads started to break away. We ran them right across the car park. They were getting tripped up and smashed about the head as they ran, they didn't even try to re-form. We couldn't believe it. This had been a proper off with even numbers tearing into each other yet they'd run. I mean, it was West Ham we were facing, not Rotherham.

As the rest of the Londoners came out into the car park for their cars and coaches, City ran at them and started battering anybody who looked like a lad. Even the fringe players and some replica-shirt boys were getting involved, and it was an evil atmosphere. I remember one tall, well-dressed black lad moaning, 'For fuck's sake, we ain't brought a mob,' before he was battered into the side of his coach and kicked senseless. A few got nicked on each side and the local paper's reporting of the court case told it all. The Londoners were all in their late thirties or forties and had occupations like surveyor, accountant, etc, while most of the Hull lads were early twenties and unemployed.

For the return fixture later that season, strangely the number of City's lads willing to take on the Hammers dropped to one coach. The word had obviously gone round regarding liberties taken and there was a fearsome mob numbering hundreds at the Boleyn Ground that proceeded to batter and terrorise the Hull lads throughout the day. This is a balanced view of both matches, and goes to show that if you are not prepared to travel in numbers to places like Upton Park, victories gained on home soil won't mean as much.

* * *

It wasn't until the mid-nineties that things started to take off again at Hull. The catalyst was a final game of the season against Bradford City in 1996. We had been relegated (we won only five of 46 league games that season) while Bradford were pressing for promotion to the First Division. That, along with the decision by the match commander Inspector Callum to give the away supporters Hull's traditional end, made for an explosive situation.

Before the game, Bradford's fans kept a low profile and the

small group of lads who travelled by train were destroyed by a heavy Hull presence in the city centre. Inside the ground, the incoming mass of Hull fans invaded the pitch, with up to 200 lads heading towards the Bradford supporters. They were met this time by resistance from the BCFC lads, but the police soon took charge and those not arrested made their way back into the North Stand. Officers then took control of the North Stand perimeter, and a further two attempted invasions were repelled with truncheons.

The game was won by Bradford 3–2. As we streamed out, all eyes were still on the pitch as the police expected another invasion by the Hull fans to protest against our hapless board of directors. Instead about 50 of us ghosted towards North Road and the jubilant Bradford fans. The Hull firm spread across the road as we approached their boys and the first ones that were met soon back-pedalled.

One lad came bouncing over and challenged me with the immortal line: 'Who are yer?'

'FUCKING HULL' I shouted as my fist glanced off his forehead.

He backed off and pointed to a lone officer. 'Did you see that? He hit me.'

The officer stood with his right leg forward, taking his full body weight, and held his baton out in front of him (his stance reminded me of Corporal Jones in *Dad's Army* during bayonet practice). 'Move away, move away,' he shouted, but I took no notice and pursued my target, who ran off into the crowd.

The Bradford lads were trying to egg themselves on with shouts of 'OINTMENT, OINTMENT,' but each surge by them was run back. The Hull mood was such that the police presence was brushed aside. They moved along North Road and cut off the escape route for several thousand Bradford fans.

This scenario lasted for 15 minutes. Each time Bradford

mustered their forces and ran at us, their attempts petered out as they came to the thin line of Hull lads. It didn't matter to us that we were outnumbered; you could tell they didn't have the stomach for it. Their attempts at running us had little conviction, yet all the time they carried on with that pathetic shout.

We drove them down the street. A few tried to climb through gardens to escape but ended up worse off as they were cornered and attacked with no mercy. I had never before been involved in something as vicious as this and there was no let up until the police drafted in a squad of officers in riot gear and also sent the horses in. The Hull lads gradually moved back and took up positions at the top of Boothferry Road, waiting for the train crew to pass by, but they took another route home.

The police now moved us on. It was over. As we walked back towards town, one of the Bransholme lads turned and said, 'How's this for a souvenir?' He took out a hankie, opened it and produced half of someone's ear. That's how intense it was down North Road.

The aftermath of this game was such that a media witchhunt was undertaken by the local press, urging people to ring in with information about photos printed on their front page. From this joint effort by the press and police, 50 people were identified.

★ ★ ★

Suddenly faces not seen at Boothferry Park regularly in years were back. A Hull lad returning from an 18-month stint at Her Majesty's Pleasure commented, 'Fucking hell, we only had fifty lads before I went in, where's this three hundred come from?' But it wasn't just the hooligan elements that were fired up. Ordinary supporters had been disgusted with the decision to give away fans our end and many sympathised and understood why trouble occurred. Years ago, these same supporters had often cheered us as we battled on the terraces. They often played their part by refusing to point us out, and in some instances help conceal us as we ducked and dived to escape police detection. These same people worked alongside us during the week. They liked to know what had been happening and took pride in our exploits.

These fans had begun following the Tigers as young lads, no different from us but they happened to miss the hooligan calling, so to speak. Many of them in my age group would dress the same as me circa 1975 and were always on the edge of skirmishes but as the City Psychos entered the scene they began to distance themselves from those 'wanting it'.

One of these lads, Steve from Orchard Park, can explain better then I:

STEVE: 4 January 1969, FA Cup round three, Hull City 1, Wolverhampton Wanderers 3. My first game at Boothferry Park ended in defeat, a trend that was to continue for the next 30-odd years. I was eight years old at the time and my oldest brother had taken me along with a couple of his mates. We stood in the Well in the pouring rain and watched Derek Dougan, the lanky Irish geezer with the Mexican 'tache, score a couple of goals for Wolves, but I was still hooked. I never did become a 'lad' though. I suppose you could call me a 'normal' or a 'scarfer' although I've never worn one.

For the next few years my visits to Boothferry Park were limited to when I could get our kid to take me, which wasn't very often as he was six years older and didn't want me tagging along. When I was old enough to go without him, most of my mates weren't into Hull City. This was illustrated perfectly the day that me and a couple of mates twagged off school and took a train to Bridlington. We were about 14 and our intention was to get a tattoo; we'd heard there was a guy there who didn't ask for proof of age. His shop was closed but he'd left a phone number on his door, so we rang and he came round. I declared my football allegiance by having M.U.F.C. tattooed on my forearm (Man United were popular then as well), one lad had Popeye complete with pipe and sailor's hat tattooed on his shoulder, and the other had 'I LOVE FATTY BUM BUM' tattooed on his arse. Enough said.

I managed to get to quite a few games and the one against Man United in 1974 was my first recollection of real violence. I was behind the goal low down on Bunkers with a mate who was also a United fan, but we were both supporting our hometown club that day. I remember the Red Army encamped in the East Stand (Kempton) and several lads getting onto the pitch before the game to kneel Muslim-style in front of the massed United fans. It was half-time when a solitary lad from the United ranks ran across the south-east corner of the pitch and charged towards the City on Bunkers Hill. This prompted another group of United, who had been mingling in the City end, to commence their attack and widespread fighting broke out. I remember a big black guy (United) with fists and boots flailing wildly before disappearing beneath a flurry of punches and kicks. It took a good five minutes for the coppers to restore order. Funnily enough, the single invader was actually from Hull and lived on my estate; at that time Orchard Park was a breeding ground for the Red Army.

A few weeks later we were on our way to a night match against one of the London teams, possibly Fulham. A lad called Billy had tagged along with us. We knew him from school; he was a big lad but slightly lacking in the brain department. People used to take the piss out of him at school, so we took him under our wing. When he got mad he had a habit of baring his teeth like a rabid dog, and if he got really pissed off he would lose it completely. We decided to have a bit of fun, and on seeing a group of Fulham fans sitting on a wall eating bags of chips, I nudged my mate. When we'd got a few yards past them, he said, 'Hey Billy, one of them lads just phlegged on your back.' Billy stopped and twisted his neck round to have a look. I said, 'Bill, it's right in the middle, you can't see it but it's thick and green.'

Bill's top lip started to go. He strode back to the Fulham lads and without bothering to ask which one did it, smacked the first one on the chin, sending him flying backwards off the wall and into a front garden. Without hesitation, Bill jumped over the wall and dived on top of the poor lad, who had bits of fish and batter all over his face. The other lads just sat on the wall, watching open-mouthed, while Billy proceeded to smash the lad's head up and down on the concrete path. Billy's lip had peeled back now, exposing a row of uneven yellow teeth and a low growl was coming from his throat. What the poor lad said next had us in stitches for days after: 'For fack's sake . . .' the words came out in time with his head being banged on the floor, '. . . someone call the R – S – P – C – A.'

Orchard Park Estate was and still is rough, but that's no different to most places in Hull. Fashion-wise, in the mid-seventies the estate was in some sort of post-hippy timewarp. Denim was in abundance – that's jeans, shirts, jackets *and* waistcoats – along with suede desert boots and Afghan coats. Musical tastes were predominantly heavy rock with the likes of Led Zeppelin, Bad Company and Black Sabbath all popular, and 10pm at the Voodoo heralded the weekly head-banging session with air guitars, usually to the sound of 'Caroline' or 'Down Down' by Status Quo, or 'Alright Now' by Free. This was until Punk came along and blew away the cobwebs.

This contrasted sharply with the more central inner-city areas of Hull, where the Soul Boy scene had really taken off. Perhaps this was one of the reasons that I never got into football violence. It wasn't a conscious decision, and I probably would have got involved in different circumstances, I just didn't mix in the right circles. In the late seventies, most of my fighting was done in city centre pubs and clubs. A lot of this was similar to football violence in the sense that it was gang/

group-orientated. Orchard Park lads would meet up with Boothferry lads, with the inevitable results. Also at that time Hull City were in decline and both rugby clubs were starting to prosper. This led to many a melee in the bus station between groups from West and East Hull.

City did still have a reasonable following though, and in the late seventies and early eighties most people, although not directly involved in the hooligan scene, did sympathise with it. When fighting broke out on the terraces, most people would applaud and cheer on the City lads, and chants of 'City aggro' would ring out – unlike today, when anyone remotely resembling a hooligan is treated like scum, both by other fans and especially by the police. I can testify to this, as I have witnessed over-the-top policing at City games home and away, but mainly at Boothferry Park, where even families and pensioners have to run the gauntlet of lines of riot police and snarling dogs, or are made to take ridiculous diversions to avoid coming into contact with other fans. Twenty-odd years ago, although the potential for trouble was greater, the policing seemed to be much more low-key. Also, the segregation inside grounds was not very effective.

I can remember a game at Sheffield United when, halfway through the first half, I realised I was surrounded by a group of United lads in the City end. When you go to a lot of away games you get to remember faces and I didn't remember these. I was just waiting for something to kick off. It never did though; they must have realised they would have taken a beating from the numerous City lads in the stand. After the game they resorted to throwing coins and bricks over the wall as we were kept back for ten minutes. Stone/coin throwing is one aspect of the football hooligan's make-up that I can't stand: two guys going for it toe-to-toe, no problem, but throwing stones? To me it signifies cowardice.

Another example of a lack of segregation was at Boothfery Park against Chesterfield when it kicked off in the corner of

Kempton. The fans of both teams were freely mingling and I think the O.B. had underestimated the potential for trouble from the small group of Chesterfield fans, most of them were wearing donkey jackets. They took a pounding. One lad of about 17 was sent crashing against an old City fan of about 65, spilling his half-time drink. He retaliated instantly with a right hook, sending the donkey-jacketed youth tumbling down the empty terracing. So much for innocent pensioners!

Not being involved in the hooligan scene didn't stop me getting targeted by opposing team's lads, especially in the early eighties. At that time, anyone of a certain age seemed to be fair game and I had run-ins with Man City at home and Walsall, Portsmouth, Charlton and Spurs away, to name a few. The Spurs game resulting in travelling out of North London without a single window in our coach. This highlights the difference to today: in my recent experience, firms only target other firms, resulting in less problems for normals/scarfers like myself. I can't remember having any problems at all in the last dozen years home or away. The only problems I have had are usually caused by policing.

This was made crystal clear in a recent game at Boothferry Park against Lincoln. The police presence at that game was way over the top, with rows and rows in full riot gear before and after the game, along with the customary nags and canine accomplices (dodging horse shit is another hazard for the modern supporter). This didn't stop the local street vagabonds from trashing my car which was parked a few streets away. This is a common occurrence at City's home games, another example of the police ignoring the real problems on our streets.

Today the rank-and-file supporters are less tolerant of the hooligan element. There are probably lots of reasons for this, but for me the City lads' exploits are always the second result that I look for. I may not be involved personally but I'm with the lads in spirit, and I look forward to the Monday morning reports either from the horse's mouth or via the Internet. After all, an

Englishman's home is his castle, your home town is just an extension of this, and to those that condemn football violence, put it into perspective and look what else is going on all around. Does it still seem so evil?

* * *

The Bradford incident had fired up support again. Not just ordinary fans but old school hooligans had returned, incensed by the decision to give Bradford the South Stand. The day's events brought back the emotions and adrenaline that we thrived on ten years before. Now, however, we were two divisions lower: no Boro, Blades, Stoke or Zulus to test us, instead we had the pleasure of meeting the Rotherhams and Halifaxes of this world. But things were beginning to stir in the lower divisions.

Slowly but surely, signs were emerging. Mobs were again 'firming up' after the early nineties 'slump' and the Nationwide teams were leading this upsurge. This was the last thing the authorities wanted to hear, not with Euro 96 on the horizon. Luckily for them, the tournament was a great success and England's march into the semi-finals caught the imagination of the public. Unfortunately for them, the night was marred by riotous behaviour up and down the country after another defeat by Germany. Hooliganism was making the headlines, and some of us smiled.

Our first season back in the Third Division (old Fourth) and the vast number of lads who had turned out for Bradford were again in evidence, apart from the 50-odd with banning orders. Our numbers were good, especially by this division's standard, and matches against mediocre opposition would see 200-plus frequenting the now-notorious Silver Cod pub. The away bug hadn't kicked in yet; Saturday away trips were reserved for the diehards, as the team's fortunes on the pitch didn't leave you tingling with anticipation.

A vanload of lads on a day out to Mansfield met with some opposition from disgruntled locals, upset that Hull lads had set up camp in their main pub. The brief, violent encounter brought about many mobile phone threats, with Mansfield fans periodically ringing Silver Cod goading us, calling us a second-rate firm who dare not travel. They assured us our next meeting would result in them 'doing you once and for all.'

These antics ensured that three coachloads attended our next visit. We had 150 lads on these and others following in vans and cars. The police collared us on the outskirts of Mansfield and said they would escort us to the ground and the one pub designated for away supporters, but the minute we reached a roundabout, the leading coach emptied from the front and back doors. This was the signal for the other two do likewise and in the confusion 150 lads headed back towards the town centre.

During mobile phone conversations with Mansfield, we had told them our numbers were around 50. We rounded a corner and saw one of their spotters. He was on his toes straight away but had seen only the first few of us, so the element of surprise was still in our favour. We quickened our pace in anticipation. The Mansfield lads were in a pub down a side street and the Hull at the front were met by a barrage of glasses and bottles. Mansfield streamed towards us but their faces were a picture as the first wave of Hull boys was followed by more and more, and after a brisk exchanges of punches, they turned and ran into the pub, leaving some unconscious mates behind. Further phone conversations weren't as boastful, and their caller remarked that we were in a different league to them.

One team who came and surprised us were Scunthorpe. Normally when we play them they gob off inside the ground but disappear afterwards, but on this day they were up for promotion and brought a firm of around 75. They made

Fiveways pub their own, staying in there till just before 2.45pm, around the same time a mob of 350 lads had left Silver Cod hoping for a meet as they approached the ground. It had been impossible to get to the Fiveways before this, as Cod was surrounded by police and they were restricting our movements.

As the Hull lads reached North Road, they tried to break through the police cordon, but only around a dozen got through. Still they walked towards Fiveways and the advancing Scunny lads. I was down Boothferry Road but on the other side of the intersection, and the Scunthorpe lads ran at us well up for it. We were outnumbered six to one but nobody ran and after a brief encounter, in which I managed to down one of them, a few O.B. arrived and the Scunthorpe lads moved away – leaving me, I hate to admit, out for the count after I'd been twatted by a bottle. After an embarrassing ride to hospital in an ambulance, I made my way back to the ground and managed to see the second half and Scunthorpe win.

I heard that Jacko had been arrested on the front car park. Apparently he was going mental after I'd been sparked and took it upon himself to mount a one-man attack on the Scunny lads. After the game, hundreds of Hull headed back towards Fiveways but the Scunny lads reverted to type and disappeared. I was gutted. I'd lost one of my front teeth and was covered in cuts and bruises. To add insult to injury, my dental bill was £310. Mind you, paying for the treatment was the lesser of two evils; if I hadn't bothered I would have spent the rest of my days doubling for Shane McGowan.

In all the years I have been involved, this was only the second time I had been incapacitated. The first had come all those years before when, plastered in Nivea Cream, I suffered a beating from my own supporters for smelling like 'a puff.' I was only 13 then, and it still pains me to think about it. How funny life is: just a decade later, every lad at every football ground in the country was walking around stinking like a whore's armpit. Some lads sprayed themselves with so much aftershave that they didn't need to hit you; you choked on the fumes of their Paco Rabanne. That's progress for you!

CHAPTER TWELVE

The Silver Cod Squad

ONCE IT BECAME known that we used the Silver Cod pub, some mobs would try to get in there early on match days before we had numbers, in order to brag that they had 'taken' our boozer. Let's face it, if a coach or a few vans are outside spot-on 11am, they can claim the territory before the home fans arrive in dribs and drabs, unless it's a top game and everybody meets early. One such occasion was against Plymouth. They had been promoted to the Second and brought nearly 100 lads to Cod at opening time. There were about 30 Hull in, but nothing happened and, as more City started coming in, the Plymouth lads decided to move on. Fair play to them, they came and drank in our pub.

Another was Crystal Palace, who were having a beano for their last away game of the season. Both sets of lads were yarning and getting on okay, no trouble, but during the match there must have been a mood change, as afterwards there were some ugly scenes outside the Three Tuns pub. City wasted a lot of the Londoners they had been drinking with hours earlier. Weird.

The worst spot of trouble in Cod was against Stoke City. We'd not played them since 1977 and we knew that if any team was likely to test us, it would be Stoke. They arrived early and a lot of their lads were drinking in the bar as the City lads started to come in. A few insults were hurled, then a few bottles, and it went off big time, with Stoke sandwiched

between Hull lads already in the bar with them and those in
the lounge. A few got injured, and we heard later that a Stoke
fan had been blinded in one eye when a heavy glass ashtray
smashed. If that is true, it's bad luck, and certainly wasn't
intended, but it could easily have been a Hull lad suffering
serious injury. They were game but eventually were chased
out by superior numbers, with pool balls whistling past their
ears.

There was animosity between the two sets of supporters
for a few years after that, with rumours going round that they
would bring a mob of top lads seeking revenge – not youngsters
but a mob from their mid-thirties upwards, coming to show
us you didn't take liberties with Stoke and to smash the pub
up. So when we next played them, there was a good mob in
Cod. Stoke were spotted and the lads streamed out. A short
stand-off was broken by a young Hull lad running into them
with a pool cue. The rest of the City lads followed his lead and
Stoke were soon on the back foot. As any lad knows, a firm on
the back foot has already nearly lost the battle. They were
shouting, 'Stand,' yet you could see them arguing while
running away. On that occasion they didn't get as near to Cod
as they would have liked. I think some of them underestimated
our numbers and were shocked by the sheer violence. His
mates abandoned one of the Stoke lads and he got a battering
by the pelican crossing before some older Hull called the mob
off.

Blyth Spartans, who we played in the FA Cup, are a
famous non-league side from Tyneside. Everyone thought it
would be a non-event but they maybe had some Newcastle
with them, as they drank in Cod and dished out a few slaps.
When word got out, City went down there in numbers and a
little set-to occurred in the pub doorway, but the Geordies
were firmly entrenched and were later escorted to the ground
for their own safety. It just shows how foolish it is to
underestimate ANY team.

For the past eight years at least, Silver Cod has been our main meeting place and I can say, without fear of contradiction, that it is one of the most intimidating football pubs in England. And no, I'm not advocating that any rival mobs now make a beeline for the pub; I'm just explaining that it is what it is – a lads' pub, and there is pride in this. Because of better policing and surveillance, taking someone's end became well nigh impossible and almost bound to result in dawn raids and custodial sentences. Lads continued, however, to make the effort to take their rivals' pubs, and that is why Cod has been defended so vigorously. I know some teams have turned up during our quieter periods and drunk in Cod, but it has been many years since anyone got a 'result' there. And you can rest assured that the police know all about it on match days, boys – so don't bother trying.

Anlaby Road itself has seen better days, and the vista of boarded up shops and run-down Victorian housing adds to the picture. A Peterborough lad who'd arrived by train remarked that it was like walking through a minefield, and he felt so unnerved by the experience that he left at half-time rather then make his way back through the crowds. The pub holds prime position; you have a clear view up and down Anlaby Road and other firms have great difficulty in approaching unannounced.

How fiercely Cod is guarded is illustrated by the story of what happened when 20 Hartlepool lads foolishly disregarded warnings not to cross the threshold.

MANNIX: It was an end of season match, one of those days when you get brilliant spring sunshine. I was a little bit gutted, as I had promised to take my eleven-year-old son, and I knew all the lads were meeting in town for an early drink. One of my best mates, Lemmy, a face at City, was with me and we got to Silver Cod dead on 11am. We got a drink and went to sit outside in the heat, when we saw 20-30 lads walking up Anlaby

Road towards town. We didn't recognise any of them, so a simple deduction said they were Hartlepool. They weren't top-quality boys, but neither were they scarfers.

'Get ready, L,' I said, and we prepared to stand our ground, but as they got nearer it became apparent they had split into two groups, one walking towards the city centre on the opposite side of the road, the other heading towards Cod. My lad was sat on a bench, and we positioned ourselves either side of the door.

'Morning lads, wouldn't drink in there if I was you,' offered Lemmy helpfully. They just stared and walked past into the bar. One of them, a skinhead with shades pushed up on his forehead, grinned. Must be some scalp for them, a pint in the Silver Cod unhindered.

One quick phone call to a town centre pub, and ten minutes later a few taxis pulled up. With no more verbal than a 'Which side are they in?' 15-20 very old, decent Hull walked in, straight into the bar and shouted, 'Lets have it then.' My lad was playing the video golf game by the door and was frozen with fear as grown men ran past him into the hapless monkey-hangers, who, although I may have been mistaken, had lost their earlier ring of confidence.

They made an effort to stand their ground but were absolutely battered. I remember a main Hull face when I started on the scene in '78 almost foaming at the mouth as he repeatedly smashed a bar stool over the head of one of the Hartlepool. This continued for about 30 seconds before the Hartlepool managed to start escaping. They were running to the exit, where a handful of other City had just arrived. These lads also flew into them. They were now bloodied and literally crawling out of the pub whimpering. There was no need for overkill, so Lemmy and myself sat watching the proceedings. It was no bullying though, as there were equal numbers in Cod at the time. A number of these 'Pool lads were later seen bandaged mummy-style and hiding behind plod outside the away turnstiles.

By 1pm there must have been 300 lads inside and outside Cod. It was near the end of the season and a lot had come out of the woodwork for that match. As we were walking to the ground, a mini-van of Hartlepool came out of Hawthorn Ave and turned to go towards the ground. This was missed by most Cod lads, who by that time were well cordoned in by police, but there were ten of us walking to the ground and when one of the 'Pool fans started gesturing about running, we went for the van. They wouldn't get out, so it was limited to us kicking the van (why do we do that?) and a lad from the Avenues area chinning the driver through an open window.

One decent Hartlepool lad later stated that the mob outside Cod was the best he had ever seen from a lower division club. There was no way we were going to be touched that day, but they did sell their allocation of tickets as they were doing well, and they must have had some lads, because six decent Hull got the wrong side of the police cordon and had an off with them down North Road. Eventually the Hull lads backed off in the face of much greater numbers. Just a pity they weren't keen to look for it.

As we were going home after another couple of drinks in Cod, my lad started laughing and said, 'That was great dad, did you see them crawling out screaming.' I do not condone this attitude but neither do I apologise. Without any prompting or cajoling from me, he had experienced the 'buzz' that physical violence can give, and was already far more qualified to explain the phenomenon than the legions of tweed-jacketed sociologists and 'experts' that the media look to for explanations. He had learned that the will to fight will always be there in some men, and that there had been more savagery at the most expensive boxing match of that time, Tyson v Holyfield, than had occurred in the Silver Cod. He had seen brotherhood and friendship under challenge, the endurance of suffering, the facing of fear and the discipline of achievement. He may come to realise, as I

have done, that fighting will be around in one form or another
as long as there are men to fight.

★ ★ ★

The first game of the 1999/2000 season saw us at Exeter.
Over 150 lads arrived as early as 9.30am. Now Exeter are
another of these teams who boast they do everyone that goes
there. Bollocks. We were there all day and apart from a token
gesture after the game they were running scared. The reason
for this wasn't just down to our numbers, it had more to do
with the ages of the respective firms. The Exeter boys were
just that, boys, who had probably read some of the new
hooligan books, had begun to throw their weight about against
smaller teams, and were now convinced they were the business.
We had an average age of 35, with some of us well past 40,
and numbered over 100 lads in this age group.

In September 1999 we were pitched against Liverpool over
two legs. At home they outplayed us (of course) and had a
good aggregate advantage going into the Anfield fixture. The
absence of the Liverpool fans at Boothferry Park was disappointing but we made up for it by taking 6,000 to Anfield.
Liverpool won the game but we'd fought back from 2-0 down
to 2-2 and we had our 15 minutes of fame.

Before the game, 100 lads met in the Rat and Parrot in
Liverpool city centre and for two hours we lorded it up in the
pubs around the Beatles' old haunts, with our numbers
swelling all the time. Even Man Utd's boys don't take these
sort of liberties up the East Lancs Road. It could be argued
that they didn't rate us so didn't turn out for the game, but if
you're playing some team who are bringing 6,000 then you
would expect there to be at least a couple of hundred lads, so
an off would be on the cards for those who wanted one. The
same scene was being played in all the pubs next to the
ground, and normal LFC strongholds were resounding to the

'Humberbeat', much to the annoyance of the locals, who had to sit grinding their teeth, hopelessly outnumbered.

We were again drawn against Chelsea in the third round of the FA Cup. This game came days after an undercover TV exposé of Chelsea fans had been aired. The pubs around town were heaving with lads hoping for a crack at the Headhunters and this seemed to be on the cards, as the police requested that all the pubs down Anlaby Road shut after noon. But their intelligence reports must have been way off the mark, as only 200 Chelsea shirts turned out. A couple of Chelsea fans came up as guests for the weekend and were extremely embarrassed by their poor turnout. By all accounts they were very impressed by the numbers we had waiting and gave us a glowing report back home in The Smoke.

Lincoln away produced the highlight of this season, with the police playing games with us by escorting us over four miles away from Lincoln after telling us they were taking us to a pub near the ground. Two coachloads of us ignored the escort and began to walk back towards town rather than be sat in a bar with the Lincoln Poacher out in the sticks. Luckily we had set off early, so the forced march still gave us time to hit the pubs on the outskirts before carrying on. Word got round that some Hull lads who had gone by car had been fighting down the High Street, so everyone drank up and jogged the last mile towards the sound of sirens. I think we surprised the local lads by turning up mob-handed from seemingly nowhere, but the police had taken control of the situation and, with the dreaded dog section, they soon moved everyone on.

We entered the ground and took up prime position next to their side stand, but around six Hull lads decided not to go in and went for a drink instead. After a dour first half, things changed for the better. One of the lads in the pub rang to say they'd been attacked by some Lincoln and these lads were tooled up. Over 100 of us got out and had a wander towards the scene of the attack. Our mob split into two groups and went different ways, the first group meeting up with equal numbers who had streamed out of a pub brandishing weapons. They stood there with an impressive armoury: coshes, bats, pool cues, chains and metal bars. They were out do real damage.

Now I think they expected us to do a runner. We did – straight into them, and after some fierce fighting, which at one point stopped to let some of the Lincoln lads drag away two of their comatose mates, we had them backing off. Lemmy ran into a small group and rugby tackled one of them; the rest ran, leaving him on top of the tackled lad, who he pounded to bits. Demoralised and bruised, the Lincoln limped back to their pub and locked themselves in.

We carried on down the street hoping to meet up with any leaving the ground. Unbeknown to us, the Lincoln boys had rushed back out of the pub to help their stricken friends when they were set upon by the second group of Hull lads and done again. Not their lucky day.

★ ★ ★

The traditional migration by City fans on the first day of the 2000/01 season continued at Blackpool. The pubs on the Golden Mile were packed to the rafters with optimistic supporters. We all hoped this would be 'our year'. Today's support was boosted by a contingent of Dutch supporters over for the weekend with some Hull lads who live and work in Holland. These lads were Top Oss supporters and were soaking up the atmosphere and enjoying the hospitality of the Tigers fans. They couldn't believe that an English Third Division club would take so many fans to an away game.

Years ago, an away fixture at Blackpool would have guaranteed trouble, but not now. The Blackpool lads were nowhere to be seen and any football fans staying overnight had more chance of an off with the many stag parties that filled the public houses and night clubs. The police seemed nervy throughout the day and monitored closely the movements of our boys before, during and especially after the game.

We once again trooped out of the ground feeling slightly deflated: another first game of the season, another defeat. A few misguided Blackpool fans began taunting and throwing bricks at a large mob of pissed-off lads, who tried to reach the Seasiders stood safely behind a wire fence near their clubhouse. The police reached the fuming City fans and beat them back with a baton charge, abetted by the mounted division. The Dutch lads snapped away, photographing everything that moved. The police pushed us back across the massive car park towards the small, slightly seedy back streets behind the seafront. They then began to panic; the last thing the police wanted was for us to cause trouble on the front. It would be bad publicity and would tarnish the resort's image (like fuck it would). They tried to head us off, but we split up, which added to their problems. They decided to follow a group of 30 who had turned down a side street full of bed and breakfast accommodation. A police van hurtled down the street and cut off the exit, while officers on foot ran behind the 30 lads. As they caught up, they were absolutely gutted to see everyone turn and enter two B&Bs mid-way down the street. The police were left open-mouthed in an empty, cordoned-off street.

Chesterfield 2000/01

The double-decker pulled up outside YEB and 75 lads patiently boarded. Many were veterans, old-school casuals who had been on similar buses 20 years before and had managed to stay together through the years. They still felt the same rush of anticipation as they arrived at their destination, but the wedge hairstyles had been replaced by grey or thinning hair and the waistlines had grown a few inches. There was another significant difference: when a punch was thrown, it was the punch of a man, not a youth.

Years before, we had been young men battling older, harder opponents. Now the roles were reversed – and I know which side of the fence I'd rather be on. Age does make a difference. Younger firms will only stand a chance against an older foe if they outnumber them and even then it would be touch and go. We found the best way to tackle older groups was to try to break them up, isolate a few and then attack, but it is hard to do that to a firm like Hull's. We stay together and fight together; we're in it together. That comes with years of experience and knowing who is by your side, and if you've experienced that you are a lucky man.

The double-decker was hired to take us to Chesterfield, a team we'd not played for a good few years. We knew a reception committee would be waiting, so the plan was to hire the bus to Sheffield, then continue by train. The Transport Police began flapping as we appeared from nowhere on the platform, hurrying over the bridge with garbled radio messages of who we were and where we were going. We'd caught them on the hop. Outside the station at Chesterfield, a harassed van full of Old Bill jumped out and tried to head us off, not wanting us to make for the town centre. A few bemoaned the fact that, in their words, 'You wouldn't believe the amount of videos we've had to watch of you bastards this week.' They were already sick of the sight of us.

We knew a coachload of our boys was already in a town centre pub, the Blue Bell, and it was there we aimed. The road from the station rises towards the main street and a group of 20 made a break across a car park running towards alleys, which would bring them out near the hostelry. The police broke ranks and lost the plot, leaving the rest of us to march to the pub without further hindrance. It was probably easier for the O.B. to monitor our movements if we were all together, but that wasn't their original plan.

Entrenched in the town centre, our numbers grew as text and mobile messages passed on our whereabouts. Soon the number in the pub reached 150-plus. The police were happy enough to let others in but weren't going to let us out, not till they were ready. A push through the front door by a group of eager lads was met by dogs and batons. The older, wiser members didn't get involved. No need for confrontation yet, the gesture was futile. Those fighting by the door would learn that the hard way, but they'd learn.

An inspector informed us that we would be taken to the ground. We were marched through the streets, uniformed coppers striding purposefully beside us with batons held resting on their shoulders or dug into your back if they thought you were slowing down, and maintained a constant bark:

'Keep moving.'

'Stay on the path.'

As we walked through Chesterfield town centre, we saw our first glimpse of opposition, if you could call it that: squashed faces contorted in anger and the sound of fists banging on the pub windows, but that was all.

We spent a cold, miserable hour and a half on open terraces watching an in-form Chesterfield run us ragged. The proceedings were enlivened only by a small altercation in a side stand when three City fans surrounded by Chesterfield lads launched themselves into the mob. Another Hull fan jumped into the melee after sprinting across the corner of the pitch and all four then fought their way down and over onto the other side of the pitch. Everyone else was kept in by the fence. The City lads were dragged off but only one was arrested, the other three successfully arguing that they'd been well away from any troublesome Chesterfield fans until a group of 50 stood around them. The sight of three of our number coming out of that situation virtually injury-free and without punishment was good.

As we made our way out through the darkened streets, we had to split up, with the lads on coach going one way and the rest of us force-marched back to the station. I say force-marched but it was more like a jogging session; the police wanted us out and quick. We could see Chesterfield trying to reach us and at one point 20 Hull ran past the police and up a side street towards the approaching locals, but they were headed off by a screeching van of riot coppers, who proceeded to beat them back. The police were well pissed off by now and a few lads were struck across their backs as they complained about the pushing and shoving. The OB were glad to see the lights of the train, which had been made to wait for our arrival. Minutes later we were on our way back to Sheffield.

The driver of the double-decker was waiting for us but it was still early doors and we wanted a few drinks before leaving for home. A whip-round kept him happy and guaranteed us three more hours. We moved around a few pubs hoping to meet up with some locals but it was surprisingly dead. Sheffield Wednesday had been at home to Norwich but there was no evidence of them anywhere. We didn't expect to see any Blades, as they had been to Burnley, almost certainly firmed up. Maybe we'd meet them later? By 7.30 it was evident nothing was stirring. Seventy-five lads had been drinking for two hours in the centre of Sheffield without any opposition. It was time for a walk, so we headed off down the Sheffield United stronghold of London Road, which is lined with pubs.

We were in one boozer when a bloke walked in with his missus. He was well into his forties but had that 'in the know' look about him. Nods were exchanged, questions asked and, as we left for the bus home, we heard, 'Don't worry, I'll let the lads know you've been.'

Carlisle United 2000/01

The season was coming to an end – and what a rollercoaster of emotions it had been. The team had been locked out of Boothferry Park for non-payment of rent and had (again) been put into the hands of the receivers. To top it all, the players and staff hadn't been paid for weeks. Amazingly, we found ourselves in a play-off position and were desperately hoping for a day out at the Millennium Stadium in Cardiff – and so were their mob, the Soul Crew. The result at our final away game would determine where we finished and which team we'd be up against. So interest in the Carlisle game was huge.

We were dropped off near the ground and the expected police round-up didn't materialise. Our walk into town was uneventful; we were aiming for a Wetherspoons where we knew a few Hull lads were already drinking. As the first few rushed through the doors they just had enough time to see six Carlisle lads scamper out through the back.

The beer garden soon filled up, with over 100 lads drinking and chatting, while others stood with mobiles stuck to their ears, directing more to the pub. The back gate opened and a Carlisle lad shouted abuse, then ran off. Three of ours followed. He was backing off down the alleyway, yet giving them the 'come on' gesture. K** ran at him, and he was off. All three continued down the alley and stopped at the junction of a busy road. Coming towards them were two lads on pushbikes. They pulled up and made contact, and were adamant that their Border City Firm had enough lads for a 'meet'. They tipped us off on how best to get to them and it was suggested that we leave by the back way to give us vital seconds before the Old Bill could react.

We set off at the agreed time, bypassing the police by running over some waste ground. Carlisle were true to their word; we could see them further up the road. We ran on but the police caught up with us, eventually using dogs to stop us.

We could see that their Border City Firm were also contained. It was more or less over before it started, although after being directed down a nearby street we tried to reach them again by running through some connecting alleys. The police had already blocked off all access points.

The game was a dour affair and finished a disappointing 0-0. The final whistle saw dozens of Carlisle fans encroach on the playing area and before long the police were holding back a couple of hundred fans. We stood laughing at this pathetic gesture, especially as the majority were teenagers bedecked in scarves and shirts. The invasion managed one thing though – it occupied the police. Fifty of us drifted outside.

We knew the home end was at the bottom of the track and hoped to get onto their terracing and greet the BCF as they made their way off the pitch. As we neared the open gate, one of the cyclists was spotted; he clocked us and, along with his mates, ran back inside, closing the gate. Not so keen on arranging things now, eh? A few of the lads had ventured onto the street and met with a very game bunch of BCF. We could hear the barney and eagerly joined in. These Carlisle lads were well up for it. One of them picked up a weighted advertising sign and ran towards us. A Lemmy uppercut and the lad and the sign were sprawled out in the middle of the road.

Carlisle's 'famous one' was grappling with one of ours and was pummelled to the floor (you picked the wrong one there, Mr Dodd). They were beginning to lose heart and started backing off down a side street. I can't call them for that, as more and more of our lads could be seen running down the track. At the same moment, a police van pulled up and out they jumped. One Hull lad was bundled inside and the rest of us were politely asked to move on. Another van whipped by us and careered down the street after the locals.

Our attentions turned to some more of their lads now coming out of the ground. Finding themselves right amongst us, they bolted back. I was in a chasing group who failed to reach them before they found the safety of the terracing. For my sins I received a double whack across the back of my legs from the baton of an angry constable. I'd been giving plenty of verbal, so in hindsight he did me a favour; I could have easily been following the other Hull lad into the back of the van. We were left by the side of the road, with the police running round trying to find the drivers of the two coaches, and it wasn't long before we were on our way home.

Six Carlisle lads, including Paul Dodd, were arrested and charged with affray, and were bailed along with a Hull lad. They were sent to Crown Court under a blaze of publicity, yet five of them walked (including the Hull lad) for lack of evidence. The 'unfortunate famous one' was jailed for four months while a colleague ended up with community service. The biggest crime in all this was the amount of money it cost bringing these flimsy charges to court: an estimated £250,000. The people of Carlisle will sleep safer in their beds now.

Shrewsbury 2001/02

Fifteen of us decided to hire a minibus and have a night out watching the Tigers down at Shrewsbury. I volunteered to drive for this Friday fixture and we set off at 2pm after a couple of hours in Cod. We should have had a fucking bucket with us; I lost count on the number of times I had to stop for weak bladders. The Greek One was the worst culprit and took some stick from the others; serves him right.

This would be my first visit to Shrewsbury and we didn't expect any bother, as there was no history between our firms, but we were to be surprised. I'd heard that England's Border Front, as their firm is known, were fervent England followers and had been active in the South West and Midlands for years, but I'd never heard of problems when Hull lads had visited Gay Meadow.

We parked on the club car park and wandered into town.

First impressions were of a tidy market town of traditional public houses, small antique shops and art galleries, the perfect place for a weekend break (I sound like Judith Chalmers). We strolled up the road and passed two lads, who turned, shouted and gestured for us to follow down a small street. We duly obliged. Halfway down stood a small pub, and from the side doorway we could see a number of local lads waving us on. We moved towards them. Three tried to scramble back into the pub and the rest quickly moved further down the street, shouting, 'It's camera'd up, come down here.'

The three in the doorway weren't quick enough. One of our lads got in amongst them and literally went berserk. He hit one, who crumpled in a heap, and the other two couldn't pull open the door as their mate was blocking it. They just stood shielding their faces as Lemmy tore into them both. One of these lads was dragged out of the pub by his hair and thrown onto the ground. He pleaded with us to leave him alone (a minute earlier he'd been brave as a lion).

The Shrewsbury boys further down began to throw bricks, but as we approached they shot off round the corner, leaving one lad to face us, a local piss-head still in his work clothes. He hadn't noticed one of our group come in from the side and took a massive forearm shot to his head. The poor bastard was out like a light and, as he fell, he hit the corner of a brick wall square in the face. A couple of the locals reappeared but kept a safe distance. A lone police car drove up, so we turned and walked past it. There was no point in hanging around: reinforcements would soon arrive and it would be us who took the shit from the local bobbies.

We carried on past the ground, where a pub was found. All talk was of the doorway incident, with Lemmy taking centre stage. He laughed as he described how all three had panicked in the cramped space and began pushing the door instead of pulling. 'Mind you, the cunts couldn't open it once I'd laid one of 'em out!'

A few of the lads began ringing round. It was only a small off but we wanted to rub it in to those who couldn't be bothered going. Amazingly one already knew; an EBF lad had rung an acquaintance from Newcastle who then passed the information on to one of ours. That's the power of the hooligan network these days. There was something else.

'What you on about, what knife?'

'Listen to this lads, they're saying we've used a blade.'

Apparently, the Shrewsbury lads had come to the aid of the decked piss-head and took the facial damage from the wall as a 'slashing'.

'Fuck 'em, let 'em think it.'

It's amazing that someone sat at home in Newcastle knows about an off we have in Shrewsbury ten minutes after it's happened. The problem is that it's not always the truth that gets touted around.

As we sat by the window, we had a good view of the EBF, who were now streaming down the road. They gave us the cutthroat sign and began to bang on the windows. We were up and out, facing them in the street; at one point there was only five of us out but we went straight into them. In total only a dozen of us actually got out, fronting about 50 EBF. We clashed with their front-runners and fought one-to-one. A couple were put on their arses and a few of us moved in amongst them. They didn't seem too cocky now. I could see that three of their lads were laid out, not moving: Lemmy's right-hander was working overtime. He was enjoying himself tonight. As I ran forward, I saw one of the locals stood by a bus stop; he was trying to look indifferent and detached from the brawl around him, yet I'd seen the same bloke minutes earlier banging at the window. He realised I'd noticed him and, as I ran up, he pleaded with me, 'I'm not with them, I'm not with them.'

We ran them up the road and on past some approaching police vans. We gradually broke off from chasing them and returned to the pub, walking by the three lads still out for the count. The landlord greeted us back inside. I think he realised that our actions had saved his pub from a trashing. Lemmy had us laughing again; he'd been the first one up when the EBF had arrived and had met the landlord barring the exit.

'Don't worry mate, they can't get in,' said the landlord.

'Can't get in? Fuck 'em, we're going out!'

We watched out of the window as an ambulance crew sorted out the stricken lads on the road. The Old Bill had a watchful eye over the rest of our stay and no further meets occurred. We'd met with some opposition, managed to mix it with them twice and saw City equalise in the last minute. Perfect. As we drove home, the final tally read: run them twice and sent five to hospital (Lemmy had personally sent four to Out-patients). Not a bad night's work for 15 of us.

Luton Town 2001/02

Here was a game everyone was marking off the calendar. Luton's MiG (Men In Gear) Squad had been posting boastful Internet messages all season. We played at Kenilworth Road on a Tuesday night when only a few lads managed to go and they came back stating that there wasn't 'much about'. This didn't surprise us, as we'd gone there a couple of years previously in the cup and they'd offered nothing. I'm not claiming Luton don't have any boys, just that we didn't come across any on two visits. We knew they could turn out the numbers, as Mansfield would testify, and hoped they'd venture a bit further up north.

We arranged an early morning meet – they weren't going to catch us unawares – and by 10am had a good 60 lads out. A call to one of the MiGs at eleven confirmed that they were on the way. We were told they had a coach and a few carloads. In their own words, 'We've just passed Mansfield, we'll be there in just over an hour.'

We later heard from a reliable Hull source that a coach of

lads had got off near the ground. Are they looking at taking it to Silver Cod? Nope, instead they walk the other way to Fiveways. This was confirmed when a few of ours spoke to a carload of MiGs at a pre-arranged city centre debating point: 'They haven't the numbers with them to entertain the idea of a city centre quick-step, they inform us that they went to Fiveways instead.'

Okay, we'll come to you then. We decide to move in with smaller numbers, some lads stay up town, others go to Cod, while about 50 take taxis to Fiveways. The logistical nightmare of moving 50 lads to another pub over four miles away, to arrive together, proved impossible. But the first few arrivals, instead of waiting for numbers, walked straight into the pub.

There was a definite MiG presence in the lounge and yes, there were women, children and scarfers in there as well. One distinctive-looking member of this elite squad, a skinhead with a cross tattooed on his head (you know who you are), turned to his friends and was heard to say, 'C'mon, we can do these cunts.' He should have kept his thoughts to himself and his mouth shut, because at the same time more Hull poured into the pub. The atmosphere turned, and the Luton fans were left feeling totally intimidated. All non-dancers were politely asked to move away from the dance floor. One actually said to his mate, 'We're alright, they're not after us.' He knew who we were after. We mingled in with the Luton lads, but they sadly declined any offers put to them. 'We're only here for the football lads, honest.' The police had been about 40-handed outside and the MiGs couldn't believe we'd just walked through them.

Now, contrary to the opinion of some, we are not bullies, and we carried on drinking in Fiveways and chatted to the deflated visitors. We didn't need to show our strength by hitting any of these MiGs, the point had been made and they were relieved. A small incident did occur in the bar, when a member of our early expeditionary force came face to face with cross-head. His earlier remarks had been remembered and he ended up with a very sore, if not broken, nose for his troubles. To cap it all, a pool ball bounced off his head and the ricochet hit a Hull fan, who rounded on the thrower and asked, 'What the fuck are you up to?' He calmed down when he realised what had happened. 'As long as it hit that cunt first, it's alright.'

One Luton lad admitted to me they were 'chaps' but couldn't compete with us, which is fair enough, but they shouldn't have called it on in the first place. On the way down to the ground, a few of the same lads were targeted by a group of MYT (Mad Young Tigers) and took a few slaps. We had nothing to do with that, just young lads making a name for themselves (we've all done it).

After the game, the Luton supporters ran the gauntlet of Hull boys along the full length of Boothferry Road. No punches were thrown; we left it to their imagination and got into their heads (true Psycho style), so much so that they asked for the police to ride shotgun in their vans until they'd left the area.

CHAPTER THIRTEEN

Into The Valleys

MANY OF THE teams we came up against in the Third Division claim that we don't travel. I can understand that to some extent. To lads at clubs such as Lincoln, Scunthorpe, Hartlepool and Darlington, a game against us is probably one of the highlights of their seasons. But over the past few years we have turned out time and again at these clubs and often left disappointed. Lincoln apart, these teams shout a lot but don't back it up, and so it can be hard to raise any excitement at the thought of visiting them. We pick out certain games each season and make sure we don't miss them – we might give Scunthorpe a miss for a few years, then turn out unexpectedly. You'll never know.

Cardiff and Swansea will testify to this, and on a Friday night both times. During the 1998/99 season we played the two South Wales clubs but no real trouble materialised: at home Swansea didn't show, and Cardiff played us at Boothferry Park on a Friday night, not ideal for travelling fans. Our game at Cardiff was played during the Easter weekend and two coaches had been booked and filled, not bad for a club languishing at the bottom of the Division Three. But on the Friday night, the coach operators cancelled, saying the police had advised them that potential troublemakers would be on their vehicles. So the lads who organised the trip had the task of trying to let everyone know what had happened as well as arrange alternative transport, which was impossible at such short notice.

The outcome was that only 18 managed to make their way to Cardiff, and after the game an impressive firm met them on the car park. They stood their ground but, to be honest, there was nowhere for them to go, so all they could do was front it and not panic – not an easy task given the circumstances and the numbers in front of them. Suffice to say, the 18 Hull were given a day's pass.

The Swansea away game was on the last day of the season and the Hull lads met some Cardiff on their way to Mansfield. This time the numbers were reversed and the Hull boys showed they had not forgotten being let off a good hiding and conversed with the Cardiff lads rather than kick them in – mutual respect in evidence. Swansea would later claim that they ran Hull's boys inside the ground, but all they did was get on the pitch and make a half-hearted effort to come down to the away end. With a fence separating both sets of fans, it was pretty laughable. We had turned out at their place. Could they say the same?

After they'd been relegated in 2000/01, we hoped they'd at least return the favour and travel to ours. They managed to get to Goole and caught the train to Hull. We heard from a lad who works on the trains that they numbered around 50 lads. The police took over and told them they were being marched to the ground, so apparently 15-20 of them decided to get the next train out. The escort had only got as far as Great Thornton Street (a council estate on the edge of town) when they were confronted by a mob of Hull. The police baton-charged the locals but the escort was stopped in its tracks. The Swansea were held for nearly an hour before a bus arrived to take them to the ground.

They were animated enough inside, safe in the knowledge that the bus was waiting to take them back to Goole. Like their South Wales neighbours, they'd have to wait and see what a Friday night would bring. Nick will take it from here:

NICK: A Friday in March and 45 make the trip to Swansea. In the second year of the third millennium, the transport is a coach with TV (with choice of films) and toilet on board. Long gone are the days of the KHCT double-deckers of the late seventies and early eighties – cheap, conspicuous and uncomfortable. Given the distance and the inconvenience of the Friday night fixture, it's a good turnout.

In May 1999, Swansea had invaded the pitch before their crucial end of season game against City, throwing golf balls and umbrellas into the away fans' end (where various King Billy flags were draped) without ever really coming into contact with the few from Hull who'd attended. Not many had made the trip down, as City had assured their own survival the previous week after a traumatic season, Swansea was a distant team with no 'history' and the game meaningless after months of 'cup finals'.

This game changed that. The *Hull Daily Mail* printed a colour picture of City up on the fence with Swansea scuffling in front of them. With the advent of the Cyber Thug and the website forums dedicated to football hooliganism, it wasn't long before Swansea started to gloat about this 'achievement', bringing it to the attention of a wider audience. Thus all subsequent games between us have been preceded by Internet hype and hot air. This one was no exception, except it was rather muted and one-sided.

The bus travelled down with *A Sense of Freedom* followed by *Scum* on the video. Just the sort of films to get you in the mood. Add to that cans of Stella, 'herbal' cigs, some white powder (possibly Daz or Persil) and the odd sniff of amyl nitrate, and the party was in full swing as the bus crossed the border into Wales. The cans of Long Life and Skol, and packets of Player's No.6 from the innocent seventies, seemed a long way off.

Surely the Swansea police will be waiting on the motorway, as they were the year before at Cardiff? But they are not. The bus slips off the motorway and into the darkness of Swansea. The driver seems to have a vague idea of the way and before long the floodlights are sighted in the night sky. We head towards them. Still no sign of blue flashing lights alongside the bus.

We get to a junction about 200 yards from the ground, and the driver lets us off outside a pub called the Swansea Jack. It's a quiet pub and after a quick 'discussion' with the bashful clientele, we are directed further up the road. They have sent us towards the Garibaldi and the Singleton – two pubs which are regularly mentioned by name on the Internet as main Swansea boozers. Two police are on horseback across the road as the group heads towards the pubs. This is an unreal situation: at the main Swansea pub, having slipped into town undetected by the police and the supposedly vigilant thug hordes of waiting Swansea, despite using the main roads an hour before kick-off. What now? Are they all suddenly going to come round the corner with bottles and bricks? Where are they? Why is it so quiet?

The group decides not to wait to find out, and tries to enter the Garibaldi. The locals quickly suss what is occurring and attempt to repel the incursion, with blows being exchanged in the doorway – and the door is quickly closed. Despite the noise and shouting, no one comes out of the two pubs. Someone in the Hull group decides to put the windows in, at which point the two mounted police quickly arrive, followed immediately by a couple of vans of Swansea constabulary. Confusion reigns. The locals now want to come out and attack while the police want to move the Hull away to the ground through the dingy, narrow streets.

The Hull by now are enjoying it and are reluctant to move. The Swansea are getting agitated, with more of them arriving all the time as word spreads fast about this daring raid in the heart of their territory. The police finally move the Hull to the nearby ground, with various enraged, mustachioed, Welsh, Stone Island thirtysomethings offering out the group from a safe distance behind the police horses.

Twenty minutes before kick-off and the night's 'fun' is over.

It lasted about 15 minutes and the balance sheet reads: one medium-sized pub window broken, lots of shouting, a bit of 'handbags', three pubs visited. Nevertheless, it is seen as a result for the visitors: against all odds they have managed to arrive in the heart of a no-go area for away fans, have strolled around and struck a propaganda blow hundreds of miles from home on a Friday night against a team who had been calling it on and were waiting for them, and with a vigilant local police force (aided by intelligence from Hull) doing their best to scoop them up. A couple of mobile phone calls later and details of the Garibaldi incident are on several websites before the first half is over. In 2002 the whole world knows about it when a backstreet boozer in Swansea has a window put in.

On the Internet the next day, Swansea are furious: accusations of help from Cardiff (my enemy is your friend), attempts at damage limitation ('it was only a window'), fictitious accounts of fighting before the game, denials that the pubs concerned had any Swansea in them, etc. All this from people who had been inviting it for several weeks on the same websites. The truth is that the incidents themselves were minor, but in 2002 just getting to some games is a result in itself. Anything beyond arriving is a bonus.

The Internet is where the action is now, not, as laughably stupid and lazy journalists think, to cause and organise trouble, but to reminisce, chat, exchange opinions, jokes and memories, often with 'enemies'. The book you are reading now is a by-product of this, as is the recent *Storm over Europe* computer game which features football hooligans battling against European police forces. As technology and police surveillance grow more sophisticated, old-style shenanigans at football become less and less worthwhile; the ersatz message boards and forums become a user-friendly alternative, a bit like a blow-up doll is for people who are worried by AIDS and are tired of 'difficult' birds. Nowhere near as exciting as the real thing, but much more safe and convenient . . .

The Cardiff fixtures provided better entertainment all round, though the Soul Crew boys also suffered police interference as they arranged a visit to Hull. A South Wales acquaintance, Pete, can embellish:

PETE: Young Taffy arranged our coach for the trip to Humberside and it was full to the brim of Rhonnda and the surrounding area's finest. Old Taffy had arranged two coaches which were full of the Cardiff boys. We thought everything was sorted, but South Wales Boys in Blue had other ideas.

Late on the Friday night before the trip, Old Taffy was informed that the coach company had pulled out due to police orders. Calls were made to various lads, producing panic about the next day's travel arrangements, as there was now only one coach going up. This wasn't too good, as we knew the locals would be giving us the warmest of welcomes. Fair play to the lads, they managed to get a Transit and cars together at short notice. We set off on the Saturday morning at about seven o'clock. We weren't feeling too confident; we only had about 75 lads en route to Goole, which we had pre-planned as the meeting place for all Soul Crew.

We got to Goole about midday and met five lads from a certain Scottish team in the pub next to the train station. After a swift beer or three, we decided it was time to go and make our presence known in Hull. To our total amazement as we left the pub, Old Bill came from everywhere. The day was fucked up there and then. We got escorted the 100 yards to the station and kept on the platform for an hour or so. When the train finally arrived, it was the slowest journey ever. We were told there was a cow on the line. Bollocks, it was all delaying tactics. When we arrived in Hull it must have been 2.50pm. We then get the slowest police escort you could imagine, the type when your legs ache and you want to burst into a sprint but can't. I later found out they took us the longest possible route to the ground.

At last we see the Boothferry floodlights. You know the buzz you get when you see them, knowing that you're finally near the ground. As we approached through a residential area, we could see a nice-sized mob waiting for us, which we were a little surprised at, as it was now half-time. We got closer and things suddenly got exciting. About 80 Hull were coming at us from the front and sides of the escort. We gave as good as we got but don't recall any major punches thrown, just a few handbags through the police lines. Things could have been really naughty, as both mobs totalled 80 and were going mental. One Cardiff lad was literally frothing at the mouth. We managed to get at the turnstiles about ten minutes later and the Hull lads inside the ground came down for a go. We charged at the fence and so did Hull. I thought it was going to go off big-style there, but it all died down. It nearly went again as Hull tried to get on the pitch, as well as Cardiff, but the police and stewards kept order.

It was the usual bollocks during the game; we lost 2-0, which was a good result for them as we were pushing for promotion. Afterwards we went into the car park and Hull had around 350 lads waiting outside the pub near the bridge, but there were loads of police whacking them back up the road. We had a little go at trying to get over to them but the Old Bill were smacking fuck out of us as well. We wouldn't have done much if we had managed to get on the road, as there were hundreds of them.

Then it was game over, back on the buses on the long trek home to South Wales. The main topic of conversation was how we were impressed by the Hull turnout and how up for it they were. We put Hull up there in the top three firms we'd come up against in the past ten years: Millwall, Middlesbrough and Hull, no doubts whatsoever. Hats off to Hull, they've gained massive respect from that day on.

The return was a Friday night fixture and we were completely taken by surprise. It is one night we will not forget. Not many would expect a firm numbering 120 to travel all the way down from Humberside to South Wales on a Friday, especially as Hull weren't doing too well in the league and you wouldn't expect a lot of lads would give up work for it, but they had planned this fixture particularly well in booking time off and arriving unannounced.

The previous time we had played them at home, they only brought about 18 lads, and we had turned out proper that day and were a little disappointed, but we gave Hull a pass. They were surrounded by about 200 Soul Crew in the Ninian Park car park. A few of ours wanted to get stuck into them but all the main faces told them to fuck off, as we would look like bullies. It's not the Soul Crew's style that, 200 onto 18, Brighton do them tricks. We did find out that Hull had the same problems that day that we did: the Old Bill had stopped a couple of their coaches. I've got to say hats off to the 18 that did show in cars, brave fellows them.

We have to admit Taffy was told the night before the Friday game that Hull were bringing a firm, but because of the time before and so many other occasions that alleged firms didn't turn up, we simply didn't believe it. We turned out at about five o'clock in the city centre, reckoning that about 40 lads would be enough. After a few beers and a few scouts having a little nose around, the 40 decided to make their way to a pub near Ninian Park. It was about 6.30pm, and this was when Hull's firm was spotted by the Mad One, much to his complete shock. He had taken a taxi from town and for some reason the taxi had gone straight past Ninian Park and there, outside the Grange End terrace, were 120 of Hull's finest, pushing and shoving the many Boys in Blue. The Mad One could see that Hull did not want to be forced into the ground and were trying to go for a drink. The Mad One got to the pub and told everyone but nobody would believe him, much to his annoyance. By the time he managed to convince everyone, it was too late and Hull were in the ground.

We took up our positions at kick-off in the Grandstand upper section; all the other not-so-main lads were at the bottom of the stand, to Hull's left. The wiser members of the crew studied Hull's firm throughout the game, and it has to be said they looked well up for post-match business: no youngsters at all. Hull must have thought we had about 250-300 in that stand because of all the wannabes wearing Burberry and Stone Island, but we knew ourselves we only had about 40 who were going to have a crack.

The game finished but we had left two minutes beforehand and were getting together in the car park. We could see that the ground had started to empty and the old butterflies in the guts started to go nuts. The 40 Soul Crew were halfway up the car park and then Hull's mob came out of the ground and headed straight into the car park.

What a sight that was. Hull were all close together, tight, moving as one mass towards us. Then it started to go wrong for us. We had a little pop at them and they just came straight into us and backed us off towards the top end of the car park. We tried to stand but there was just too many for us to handle. What pissed us off was all the wannabes were watching this and just throwing stones at Hull and their buses. The Old Bill got on top of everything then, and that was that. Result for Hull, not a big one mind, they know that, but still a result for them at Cardiff. The Soul Crew have got a lot of respect for Hull after that, as I'm sure Hull have for Cardiff

As we all know, people usually see incidents differently, so it's refreshing to note that our recollections aren't dissimilar to our opponents. The home match had seen the lads out before 10am. Around 100 had gathered in a bar waiting for news of the Soul Crew's whereabouts, with many offering suggestions on where they'd show, how they'd arrive and where any confrontations may take place. A few busied themselves in readiness for any such meeting; they had found some coils of thick, metallic electrical cable and, with the aid of a hacksaw, it was cut into cosh-sized pieces, ideal for close-quarter fighting.

The jungle drums were pounding out messages. Reports came in that they'd been spotted down the M18, numbers weren't known yet but it wouldn't take us long to find out. It was time to move on. We expected them to stop off either at Doncaster or Goole and get the train in, or even chance a drive right into Hull city centre. We made our way through the back streets that skirt the centre and set up camp in the Prince Regent, opposite the side entrance to Paragon Station. Though we knew the police would spot us, if Cardiff came by we'd be waiting, and the O.B. would have to deal with two sets of lads going at it hammer and tongs (and electric cable).

More messages came through. They were in Goole, 34 miles down the M62. Two lads were dispatched to pass back information on the Soul Crew's movements. We needed to know which train they'd be taking and to confirm they were actually there. In the past we'd had many false leads when expecting a firm to turn up. Within minutes, we had official confirmation. Cardiff's police spotter came through the doors and walked round the pub eyeing us. 'Is this it?' he asked. 'You'll need more than this.' His remarks were greeted with instant abuse from those within earshot and he walked out with a smug look on his face.

Our spotters had sent back information that Cardiff were holed up in The Great Northeastern public next to Goole Station, surrounded by Old Bill. Our spotters were sussed themselves and had moved on. We decided to move down Anlaby Road. The police kept their distance from us but their numbers had grown, with many kitted out in full riot gear. Eventually we made our way towards Cod and the ground. As we walked up the flyover, the police blocked off the walkways. Those stopped were searched and, for a few found with the cable in their possession, the day was over. The rest of us continued on to Silver Cod, were hundreds stood watching and waiting.

A bus could be seen edging its way slowly towards the pub. Surely they wouldn't risk bringing it by here? A shout went out and hordes of Silver Cod Squad filled the road, but it was a false alarm. The police looked decidedly edgy and the spotter from Cardiff was watching from the wings.

'Have we enough now?' His silence spoke volumes.

The police stopped all traffic and a line of riot officers complete with balaclavas and small round shields stood shoulder to shoulder along the breadth of Anlaby Road. This normally busy thoroughfare was strangely quiet – until dozens of pint glasses sailed through the air. People were getting agitated. It was 2.45pm and still no sign.

Many gave up and made their way to the ground, leaving 100 hardcore still eager for a meet. A car pulled up; they'd been sighted. The police had taken the unprecedented step of escorting the 50 or so Soul Crew along Hessle Road. With more uniforms than lads, they were well protected. We now had a running commentary on where they were, and casually walked towards North Road, past the countless white vans outside Boothferry Park. More riot officers told us repeatedly to disperse and enter the ground but no-one moved.

Within minutes we could see the blue flashing lights in the distance. The Soul Crew were moving down the road very slowly. Their chaperones kept stopping, hoping their colleagues would clear the road ahead, but we weren't going anywhere.

Before long, we were face-to-face. Insults and threats poured out from the aggressive locals. The police, three or four deep, batons raised, separated the two firms. Some of the Cardiff lads were as animated as ourselves but the majority looked on in disbelief. The five-minute walk down North Road had taken them 25 minutes.

The lads in Kempton matched the intimidating atmosphere

outside as they surged towards the fences when the Cardiff lads entered the ground at 3.45pm. Those of us left outside went back to Cod and waited. We were ready to try again later. The number of police deployed outside the ground was amazing, with CS gas, batons and shields at the ready. They began to line the full length of Boothferry Road from Three Tuns to North Road corner and it was still only 4pm.

Cardiff were kept in after the game, while the police played cat and mouse with the hundreds of City fans. Most were pushed back towards Three Tuns but enough got through to cause problems if the Soul Crew were taken back the same way. A bus was brought in and the Cardiff lads were quickly sent on their way. We'd shown these lads we were no second rate firm; we now had to go to Cardiff and show the rest of them.

The trip to Cardiff had to be organised on the quiet, with a coach company that was outside Hull. Only two people knew the firm's name or location and the police for once were clueless. We met up in a back street boozer on a small housing estate, as far from prying eyes as possible. The two coaches were due to set off at 12.30pm, giving us plenty of time to get there. Our original plan had included having two large shields made, one for each coach. They were decorated with the Prince of Wales Insignia and inscribed with the words 'The Leeds Welsh Rugby Club.' We wanted any snooping traffic cops to think we were rugby fans coming down for the weekend game and hoped it would get us into the city centre before they knew what hit them. But the foot-and-mouth epidemic put paid to that.

We made it as far as Monmouth before we were sussed. A lone traffic cop sat behind us and followed us in. The city centre slip road beckoned and when both coaches indicated and bore left, the police car began blaring out its siren and flashing its lights.

'Keep going driver.'

There was no point. At the top of the slip road was a posse

of South Wales Constabulary awaiting our arrival. We were taken to a nearby retail park and the coach pulled up behind a Sainsbury's supermarket. It was obvious they didn't know what to do with us. In my eyes, they had three options: take us to a pub (no chance); leave us on the retail park and bus us in just before the game started (too risky); take us to the ground now and sling us inside, so we're out of the way (bastards).

At Ninian Park we were told that if we didn't co-operate fully we would be arrested. A futile scuffle broke out in front of the turnstiles, then seconds later we were in. We stood freezing our bollocks off; there was a cold chill to the air and it went right through your clothes. 'Fuck, its only 6.45pm.' Hopefully things would warm up later.

A few of the lads had flags and set about positioning them for maximum effect. Several contained Loyalist references, and along with the obligatory Cross of St George, they got right up the noses of the incoming Cardiff fans. The ground began to fill and the atmosphere rose a level as they realised we were mob-handed. In total, a respectable 120 lads had turned out. A few of these lads were Mad Young Tigers but 80 per cent were in their mid-thirties to early forties.

The main topic of conversation was the mob of lads seated to our left. They were about 300-strong but we couldn't believe how young they looked. I have kids of my own that age. We constantly checked around, looking for signs of the main firm's whereabouts. They had to be in the upper section of the Bob Bank but they were keeping a low profile. To be honest, the game was of little consequence to any of us, we just wanted to get out and see what they had to offer.

Two Hull lads were arrested for incitement. We also heard a whisper that the police were waiting to see who took down the Loyalist flags and that they'd be arrested for more of the same. From what I can gather, the police weren't best pleased with us turning up, especially the Divisional Commander, who had to leave a black-tie dinner dance to take over operations at Ninian Park. We heard later, from lads who spent time in the cells, that the Old Bill had flapped a bit, as their intelligence report had stated we weren't travelling in numbers. This was sweet revenge after they'd put the dampener on our previous encounter in April 1999.

Injury time, and we began to edge nearer the Grange End exits. We hoped a reception committee would already be waiting for us, and a quick escape could catch the police off guard and give us a few precious minutes to make the acquaintance of our Welsh hosts. The referee's whistle was the signal we were waiting for. All 120 of us, silent and focused, hit the street. Police had cut off the street in front and behind. It left us one chance: we had to get everyone straight onto the car park and quick.

We rushed through the side gate and on past the coaches. We could see Cardiff in front of us and aimed straight for them. Our front-runners piled into the Cardiff lads. A few slaps were dished out, nothing major, but they just scattered. The police soon entered the fray and charged us back towards our coaches, hitting anyone in the way and began spraying gas indiscriminately.

We rounded the side of the coach and headed out towards another group of Cardiff who had gathered to the left of us. They again backed off. More riot police joined in. To cap it all, our poor driver was set upon by an over-zealous police officer; he was cleaning the wing mirrors when the officer began hitting him with a baton and screamed at him to get on the coach. This scenario was played out to a watching crowd pressed up against the fence. They were going disturbed. It was no good hurling abuse at us; their pride may have taken a knock but they only had themselves to blame. No-one slept on the long journey home; the adrenaline buzz saw to that. I reckon a good few of Cardiff's lads couldn't sleep either as they ruminated over the car park debacle. The consensus was that Cardiff had become too complacent. It was a lesson we should note ourselves.

We had some big hitters out that night and taking a backward step wasn't in their vocabulary. It was interesting to hear the view of a Cardiff bobby who returned from match duty and spoke to one of our lads in custody.

'You won tonight,' said the copper.

'No, mate, we got beat two-nil.'

'I know that, I'm on about the fight afterwards.'

The Internet message boards were hot for the next few nights and the inquest into the game lasted over a week. Many a Cardiff lad gave us respect for turning up and taking it to them. Others argued that hardly a punch was thrown. Our reply to that was: if you can't catch them, you can't hit them. We knew it wasn't a major off, not by any stretch, and we'd be fools to claim otherwise. Let's face it, how often do you get the chance these days. Let's just say it was worthy of a mention in our growing C.V.

I later had a chat with a City fan that had attended the Cardiff game and witnessed the scenes on the car park. Now this person was an original member of the Monte Carlo Mob and had been a much-respected stalwart of City's skinhead gang. He mentioned that he'd enjoyed watching the action, as brief as it was. He went on to say that in his opinion we'd pulled off something that even the old school skins wouldn't have attempted in their prime. This gave me an inner glow and an immense sense of pride; I felt ten feet tall.

I thought back to those Picadish days, when I had stood for hours looking out for away fans, hoping it would be me who spotted them. I wanted to be the one who ran up to the town lads and shout: 'They're here.' I was desperate to be part of the City crew.

Now here I was, thirty years on, chatting to one of my peers and receiving recognition for our actions on a cold Friday night in March.

Do you know what? It still feels good.

And Now The End Is Near

THIRTY-FOUR YEARS have passed since that Friday night 'friendly' when I first tasted that potent mix of fear and excitement at a game against Liverpool at Boothferry Road. I have witnessed many ups and downs with the Tigers but one thing has been constant, and that is the adrenaline kick when you are with like-minded friends on a Saturday afternoon. This is still an important part of my life. Many of these friendships have been forged over years at football grounds around the country. I can proudly say that I still stand with lads who, like myself, have been part of this sub-culture for over a quarter of a century. Yes, faces may disappear for months and even years, but on return they are welcomed back into the fold. We have long memories and any past reputations earned mean a lifetime membership of our exclusive club.

So what does the future hold? Well hopefully for the team, we will at last fulfil our potential and begin our steady climb up the divisions. The supporters deserve no less for their unwilting loyalty during the dark years in the basement.

COCKNEY JACKO: Thirty years on from the the Gordon Banks match and my Cockney accent has all but gone, but not that eternal belief that success for Hull City is just around the corner. That Wembley day, the one that is so, so overdue, is coming soon, I can feel it. These sentiments will be familiar to many people who decided to support a rubbish team when they were young. The thing is though, no matter how bad your team happen to be, you will still love them. Divorce is not an option in the world of football supporting, it really is a case of till death do us part.

The worst days of Hull City Football Club have been over the last couple of years, in which time the club has languished dangerously close to the bottom of Nationwide Three. As the threat of the end of your Football League status looms large, you might think people would off had enough. Not a bit of it. In times of crisis, a club needs its supporters more than ever. We do not let our club down in such times. It is fair to say that in the time I have supported Hull City, the supporters over a consistent number of years have outshone the team. For all the defeats the team has suffered in its sad decline down the leagues, there have been quite a few major victories off the pitch – sometimes actually on pitches. Some of the supporters of bigger clubs have turned up here in the past imagining that 'Ull' is a sort of fishing village on a river somewhere up North. An ignorant attitude like this can get you into trouble. For some it has; a couple of teams who had fans that came with big reputations left in well-soiled underwear. It's rude to name names in such matters but I must admit I can hardly stop myself whistling the tune of the song 'Are you reading Bir-ming-ham' as I remember.

Hull is geographically remote from any other city and therefore, despite a population of about 300,000, everybody tends to know everybody. It's like living in a very big village, sort of. It is this remoteness from other influences that has kept the Hull City faithful so well bonded. It is also a factor in keeping the firm from being infiltrated in the way some bigger teams were. At a club like mine, you can't just turn up and claim to be a lifelong fan that has happened to be working away or whatever. No chance. Round here, everyone knows everyone, either from school, drinking in the town at weekends, work, shared girlfriends or whatever. On match day, when everybody is gathered in the pub, you don't have time to chat to everyone you know. It's not ignorance, it's the same for everybody.

For a team of its size and league status, Hull City has a disproportionate number of hooligan supporters. I became one myself many years ago and, in the words of a famous song, 'It's a hard habit to break.' If you are reading this and you have been involved in this kind of thing, if you have been there and done it, been through the near-death experiences, felt the rush of adrenaline that can be brought on by pure fear or victory against the odds, then you will know that that there is no drug that can touch it. It's not funny, it's not clever being a football hooligan, and at the top end of 'our game' it can be extremely dangerous. But there's nothing that can touch it.

As Jacko says, Hull is set apart. You could say that we are insular but this is a definite plus when you're part of an active firm. Infiltrating is impossible, everyone knows everyone else, and we fight together and socialise together. This became one of our biggest strengths. To us it's not just a Saturday afternoon thing; we know each other inside out and never have a need to question each other. If you fight one, you fight us all.

MANNIX: Nowadays City have many older lads who fight and, without being crass, they are lads you would like in the trenches with you if your life was in danger. Amongst them are friends I have known from school for 30 years, love like brothers, and without daring to compare people perceived as criminals with my grandfathers' generation who fought in wars, I can see how friendships forged in hardship and battle are stronger than others. You look from side to side when numbers are against you and see lads standing by you, lads who are not found wanting when questions are asked. Top lads.

A fresh era dawns with the impending opening of our new, 25,000-seater stadium. My greatest wish is that I be allowed to step foot inside. This book could wreck that dream, yet I felt it was the right thing to do. Not for personal glory, fame and fortune – if I wanted that I'd have written a cookery book – but because I was given the opportunity to write about something I cared about and people I respect. I've enjoyed reminiscing with mates I'd not seen in years and sometimes sitting back in my chair and thinking, *fucking hell, did I do that?*

Yes I did, along with thousands of other lads. It probably made me who I am. For that alone I am glad. In many respects I still feel the same as I did in my late teens, but years of experience tell you, no, it's not worth it, hold back. It's a hard decision to make but it comes to us all. I must admit, though, I can't make up my mind: has it been a progressive thing over the past few years, the feeling of being too old that's made me think twice about reacting and getting involved? Or is it just down to the CCTV cameras reaching saturation point in our cities and around our grounds? I'll let you decide.

Hooliganism is still here and probably always will be. A stark illustration of this came as I was putting the final touches to this book. On Friday, 2 August 2002, Hull City played Middlesbrough in a pre-season 'friendly' at Boothferry Park. Having reached this far in my story, you will know by now of the history between the two sets of lads. The day's events are, at the time of writing, still subject to a police investigation and so my overview will necessarily be brief. However, I have it on good authority that this is what happened.

By 4pm, a good 60-70 Hull lads were drinking down Beverley Road. This was five miles away from the usual meeting points but then we weren't playing one of the usual teams. This was Boro. They always came via Beverley to avoid detection and the Hull lads sat drinking had a 'premonition' that this would be no different. However, they were wrong. Instead of the usual 'backdoor' technique, Boro

parked a number of vans only yards from the Silver Cod and
stormed 70-strong through the front doors at 5pm, to be met
by eight very surprised locals. The Hull lads were informed
by their Teesside adversaries of their next intended stopping
off point and, without further ado, Boro left the Cod and
walked 150 yards to the Tam Tam pub.

Beverley Road was soon ringing with the frantic bleep of
mobile phones and news filtered through. Cars, taxis and
buses were commandeered to take the Hull lads back to home
turf, no easy task in the Friday night traffic, especially for
those on public transport, as two buses would be needed.
Within half an hour there were around 40 lads outside Cod,
many of them seething, and because of this they threw caution
to the wind and decided to front Boro without proper back-
up.

They steamed up Anlaby Road. Before they could reach
the pub, Boro came out in force, hurling bottles and glasses.
The initial barrage and the solid show from Boro had the Hull
lads backing off; they were outnumbered and, at this point,
outclassed, yet they mustered and stood their ground 20
yards back from their original position. Surprisingly only a
few punches were thrown on either side as lads from both
firms bounced around but didn't commit themselves. This
stand-off gave the police time to throw officers between both
sets and defuse the situation. The Hull lads were pushed back
towards Silver Cod and Boro made themselves at home in
Tam Tam.

Back at Cod, more lads were arriving from Beverley Road.
Those that had taken the longest were furious that they'd
missed the fracas and remonstrated with the more impetuous
lads who should have known better than to take on Boro
without them. The Hull numbers swelled to around 300
standing around the perimeter of Silver Cod, many staring up
the road for signs of movement behind the police line. Before
long, a bus arrived to remove the Boro lads – a usual police

tactic to avoid marching them to the ground. This time the sight of the bus and its departing occupants sparked an explosion of violent disorder as a mob of Hull began rampaging the length of Anlaby Road. Armed with bricks, bottles, beer glasses and cans, they aimed their missiles at the thin line of outnumbered officers, who began to retreat. A further surge, aided by people carrying crash barriers from nearby road-works, again had the police backing off.

By now the Boro were on the bus and the under-siege police were supported by a group of special operations officers who bolstered the lines with protective shields and riot gear. A number of mounted officers appeared behind the line. A final surge petered out as this time the police line held firm. With this, many began to drift away and disperse towards the ground. The police moved in and there was a small altercation on the steps of the Cod as they pushed people away.

Anlaby Road was suddenly quiet. All local traffic on this main thoroughfare was re-routed so the debris-laden road could be cleaned up. The Boro lads were taken to a local park and made to sit out the duration of the game, with 60 police officers as chaperones, before being escorted from Hull. After the game, scores of riot police stood outside Boothferry Park, ready for any further outbreaks of trouble. All this, from a game where the police believed there was no potential for trouble because of 'no history' between the clubs. It's a pity for them that this book hadn't been on the shelves; they could have read about the bad blood we've had with Boro's firm since the sixties.

So yes, in the year 2002 football still carries the burden of hooliganism. Yet people need to look beyond the game before apportioning blame and condemnation. For my generation, football was an outlet but not the be-all and end-all. Violence was pursued with vigour on our city streets, at rugby games and around the town on a Saturday night. It wasn't purely a football disease, it was a way of expressing your 'maleness' among your peers. I know many a good lad who, years ago and even now, would have spent the whole weekend drinking and fighting but wouldn't be seen dead inside Boothferry Park. How was he labelled by the media? He wasn't. Whereas a football fan caught doing the same thing ends up with restriction notices and has to hand his passport into the nearest police station during high-profile games abroad. Where's the justice in that?

My final thoughts are these. Any older lads from around the country who met us only during quiet periods would not rate us. However I think most decent lads would acknowledge we now have the numbers and quality, and are active enough, to be rated with the top teams. It is interesting how the police have had to move with the times to keep up with what's going on. In the early days, the police ran around like headless poultry, reacting to trouble instead of taking the preventative measures we see today. I cannot say for sure, but some police still see it as silly lads' macho posturing. Most of us work, pay taxes, bring up polite children and have no non-football-related criminal record. On a Saturday, however, we are white, working class football fans, and today that puts us on a par with the lowest of the low. It has become a *cause célèbre* of the media and politicians to clamp down on this. I think most junior police ranks know us for what we are, perceived 'one day a week criminals.'

The government of the day will always use scapegoats, and the political climate over the past 20 years has seen football and its problems high up the list. I'm not getting on any political high horse; no party is any better or worse than the other in this respect, but they need to address greater issues that are around us every day. They need to get things in perspective.

They need to speak to the man in the street, or better still listen to the police officers. They are in the frontline. Yes, they also police our movements of a Saturday afternoon, but with us its cat-and-mouse and a certain amount of respect is given from both sides, although at times grudgingly. Meanwhile our city streets are filled with youths who don't give a fuck, not about you, me or themselves. It's hard to pinpoint the exact time that a change occurred in Britain but the eighties have a lot to answer for. There has been a steady change in the structure of this country, with another tier evolving within our class system. The great masses of the working class have been chipped away, with a level reaching rock bottom: no-hopers, druggies and lazy bastards who live without pride. They have no pride in their area, no pride in themselves and no respect for others.

With us, it was a culture: we wore different clothes, we were part of different crazes and more often then not, fought with like-minded people. Yet 95 per cent of us wouldn't dream of resorting to 'proper' criminal activities, ever. And that's what you, the reader, have to remember.

But then again, if you've got this far, you already know that.

Acknowledgements

This book could not have been written without the memories, help and support of a few of the lads, namely Gary C, H of OPE, Mark J, Mannix. Ian T, Skids, Gary T, Darren E, Jamie C, Ian L, Dill (photo historian), Nick T and Pete L (Cardiff). Over the years I have stood with many a different set of lads – as people drift away, others come to the fore – and I have made lifetime friends of many of them. A special mention must go out to Rob S, Alan W, Jimmy S, Derek P, John L and George P.

Another mention goes out to the 'lads' collectively: Monte Carlo Mob, Albermarle Boys, OPE Lads, Hessle Road Bootboys, Woodcock Martyrs, Bransholme Lads (including Selworthy Mob), The Avenues and Beverley Road Boys, East Hull Boys, West Hull Boys, Amy YC Lads, Hawthorn Boys, Boothferry Lads, Gypsyville Boys, Hessle Lads, Hedon Lads, Holderness Road, Elephant and Wingfield Reds (HKR), Anlaby Road, Parkers Crew and the Silver Cod Squad, MYTs and The Minority.

And individually: Sinbad, Ray S, Tony, Jacko, Huddy, Ronnie, Gerald, Peo, Woody, Dave, Andy, Dobo, The McNallies, Mulloy, Tarzan (R.I.P.), Norman E, Steve D, Steve E, Steve T, Chris D, Bunny, Alex and Sid, Ray J, Les H, Tony & Russell E, Jason & Julian S, John & Phil C, Andy C, Demo, Fez, Gordon M, Bri S, Rob Mc, Paddy Mc, Mad George, Brains, Ginner, Gary C, Wolfgang G, Gaz C, Mike W (R.I.P.), Mike Y, Steve W, Wilf P, Billy E, Sugar,

John & Col L, John S, Steve G, Chris J, Hutchie, Rob S, Les P, Alan & Terry W, Barry S (R.I.P.) Dave S, Alf H, Jimmy N, John & Neil O, Jimmy G, Mike Simmo. Alan & Ian R, Stan, Ray & Alan P, Col W, Steve & Graham P, Gibbon, Kelly B, Skelly Brothers, Charlie F, Ian B, Rich C, Steve C, Stuart S, Paddy M (R.I.P.) Steve & Danny & Joey O, The Welburn & Cochrane Brothers, John L, Bernard C, Frank, Mike W, Trevor M, Kev, George & Frank M, Waggy, Budgie, Wad, Smiggy, Wilko, Ian M, Chappy, Rob E, Steve B, Stuart O, Ray P, Loz, Ray & Steve H, Stan the Man, Gray R, Hoss, Martin H, Tony C, 'H', Fat Rat, Freddy J, Caz, Pete B, Kev B, Gibbo, Steve (Burt) M, Dave T, Bri & Dave L, Tony D, Steve W, Budgie, Jock, John C, John H, Johnnie R, Jimmy H, Steve & Dave S, Moc, Kev C, Tommy B, Dave K, Scally, Les H, Smiggy, Sheppo, Angry John, Eddie & Bri E, Shep, Lee R, Rich D, Clint, Pete, Swalesy, Skids, Gary B, Neil B (R.I.P.), Captain C, Robbo, Nige, Lamo, Baggy, Rob M, Eddy W, Doc, Gareth Mc, Wilf, Mike M, Maurice, Jamie, Tommy, Gav, Gary A, Matthew A, Shady, Lee W, Higgsy, Andy G, Phill H, Jimmy G, Trog, Mike R, Ian R, Pete R (R.I.P.),Paz, Phil H, Shaun C, Steve C, Glen B, The Gills:- Jase, Tad & Marsh, Lee L, Andy C, Danny Hat, John A, Kev, Blacky, Glen C, Charlie S, Podgie (R.I.P.), Macka, Lee C, Oxford Craig, Jimmy H, Kev C, Dave B, Col B, Gumbo, Hooper (R.I.P.), Boothy, Andy S, Gary S, Tiff, Matty, Melv H, Glen A, Boris, Turkey, M. Rock, Jimmy S, Pat S, Cookie (S), Johnno, Mouse, Joey L, Jimmy W, Skolar, Simmo Bros (Tony, Paul & Melvin) Totty, Phil T, Terry D, Andy D, Andy P, Dean P, Nelly P, Jimmy P, Barry N, Johnny O, Craig L, Bud, Matt S, Marc C, Danny C, Meg, Rich B, Spud, Fat Ted, Glen A, Marc D, Cornish John, Darren C, Jimmy S, Jimmy C, Glen R, Neil R, Darren R, Lemmy, Mannix, Peanut, Bri B, Aidy T, Steve R, Andy W, Martin, Paul M, Woody, Phil the Greek, Cooky, Charlie, John B, Eddy, Bri E, Gary B, Gareth B, Savo, Darren W, CB, Rocky, Danny C, Lee C, Tank, M. Johnno, Jamie, Oxo, Lee B, Dave N, Steve N, Les B, Gary D, Snoz, Gary T, Mad Dog, Darren C, Mike T, Paul T, Barber, Big Louie, 'T', Toggy, Charlie G, Jase I, Ammo, Jase, Ian L, Alex J, Tony M, Brett M, Tony C, Jamie C, George P, Cockney Jacko, Tony NF, Charlie S, Coll C, Pike, Kev P, Cheggers, Darren E, Brendan Bullneck, Greg C (R.I.P.), John T, Alan G (R.I.P.), Gav Jacko, Tinker, Gudgeing, Kev G, Carl G, Howard, Enoch, Dean G, Toby, Rooney(R.I.P.), Harry, Neil S, Dave A, Rodders, Derrick P, Kev S, Cav, Tony S, Tonks, Dave A, Bill & Tony H, Dean L, Paul D,

Steve W, Lee W, Mark W, Dean C, Kev P, Kev W, Shane H, Wayne E, Dave G, John A, Badger, Andy W, Ray C, Dave S, Rob S, Steve W, Skin, Shano, Leigh, Darren, Jack C, Chillo, Mark C, Jeff C, Mally P, John P, Steve S, Ian Mc, Paul J, Col A, Jimmy & Craig C, Whinney, Colly (R.I.P.), Edgar, Lee H, Chris W, Dill, Nick, Nigel H, Taffy, Pete W, Maggi, Doc, Gary B, Dave C, Benno, Wilbur, Stretch, Mike P, Tony P, Shaun P, Paul, Mickey W, Cola, Lee P, Andy D, Mark D, Barney, Oxo, Willie P, Nigel P, Rips, Puss (R.I.P.), Glen C, Carl P, Killer (R.I.P.), Fugi, Andy E, Ian L, Ian G, Jason W, Mark W (R.I.P.), Martin K, Trevor, Keith B, Bruce M, Welshy, Steve & Kev J, Barry L, Roy S, Carl H, Carl S, Terry S, Gav T, Gordon H, Maggi & Mike M, Sully, Johnny P, Timmy P (R.I.P.), Webber Bros, Nicky B, Danny G and Gav H (R.I.P.).